Privilege or Punish

Privilege or Punish

Criminal Justice and the Challenge of Family Ties

DAN MARKEL
JENNIFER M. COLLINS
ETHAN J. LEIB

OXFORD
UNIVERSITY PRESS

OXFORD
UNIVERSITY PRESS

Oxford University Press, Inc., publishes works that further Oxford University's objective of excellence in research, scholarship, and education.

Oxford New York
Auckland Cape Town Dar es Salaam Hong Kong Karachi Kuala Lumpur Madrid Melbourne
Mexico City Nairobi New Delhi Shanghai Taipei Toronto

With offices in
Argentina Austria Brazil Chile Czech Republic France Greece Guatemala Hungary Italy
Japan Poland Portugal Singapore South Korea Switzerland Thailand Turkey Ukraine Vietnam

Published by Oxford University Press, Inc.
198 Madison Avenue, New York, New York 10016

Oxford is a registered trademark of Oxford University Press
Oxford University Press is a registered trademark of Oxford University Press, Inc.

Library of Congress Cataloging-in-Publication Data

Markel, Dan.
Privilege or punish : criminal justice and the challenge of family ties / Dan Markel, Jennifer M. Collins & Ethan J. Leib.
p. cm.
Includes bibliographical references and index.
ISBN 978-0-19-538006-4 ((hardback) : alk. paper)
1. Criminal justice, Administration of. 2. Family violence—Law and legislation. 3. Punishment. I. Collins, Jennifer M. II. Leib, Ethan J. III. Title.
K5001.M37 2009
364—dc22

2008045517

1 2 3 4 5 6 7 8 9

Printed in the United States of America on acid-free paper

Note to Readers

This publication is designed to provide accurate and authoritative information in regard to the subject matter covered. It is based upon sources believed to be accurate and reliable and is intended to be current as of the time it was written. It is sold with the understanding that the publisher is not engaged in rendering legal, accounting, or other professional services. If legal advice or other expert assistance is required, the services of a competent professional person should be sought. Also, to confirm that the information has not been affected or changed by recent developments, traditional legal research techniques should be used, including checking primary sources where appropriate.

(Based on the Declaration of Principles jointly adopted by a Committee of the American Bar Association and a Committee of Publishers and Associations.)

For Wendi, my everything, my world without end ⁄⁄⁄ DM

For my own beloved children, Jake, Lily and Sam,
and for my wonderful husband, Adam. ⁄⁄⁄ JMC

For my parents, Naomi and Martin Leib, who better not count on parental support laws. And for my daughter Clementine Leib Schonfeld and my son Gershon Schonfeld Leib: I'll eat you up, I love you so ⁄⁄⁄ EJL

Contents

Acknowledgments

BOOKS DON'T JUST FALL from trees. For comments and conversations about aspects of this project over the last few years, we are very grateful to Susan Frelich Appleton, Kelli Alces, Amitai Aviram, Sam Bagenstos, Darryl Brown, Adam Charnes, Mary Coombs, Tommy Crocker, Maxine Eichner, Dave Fagundes, Brian Galle, Adil Haque, Carissa Byrne Hessick, Rick Hills, Clare Huntington, Rob Kar, Jon Klick, Erik Knutsen, Zak Kramer, Ron Levin, Wayne Logan, Melissa Murray, Michael O'Hear, Roger Park, Matt Price, B. J. Priester, Myrna Raeder, Alice Ristroph, Laura Rosenbury, Elizabeth Scott, Benny Shmueli, Jonathan Simon, Jordon Singer, Jason Solomon, Jeannie Suk, Fernando Teson, Steve Vladeck, Lesley Wexler, Bob Weisberg, Ron Wright, and Ekow Yankah. We are especially grateful for comments on the manuscript as a whole to Chad Flanders, Alyssa Lathrop, and Matt Price.

We also thank the participants in law faculty workshops held at the 2006 and 2008 Law and Society conferences; Hofstra; University of Arizona; University of Miami; Washington and Lee; Washington University; Boston College; Osgoode Hall (York University); University of Maryland; Prawfsfest!-Loyola (LA); and Florida State, where parts of this project were earlier ventilated. For helpful research assistance, we thank Katherine Kao, Eli Mark, Rich McPherson, Megan Schanbacher, Brandy Mills, J. B. Lewis, Luke McCarthy, and Will Woodlee, and our schools' librarians. We are especially grateful to the students who helped edit some of this material when it appeared in earlier forms in the ***University of Illinois Law Review*** and the ***Boston University Law Review***; we also thank those reviews for their flexibility in allowing us to draw on and revise those earlier writings for this book. Furthermore, we extend our thanks to our deans for their moral and financial support of this project; to Becky Marsey and our assistants for editorial help; and to Chris Collins at Oxford University Press, for his guidance and enthusiasm for this enterprise from the outset.

Last, we would be remiss if we failed to thank each other for our patience and efforts, and, most of all, our families, for their unflagging support and tolerance for this distraction from our own voluntary caregiving obligations.

Introduction

FEW PEOPLE ENVIED David Kaczynski. In 1996, he found some old writings by his brother Ted that were similar in tone and content to a manifesto submitted to newspapers in 1995 by a feared terrorist, known to law enforcement agents as the Unabomber. David was then faced with an agonizing choice about whether to disclose his discovery to federal investigators. He ultimately revealed Ted's name, believing that he had assurances from federal authorities that they would not pursue the death penalty against his brother, whom David believed to be mentally ill. When Attorney General Janet Reno decided, nonetheless, to pursue a capital case, David was devastated.[1] Later, Ted Kaczynski pled guilty to charges that carried a life sentence.[2] Subsequently, David Kaczynski became an anti-death penalty advocate.[3]

David Kaczynski is perhaps the best-known example in recent years of a family member who provided law enforcement officials with the critical information that led to the arrest of a loved one.[4] Bernie Madoff's sons' recent choice to turn in their father for his giant investment fraud is another headline-grabbing instance of this conflict between family loyalty and public duties. Unsurprisingly, many family members confronted with a dilemma like David Kaczynski's make an entirely different choice.

Consider the Sheinbein family, for example. In 1997, a high school senior named Samuel Sheinbein was charged with murder after police found the burned and dismembered body of an acquaintance in the garage of a vacant house in Maryland.[5] But Sheinbein was never brought to trial in Maryland because he fled to Israel within days of the murder, and Israel subsequently refused to extradite him.[6]

So how was a seventeen-year-old able to get to Israel so quickly? Prosecutors alleged that, after learning that his son was a murder suspect, Samuel's father, Sol Sheinbein, brought Samuel, who was then hiding in New York, his passport, some clothing, and a ticket to Israel. Sol also drove his son to the airport,[7] and, a few days later, followed his son to Israel, where he continues to live and work.[8] Prosecutors in Maryland subsequently filed a misdemeanor charge against him for obstructing a police investigation. But because of the nature of the charge and his status as an Israeli citizen, Sol also could not be extradited.[9]

After Samuel Sheinbein pled guilty before an Israeli court and was sentenced to twenty-four years in prison,[10] Sol gave his first interview to an Israeli newspaper. In defending his actions, Sol, a practicing lawyer, stated: "I did some simple soul-searching and I came to the conclusion that with all due respect to the law, I am first of all a father and only after that a citizen."[11] Samuel Sheinbein's mother, in an earlier statement, claimed, "any parents would go and would do what we are doing."[12]

The choices David Kaczynski and Sol Sheinbein made arise virtually every day in every jurisdiction, where family members have the opportunity to facilitate or obstruct enforcement of the criminal law. Indeed, the media recently reported stories about fugitives whose family members created alibis (including reporting the death of the fugitive) for them;[13] criminals who perpetrated their frauds with the assistance of family members;[14] and white-collar criminals whose spouses offered testimony or other evidence in exchange for a reduction of the criminal liability they themselves faced.[15]

The conflict between duties as citizens and loyalties as family members has long been explored in literature—most prominently in *Antigone*, Sophocles' play about a young woman's decision to defy the ruler Creon in favor of affording her brother Polynices a proper burial. Nonetheless, it is a relatively uncharted area in legal scholarship.[16] This is especially so with respect to how this classic tension manifests itself within the criminal justice system.[17]

*****

One goal of this book is to expose how family members and their interests intersect with what we often refer to as "the American criminal justice system."[18] For instance, we find that the state does not always impinge upon family members in the course of investigating or prosecuting crimes. Indeed, sometimes legal institutions and actors defer to the decision of family members to prioritize their duties to family over their duties as citizens. Examples of these accommodations include evidentiary privileges that enable family members to avoid furnishing evidence against their loved ones and exemptions for family members from laws prohibiting the harboring of fugitives. We characterize these state policies that treat defendants better because of their family status as *family ties benefits*—and there are many of them. For several reasons that we hope to explore in this book, we generally oppose conferring family ties benefits in the criminal justice system. This is a controversial stance because it might enable our critics to characterize us as "anti-family." But we think that, in many circumstances, there are simply too many normative costs to the criminal justice system when it gives special benefits to defendants based on their family status.

In contrast to family ties ***benefits***, sometimes the state imposes extra ***burdens*** on defendants on account of their status as a member of a family.[19] In these situations, but for family status, a person would not be found liable of a crime. Examples include vicarious criminal liability imposed on parents for the crimes of their children and "omissions liability," that is, criminal liability imposed on family members for failing to rescue their kin from harm. Because these laws impose punishment on account of one's familial status, we call these *family ties burdens*.

We believe that these burdens stand in need of substantial justification. Some of these criminal liabilities appear to be attempts to protect the vulnerable in relationships of voluntary caregiving. We think it is relatively easy to protect that interest without resorting to the current laws' discrimination against caregiving arrangements that differ from the structure of an idealized traditional family unit. It is one thing for the law to recognize how citizens organize themselves into close circles of affection; but it is another for the criminal law to take a stance on how citizens ought to organize themselves—and to discredit and disadvantage those who choose to draw their circles of intimacy differently.

With an understanding of both family ties benefits and burdens, we can stand at the crossroads between the family and the criminal justice system and see two distinct questions about the facial treatment of familial status, each of which has been given spare and insufficient attention until now. First, how does the criminal justice system in this country approach the issue of family status? Second, how should family status be recognized, if at all, in a criminal justice system situated within a liberal democracy committed to egalitarian principles of nondiscrimination?

Because of the different dynamics involved in family ties benefits and family ties burdens, we largely address them in separate parts of the book. Thus, the first half of the book canvasses and analyzes family ties benefits; the second half focuses attention upon family ties burdens. Before providing a quick summary of how the rest of the book will proceed, a few clarifications are in order.

*****

This book integrates legal analysis, political theory, and public policy. Thus, we are not merely describing doctrine but suggesting an analytical framework for thinking about the way the criminal justice system grapples with questions of family status. We are hopeful that public policy makers, lawyers, and legislators will learn from our approach to this diverse set of rules within the criminal justice system—and that they will begin to see how these seemingly independent laws need to be understood in light of their contribution to privileging and punishing family status. Although we realize that each benefit and burden exposed here must ultimately be analyzed on its own terms and from within its own context, we think revealing the multifarious ways our society goes about privileging and punishing family status will contribute to each of those separate inquiries. We cannot analyze each benefit and burden exhaustively; our hope is that developing a normative lens through which to view each of these intersections can illuminate the policy debates about each of these practices. And, at the very least, the descriptive side of our project should show just how pervasive these practices are within the criminal justice system.

Many earlier books have studied the economic and cultural effects of criminal justice policy on families. Some have even considered the impact of incarceration on families, focusing on the devastating impact that the incarceration of relatives can have on the family members left behind.[20] One study has considered how the corrections system copes with the issues related to the reproductive or family-raising aspirations of its offenders.[21] And another focuses on the issues related to prisoner reentry into society and family life.[22] There is no doubt that many of the criminal law's policies and practices disadvantage families in many ways—and without attention to this sort of disparate impact on families, policy designers risk tearing our social fabric at the seams. We agree that this lens is a critically important one in evaluating criminal justice policies. Nevertheless, this lens tends to track the ***indirect*** results of other policies. For example, although lengthy sentences for minor drug crimes result in the tragic situation of too many children growing up without access to a parent, the primary objective behind drug sentencing laws is generally not to separate children and their parents.

Our focus is different and has yet to be sufficiently addressed by the community of scholars interested in how the criminal law intersects with families. Here, we examine the distinctively purposeful practices that consciously target defendants for special privileges or burdens on account of their familial status. Scholars have been successful in analyzing the *effects* of certain criminal justice policies and practices on the family. But most scholars have not recognized the panoply of laws expressly drawn to privilege or disadvantage persons based on family status alone. Some have addressed singular instances of the larger phenomenon we chart, but we are the first to offer a synthetic approach. It seems important and necessary to pause and think through how and why our laws intentionally target family status and how the underlying goals of such a choice might better be served in some cases. This book clears that ground.

Although we have chosen here to focus on explicit legislative or judicial choices to privilege or burden individuals with family relationships, there are no doubt many other ways in which persons enjoy informal benefits or burdens; for example, if a police officer makes an on-the-spot decision not to arrest a domestic violence offender precisely because the assault was committed on a family member rather than on a stranger; or if a juror refuses to convict in a marital rape case because he believes a husband is entitled to his wife's sexual services. These kinds of subterranean choices are weighty and important, but our focus here is different. We believe policymakers need to reflect upon the explicit choices they have made, choices that have been insufficiently analyzed in a synthetic manner by academics before this project. Once we have a framework for analyzing the explicit family ties benefits and burdens, one might be able to apply elements of that framework to the unstated and more obscured informal benefits and burdens. But to develop that framework in the first instance, we focus on facial benefits and burdens.

*****

As mentioned earlier, in the first half of the book we address how the criminal justice system "privileges" family status. The first chapter provides an overview of the multiple sites in which a defendant's family status is used as a basis for extending a benefit to that person within the criminal justice system. We first explore how jurisdictions offer evidentiary privileges and other exemptions affecting evidence gathering that constrain the state from intruding into familial relationships. We then describe the efforts by some states to shield from prosecution family members who harbor fugitives from law enforcement officials. Additionally, we survey family ties benefits associated with violence in the family, pretrial release, sentencing, and prison administration.

Chapter 2 then takes a normative turn and offers a framework for assessing family ties benefits within the criminal justice system. We assess the costs that they are likely to exact and explore why these benefits should generally be rejected absent a substantial state interest. We begin with an appreciation of the important role families play in securing the conditions for human flourishing.[23] We also note the ambivalent relationship the state has with the family. On the one hand, the state depends on the family to prepare individuals for their role as citizens; on the other hand, the state must compete with the family for the loyalty of individual members. That discussion serves as a springboard for our critique of family ties benefits in the realm of criminal justice.[24]

Chapter 2 also articulates four distinct normative concerns that may arise when extending special accommodations based on a defendant's family status in the criminal justice system. We recognize that not each family ties benefit will implicate all of these concerns. We therefore begin with only a presumption of caution toward family ties benefits, rather than unmitigated disapproval. First, the historical context in which the family's relationship to the criminal law has evolved reveals that many family ties benefits often served (and in some cases, continue to serve) to perpetuate norms of patriarchy, gender hierarchy, or domestic domination. Our second concern is that accommodations to families might impede the realization of criminal justice understood as the effective and accurate prosecution of the guilty and the exoneration of the innocent.[25] Our third reservation stems from the way that family ties preferences can disrupt norms of equality that should otherwise prevail in an attractive regime of governance that does not discriminate on the basis of morally arbitrary characteristics. On this view, criminal investigations and prosecutions should treat citizens' interests with equal concern and without fear or favor. The extension of special privileges to persons simply because of their family situation bears an onus of justification, especially because the policy that extends such privileges will often have a negative and discriminatory effect on those without family ties—some of whom never made actual choices to avoid family ties. Fourth, we note that some family ties benefits can have the unsavory effect of incentivizing more criminal activity—and more successful criminal activity at that. To the extent the law effectively signals messages to the public, some family ties benefits encourage family members to keep their criminal enterprises in the family. For example, if sentencing policies serve to create a class of persons who are immune from incarceration or who receive heavy discounts in their prison terms, then those persons will be the most sought after to serve in criminal enterprises—or they themselves might seek out criminal activity.

We think these four considerations, taken together, suffice to create a presumption against family ties benefits in the criminal justice system. We do not make the constitutional claim that family status is a suspect classification worthy of strict scrutiny when the criminal justice system discriminatorily benefits or burdens individuals on the basis of family status. But we do believe that, as a policy matter, the government should view the use of family status skeptically. Thus, policymakers, whether in the legislature or elsewhere, should consider our framework for analyzing family status.[26] To use the language of equal protection analysis without making the constitutional claim, the objective of the government should be at least "important" and perhaps "compelling," and the means adopted to pursue that objective should be "narrowly tailored" to achieve that objective, looking especially to see whether alternative measures might be as effective.

In the context of family ties benefits, a presumption does not entail eliminating all accommodations of family ties. Instead, we propose that such benefits undergo a set of searching inquiries. First, to what extent does the family ties benefit in question contribute to one of the four normative costs often associated with family ties benefits? Second, assuming the benefit implicates one or more of these concerns, to what extent does the benefit vindicate a substantial state interest that justifies the use of the benefit in the criminal justice system? Finally, are other less troubling means—means that can be crafted in terms that are neutral to family status—available to protect the interest underlying the benefit? To be sure, this kind of scrutiny will not resolve all questions: we will inevitably have disputes about the strength of competing claims. But it will do some important work in helping us think more clearly about the problem before us and, in close cases, will alert us to some of the potentially hidden costs of family ties benefits.

In Chapter 3, we apply the normative framework developed in Chapter 2 to assess some of the benefits we identify in Chapter 1. We find good reason to eliminate or curtail substantially some benefits, including evidentiary privileges, exemptions from prosecutions, and sentencing discounts in most cases. In other instances, where there might be good reasons to extend the benefit, we suggest policies neutral to family status that can be used to achieve the underlying goal of facilitating caregiving without encroaching on the core values of the criminal justice system—and we demonstrate how those policies could work in particular instances. We conclude this initial inquiry into family ties ***benefits*** with some reflections relevant to future theoretical and empirical work in this area and then turn, in the second half of the book, to an analysis of how the criminal justice system punishes persons on account of their familial status through family ties burdens.

Family ties burdens are the special burdens placed on defendants within the criminal justice system on account of their familial status. Thus, to parallel the inquiry in the first half of this book, we first ask which of the burdens in the criminal justice system imposed on individuals are attributable to their familial status and then, second, we ask whether such burdens can be justified, and if so, under what conditions?

Chapter 4 surveys particular examples of family ties burdens. We focus on efforts by states to impose criminal liability on individuals for crimes if an element of the crime is a defendant's family status. Examples of these substantive crimes include parental responsibility laws (based on vicarious and strict liability theories of failure to supervise); filial responsibility laws (duties to support indigent parents); omissions liability (duties to rescue family members); bigamy; incest; adultery; and nonpayment of child support.

Once we identify the practices properly characterized as family ties burdens, Chapter 5 presents a normative framework for analyzing whether such burdens can be justified. We first address whether and to what degree the normative considerations we identified earlier—patriarchal domination, inaccuracy, inequality and discrimination, and crime creation—apply to the context of family ties burdens. As it turns out, some of these considerations—crime creation and inaccuracy—are generally inapplicable in the context of the burdens. In other words, unlike family ties benefits, burdens rarely trigger concerns that they will create more crime or impede the accurate prosecution of the guilty and the exoneration of the innocent. But many do seem to raise concerns about gender and discrimination.

We then examine which additional factors may warrant consideration in the particular context of family ties burdens. We develop the claim that the use of family status to allocate criminal liability causes substantial problems for the liberal state, both because it can burden relationships that persons have had no autonomy in creating or rejecting and because it risks infringing upon citizens' liberty without sufficient justification or narrow tailoring between the goal and remedy. As we hope to demonstrate, we think that some of these family ties burdens run afoul of principles that should constrain the use of the criminal justice system in a liberal democracy.

We emphasize here that many of the family ties burdens we find in the law occur in the context of relationships that have a voluntary or "opt-in" nature, meaning that the individual who faces the burden imposed by the criminal justice system has consensually entered into the relationship of caregiving that serves as a basis of liability. We find that this pattern has some normative valence and explain its dimensions, limits, and implications for policy design within the criminal justice system.

Specifically, we propose that family ties burdens undergo a form of scrutiny similar to that which we advocated with respect to family ties benefits. Our general approach is that a presumption against special burdens based on familial status is also warranted. Perhaps unsurprisingly, just as we exhibited a tendency to be skeptical toward family ties benefits, we are also inclined to protect individuals from burdens based on familial status. However, because we are sensitive to the caregiving contributions that might stand in need of special protection from the state, we believe that at least some of the concerns we have about family ties burdens can be addressed by redrafting these laws in a manner that avoids a reflexive resort to familial status alone and instead focuses on voluntarily assumed obligations of caregiving.

Of course, we recognize that an analysis of a family ties burden needs to be viewed in its particularized context and that, in some classes of cases, the unusual burdens currently placed on family members may be proxies for promoting some of the distinctive purposes of the criminal justice system. Thus, our presumption against family ties burdens does not entail eliminating all family ties burdens; instead, we propose that such policies undergo a set of searching inquiries.

First, we propose that those seeking to impose a burden ask whether the burden falls on persons who had voluntarily assumed some duty of caregiving. Second, we explore whether the burden impinges on some liberty that should be recognized as deserving of protection in a liberal society. Third, we examine whether the laws can be drafted so as to be narrowly tailored to the governmental objectives. Fourth, we look to whether there are non-criminal measures that could be equally effective in achieving these government objectives, assuming these government objectives are sufficiently compelling or important to vindicate through law. Last, we examine whether the existing family ties burdens contribute to concerns about gender inequality and discrimination. As with family ties benefits, this scrutiny will not, to be sure, resolve all questions; inevitably, disputes about the strength of competing claims will persist. But, it should do some important work in helping clarify the problems under consideration.

Finally, in Chapter 6, we apply this framework to the various issues highlighted in Chapter 4. Having identified seven distinctive family ties burdens, we demonstrate how our normative framework helps illuminate analysis of these burdens. We conclude that, in each case, the kind of scrutiny we deem appropriate presents at least some challenge to the relevant burden. In all but one of the family ties burdens, we are inclined to recommend either full or partial decriminalization. We recognize, however, that some might disagree with those conclusions, that some might want better empirical evidence to be pursued in order to refine our means-testing prong, and that some may think some of our conclusions politically unfeasible. Thus, our second-best solution in many of those instances is to require the state to impose the burden in ways that do not simply embrace a traditional conception of the family. Rather, the burdens should be expanded to other relationships that involve voluntarily assumed obligations of caregiving. Given that the promotion of voluntary relationships of care ultimately is the justification for the burdens in the first place, we conclude that nothing else justifies limiting the burdens to the family as such; even the purported ease of administration associated with targeting family status in particular does not justify laws that impose special burdens triggered by family status exclusively. Accordingly, we endorse reorienting the criminal law of family ties burdens around a conception of voluntarily assumed obligations of caregiving. This will mean that at least some family ties burdens can withstand scrutiny, but only once they are redrafted so as not to align the criminal justice system with any particularly partisan conception of what the family is and who belongs to it.

We conclude with a coda, which reflects on what we hope the book can offer to policy makers within the criminal justice system. The coda extends special attention to domestic violence issues, and serves as an occasion to think through some useful ways to tie together insights from both halves of the book.

PART ONE

Privileging Family Status
A Roadmap

THE GOAL OF THESE FIRST THREE CHAPTERS is to explore how the American criminal justice system privileges a defendant's family status such that in the absence of that defendant's family status, he would not experience the same benefit.

At the core of this inquiry stand two basic questions: when does, and when should, the state use the criminal justice apparatus to treat a defendant's family status as a basis for positive differential treatment? While answering these descriptive and normative questions separately, we characterize state policies that use a defendant's family status to improve his situation as *family ties benefits*. If we say the state extends a benefit because of family ties, we are using that term to refer to situations in which the state extends a privilege to (or forbears requiring something from) a family member *on account of his being a family member* with someone else.[1]

Chapter 1 does the descriptive work of spotting these benefits. Chapter 2 builds a normative approach to furnish a way to think synthetically about these benefits. Chapter 3 analyzes the benefits explored in Chapter 1 through the normative lens developed in Chapter 2.

ONE

A Survey of Family Ties Benefits

AS WE DEMONSTRATE IN THIS CHAPTER, there are a number of sites within the criminal justice system in which a defendant's family status is explicitly considered by judges or legislative or executive policy makers to be a basis for relieving or mitigating the extent of one's criminal liability or, alternatively, to ameliorate the conditions of one's punishment.

A. Evidentiary Privileges

In 1993, Kenneth Taylor, a New Orleans police officer, brutally beat his girlfriend over a period of many hours. He beat her with his fists, his police flashlight, and his service revolver, and several times put his gun in her mouth and threatened to pull the trigger. His girlfriend had to be hospitalized for several days to recover from her injuries. Shortly before the defendant's trial was to begin, the victim married the defendant and refused to testify against him, asserting a claim of spousal privilege.[1]

One way in which family ties permeate the trial process is through limitations on the government's ability to present all relevant evidence. Testimonial privileges are widely recognized exceptions to the common law principle that "the public has a right to every man's evidence."[2] Because the public has a compelling interest in the efficient and correct administration of its criminal justice system, even the few privileges recognized by the law are not to be "expansively construed," since they "are in derogation of the search for truth."[3] Nevertheless, the law recognizes a small class of relationships held to be inviolable by prosecutors and other litigants, allowing witnesses with relevant and probative evidence to claim a privilege not to divulge the information they know even though it could be useful in the administration of justice.[4] In a number of cases, as explained below, the defendant is empowered to block the testimony of a willing family member, usually a spouse.[5]

The testimonial privileges immediately relevant to our analysis here are the spousal privileges and other claims of intrafamilial privilege as applied in the criminal justice context. We focus here on the spousal or parent-child privilege but the analysis could be applied to other intrafamilial privileges a legislature or court might choose to create, such as between brothers and sisters, nephews and uncles, and the like.

1. Spousal Privileges

In the common law, there are two categories of spousal privileges, and all states and federal courts have adopted one or both of them in some form. They are the spousal immunity and the marital-communication privileges. The *spousal immunity* (sometimes called the adverse testimony privilege) operates in criminal cases and generally protects spouses from testifying as witnesses against their spouse-defendants during a valid marriage.[6] Different jurisdictions apply the immunity in different ways: some insist on complete disqualification of spouses; some allow a spouse-witness to testify if he or she wishes; some allow a spouse-defendant to prevent the spouse-witness from giving adverse testimony; and others allow a spouse-defendant to consent to adverse spousal testimony.[7]

The immunity evolved from the old English common law rule of complete disqualification, according to which, in the first instance, a wife was not allowed to testify against her husband.[8] Eventually, the disqualification rule became gender neutral—and was finally abolished in England in 1853.[9] The United States also recognized a disqualification rule in the federal courts until the Supreme Court refined the immunity in *Funk v. United States*,[10] which found spouses competent to testify at one another's trials—particularly *for* rather than *adverse* to one another.

The US Supreme Court once recognized very broad spousal privileges for the federal courts in *Hawkins v. United States*.[11] There, the Court held that the privilege was a "rule which bars the testimony of one spouse against the other unless both consent."[12] To justify such a powerful privilege, the Court argued that "the law should not force or encourage testimony which might alienate husband and wife, or further inflame existing domestic differences."[13] But in *Trammel v. United States*, the US Supreme Court reversed course and concluded as a matter of federal law that "[w]hen one spouse is willing to testify against the other in a criminal proceeding . . . their relationship is almost certainly in disrepair; there is probably little in the way of marital harmony for the privilege to preserve."[14] Accordingly, the Court modified the spousal immunity in federal courts, allowing it to be waived by the spouse-witness. Many states have followed a similar pattern of having once allowed the spouse-defendant to prevent the spouse-witness from adversely testifying but now "liberalizing" to allow spouse-witnesses to testify if they wish—even if the testimony is only to reduce their own potential sentences.

Unlike spousal immunity, the spousal-communication privilege survives the dissolution of a marriage and prevents a spouse from divulging any kind of confidential communication in a civil or criminal case; it is waivable only by the communicant.[15] The privilege is limited to communications (not acts) that transpire during a valid marriage—and it is deemed waived if the communications are disclosed to third parties. The spousal-communications privilege, with its roots in the common law, was recognized by the Supreme Court in *Wolfle v. United States*[16] and *Blau v. United States,*[17] and remains largely unmodified and undisturbed. According to its proponents, the privilege ensures free and frank communication between spouses; the idea is that without such protections, marriages would lack the open conversation appropriate for a confidential relationship.[18]

2. Other Intrafamilial Privileges

In contrast to the spousal privileges, federal courts tend not to provide any similar protection for a parent-child, sibling-sibling, or other intrafamilial relationship—regardless of whether testimonial immunity or a confidential communication privilege is at stake. A parent-child privilege is the one most often claimed (and discussed in the secondary literature)[19]—and most often flatly rejected by courts,[20] with a few exceptions.[21] It is true that the US Supreme Court, in *Jaffee v. Redmond,*[22] opened the door for federal courts below to recognize new privileges under the Federal Rules of Evidence, and specifically Rule 501. But federal courts have generally continued to reject the assertion of additional intrafamilial privileges.[23]

The story is somewhat more complicated at the state level. A majority of states reject intrafamilial privileges beyond spousal relations.[24] However, Idaho,[25] Connecticut,[26] Massachusetts,[27] and Minnesota[28] all have some limited form of parent-child privilege conferred by statute; additionally, New York courts have judicially carved a limited parent-child testimonial privilege.[29]

Moreover, Virginia and Texas appellate court judges have written strong dissents arguing for state recognition of a parent-child privilege.[30]

Each of the jurisdictions that recognize the privilege gives the parent-child privilege different contours. The Idaho law seems to give the privilege to parents so they do not have to testify against their children, but it does not give symmetrical treatment to children who do not want to testify against their parents.[31] Connecticut limits its grant of the privilege to "juvenile proceeding[s] in Superior Court."[32] Massachusetts limits its parent-child privilege to "unemancipated, minor child[ren], living with a parent," ruling out application of the privilege to older children.[33] Like Idaho's Law, Massachusetts' law is asymmetric, but in just the opposite way: in Massachusetts, parents can be forced to testify against their children, just not the other way around.[34] Minnesota, although supporting a symmetrical privilege, limits its grant of privilege to cases involving "minor" children, subject to waiver by parent or child.[35] In short, there is little uniformity in the states about whether the privilege exists—and if it does, exactly how and when it applies. Most states that recognize the privilege, however, recognize an exception that applies if there is a dispute between a parent and a child, a possibility of parental abuse or neglect, or a crime of violence within the household.

B. Exemptions for Family Members Harboring Fugitives

It's a choice that no parent would want to make. Kelley Thomas' 23-year-old son, Kelly Carter, escaped from a Georgia jail in April and shortly thereafter allegedly showed up at his dad's doorstep on E. Lorado Avenue. Now, Thomas has been charged with harboring a felon. What's a parent to do? It's a difficult question, even to Genesee County Prosecutor David Leyton. "The fact that he's the father was discussed by my staff, and we will take that into consideration as the case progresses," Leyton said. "It's hard to turn your back on your own flesh and blood."[36]

The story of David Kaczynski, with which we began this book, is just one of the better known examples of family members grappling with the dilemma of whether to turn a family member over to the authorities.[37] In California, a police sergeant was suspended for helping his son evade arrest after committing a series of bank robberies.[38] In Louisiana, a sheriff's deputy helped his son flee the jurisdiction, after alerting him that warrants had been issued for his arrest on child pornography charges.[39] In Minnesota, a mother arrived home just after her son had shot and killed an acquaintance in her kitchen. Instead of calling the police, the mother helped dump the body in an alley and clean up the bloody crime scene.[40] These conflicts of loyalty trigger significant media and public interest in the decisions made by the family members;[41] those who cooperate with law enforcement are often called "snitches" and are regarded as people who violate "the taboo against turning on one's family."[42]

Some of the most difficult decisions for law enforcement arise in relation to the charging decision associated with these kinds of cases. If a family member has cooperated with the primary defendant in some way, should that family member be prosecuted? Prosecutors have grappled with that question in several recent high-profile corporate crime cases, such as those involving the Enron, Adelphia, and ImClone corporations.[43] The prosecution decision is typically an easy one if the family member is involved in the crime as a principal in the classic sense of the term.[44] The difficult decisions for prosecutors lie at the margins of criminal involvement, when a family member has acted as an accessory, particularly as an accessory after the fact.[45] Typical charging options in this scenario would be obstruction of justice or hindering prosecution, harboring a fugitive, or accessory after the fact for states that retain that criminal offense.

Remarkably, in fourteen states, the prosecution of family members for harboring fugitives is not an option, regardless of the nature of the fugitive's crime.[46] These states typically exempt spouses, parents, grandparents, children, grandchildren, and siblings from prosecution for providing assistance to an offender after the commission of a crime "with the intent that the offender avoids or escapes detection, arrest, trial, or punishment."[47] An additional four states reduce liability for an immediate family member but do not exempt them from prosecution entirely.[48]

Florida's statutory exemption for family members provides an interesting example. It forbids prosecution of spouses, parents, grandparents, children, or grandchildren for helping an "offender avoid or escape detection, arrest, trial, or punishment," with one important exception.[49] The exemption does not apply if the primary offender is alleged to have committed child abuse or murder of a child under the age of eighteen, "unless the court finds that the person [claiming the exemption] is a victim of domestic violence."[50]

These statutes are significantly broader than the exemption that existed at common law, which forbade only the prosecution of a wife as an accessory but not the prosecution of a husband for aiding his felon wife or the prosecution of other family members.[51] Despite the popularity of the broader exemptions among many states, the Model Penal Code drafters rejected the inclusion of a family member exemption in its accessory provision, "in part on the ground that this is a factor that can be taken into account at sentencing."[52] The drafters also noted that "exemption rules create trial difficulties if the government bears the burden of proving that none of the specified relations exists."[53]

No federal law currently provides a family member with an exemption from prosecution.[54] A number of federal courts, however, have at least expressed sympathy with the pleas of family members charged with aiding an accused relative. For example, in *United States v. Oley*,[55] the court upheld the right of the government to charge a wife with harboring her fugitive husband. Nonetheless, the court remarked that "[i]t would undoubtedly be difficult to obtain a conviction charging wives with harboring their husbands" and that "it might be regarded as inhuman and unnatural on the part of a wife to surrender her husband to the authorities and contrary to the instincts of human beings to do so."[56]

A number of states have grappled with the constitutionality of the family exemption. For example, in upholding Florida's statute against an equal protection challenge, a Florida appeals court emphasized "society's interest in safeguarding the family unit from unnecessary fractional pressures" and applauded the legislature's decision to "confer[] immunity so that these individuals need never choose between love of family and obedience to the law."[57] The New Mexico Supreme Court, similarly, upheld its state statute against a constitutional challenge but did not engage in any sustained analysis and instead simply stated that the statute's classifications were reasonable and thus consistent with the Equal Protection Clause.[58]

More recently, United States court of Appeals for the Ninth Circuit concluded, as a matter of federal law, that it was indeed constitutional to prosecute a spouse for hiding her husband and his assets.[59] In *United States v. Hill*,[60] Patricia Hill claimed that her prosecution on charges of harboring a fugitive and accessory after the fact for helping her husband evade child support obligations to his first wife was unconstitutional because the government sought to "criminalize conduct in which she is entitled to engage under the First and Fifth Amendments to the Constitution," specifically "her rights of association, marriage, privacy, and due process."[61] Although the court noted that "basing a harboring or accessory conviction on normal and expected spousal conduct might well violate *Griswold*," it concluded that Hill's conduct in this case crossed the line past "normal spousal conduct" and into the realm of the intentional frustration of law enforcement.[62]

C. Violence Within the Family

Another important way in which the criminal justice system uses family ties to mitigate or eliminate criminal responsibility is when a defendant has selected a family member as his victim. Some of the most striking examples of the criminal justice system's preferential treatment of family relationships occur in relation to crimes committed against spouses and children by a family member. A general hesitance to intervene in family life, even to protect a family's most vulnerable members, is a deeply ingrained historical tradition in this country.[63]

In recent years, we have, of course, seen some progress in criminal justice policy,[64] such as the repeal of marital rape exemptions in many states,[65] the increased law enforcement attention and funding devoted to spousal battering,[66] and the widespread adoption of mandatory child abuse reporting statutes.[67] But the general tradition of noninterference in crime involving intrafamilial violence is hardly a historical relic.

1. Parental Discipline Defenses

In 1990, Artemio DeLeon became angry because his fourteen year-old daughter repeatedly invited friends over to her house without his permission. On May 24, when he learned his daughter had once again invited friends over, DeLeon took a belt and hit her on her legs with it for approximately ninety minutes, causing bruises that lasted for a week. He then took scissors and chopped off his daughter's waist-length hair. The Supreme Court of Hawaii reversed his conviction for abuse of a family member, concluding that his action did not rise to the level of inflicting extreme pain, mental distress, or gross degradation.[68]

Family ties recognition is quite pronounced in the context of crimes committed against children. A notable example of this kind of family ties benefit is the acceptance of the "parental discipline defense" in child abuse prosecutions. Although the contours of the defense vary somewhat among states, in general, the defense exempts parents from prosecutions for assault if the corporal punishment was used to "benefit" the child and if the nature of the punishment used was objectively reasonable.[69] This defense is available in both fatal and nonfatal cases of child abuse.[70] A recent comprehensive examination of child corporal punishment in the United States concluded that every state still uses some variant of "a justification-based defense that operates to defend parents from liability for even severe physical violence and injury to minors," as long as the parent was "engag[ed] in 'discipline'" at the time of the conduct in question.[71] The use of this special defense for parents persists even though twenty-seven states and the District of Columbia ban spanking in public schools and thirty-nine states ban spanking in day care centers.[72] Around the world, at least twenty four countries have banned or restricted spanking in the home.[73] The Model Penal Code also recognizes a variant of this defense, stating that "the use of force against another is justifiable if: (1) the actor is the parent . . . and (a) the force is used for the purpose of safeguarding or promoting the welfare of the minor, including the prevention or punishment of his misconduct."[74]

2. Manslaughter as Mitigation

Kenneth Peacock, was a long-distance trucker who "came home at the wrong time . . . [Upon return from work and being] caught in an ice storm last February while traveling from Pennsylvania to Florida, [he] got no answer when he called his wife to say he was coming home. When he arrived around midnight, his wife was in bed, naked, with another man. Mr. Peacock chased the other man away at gunpoint, and at about 4 A.M., after drinking and arguing, shot his wife in the head with a hunting rifle. He pleaded guilty to voluntary manslaughter . . . Judge Robert E. Cahill sentenced Mr. Peacock to 18 months in prison, saying that he wished he did not have to send him to prison at all, but knew he must 'to make the system honest.' 'I seriously wonder how many men married five, four years would have the strength to walk away without inflicting some corporal punishment,' said Judge Cahill, referring to the circumstances of the case."[75]

In states following the common law rule, a jury can return a verdict of manslaughter instead of murder if it finds that the defendant killed under provocation that would inflame a reasonable person to act in the heat of passion.[76] The "archetypal" common law example of "adequate provocation" turns out to be a family ties benefit: namely, if a defendant finds his or her spouse engaged in infidelity.[77] At the time of Peacock's conviction for voluntary manslaughter, Maryland followed the common law rule that "discovering one's spouse in the act of sexual intercourse with another" constitutes adequate provocation for a manslaughter charge.[78] This is a family ties benefit because the mitigation to manslaughter under common law in this context was generally available only to persons who were lawfully married in such circumstances.[79] Although the Maryland legislature later amended its manslaughter statute to preclude a spouse's adultery as a basis for mitigation,[80] the modern trend has been to expand what counts as adequate provocation.[81] So, to the extent jurisdictions have broadened the availability of the partial defense by including non-married persons,[82] then, strictly speaking, these newer laws are not family ties benefits. Indeed, under the modern version of the provocation doctrine, defendants often can reduce their liability for an intentional killing from murder to manslaughter if "the defendant claims passion because the victim left, moved the furniture out, planned a divorce, or sought a protective order."[83] Clearly, a number of those situations do not require marriage as a predicate. Therefore, whether the provocation doctrine can be strictly construed as a family ties benefit turns on whether the state in question retains traditional views of provocation or follows a more modern approach like that of the Model Penal Code.

3. Sexual Misconduct

Legislatures have also tended to privilege familial status in the context of sex offenders who victimize family members. For example, in the last dozen years or so, every state has enacted some form of scheme in which convicted sex offenders must register with the state.[84] Under some statutes, family members may receive preferential treatment because, for example, "[i]ndividuals convicted of incest are excluded from the state's online sex offender database."[85] Other defendants benefit if they commit crimes against spouses: some states continue to extend preferential statutory treatment to a sexual offender who victimizes a spouse.[86] A recent article, for example, explains these patterns in detail, concluding that "the law in more than half the states today makes it harder to convict men of sexual offenses committed against their wives," as compared to convictions for sexual offenses against an acquaintance or a stranger.[87] These benefits to defendants fall into three categories: "those that exempt spouses from sexual offenses other than forcible rape, those that maintain separate spousal sexual offense statutes, and those that impose extra requirements for the prosecution of marital rape."[88]

D. Pretrial Release

"A man released from jail to care for his seriously ill mother while awaiting sentencing for fondling a 5-year-old girl has been arrested again in connection with an attack on another child. Donald Ray Hager, 24, was arrested [. . .] after a 5-year-old boy told a school counselor about the incident that allegedly occurred on either Hager's Jan. 14 sentencing day—when he got 3 1/2 years—or the day before. . . . According to police, Hager spent part of his free time with a female friend in Dade City; the boy was the woman's son. . . . [Apparently,] Hager went into a bedroom, fondled the boy and forced him to have oral sex."[89]

Family status sometimes serves to benefit defendants in the context of pretrial release. Before a suspect is tried for his crime, the state must first decide whether to detain or release him.[90] If it releases him, the state must determine which conditions it will impose to ensure that the defendant appears at trial. If it detains the alleged offender, the state must determine what kind of access to the outside world it will allow so that the defendant can prepare his case.

Determinations of pretrial release take different forms in different jurisdictions, but they usually share at least one feature in common: decision-makers are explicitly directed to look at a suspect's family ties and responsibilities when considering whether to release the suspect, and under what conditions. For instance, the 1966 Bail Reform Act (BRA) gave federal judges guidance regarding decisions about pretrial release, expressly articulating that courts should examine the accused's family ties.[91] Many states followed suit.[92]

Additionally, some states delineate pretrial release conditions that are tied to family status. For example, in Illinois, the statute governing bail bonds informs judges that they should consider the imposition of conditions that require defendants to support his or her dependents.[93] If the victim of the crime is a member of the household, then, depending on the precise circumstances, the court may impose conditions that require the defendant to vacate the home, refrain from contact,[94] or make payments of temporary support.[95] As we explain later, the state may have its own reasons for looking at a defendant's family ties in the pretrial context.

E. Sentencing

In the case of United States v. Johnson, *two defendants were convicted of participating in the same crime and were found to have warranted the same offense level.*[96] *Nevertheless, Johnson, the defendant with caretaking*

> *responsibility of four children, received a significant downward departure from the Guidelines based on family responsibilities and was sentenced to six months' home detention and three years of supervised release; meanwhile the other defendant, Purvis, who was without children and who was also found to have played a more minor role in the scheme, received twenty-seven months in prison and two years of additional supervised release.*[97]

According to a 1999 study, over half of all state and federal prisoners have children; indeed, more than a million minor children have at least one parent incarcerated.[98] Accordingly, consideration of a defendant's family status often arises in the sentencing context. This section explores ways in which family ties influence judicial consideration about the appropriate sentence for a particular offender.

1. Federal Practice Pre-*Booker*

Prior to the US Supreme Court's 2005 ruling in *Booker v. United States*, which rendered the federal sentencing guidelines "effectively advisory,"[99] the familial ties or responsibilities of an offender were, generally speaking, accorded little significance in the federal sentencing regime.[100] Indeed, the United States Sentencing Commission (USSC) regarded "family ties and responsibilities" as a "discouraged" factor, and thus downward departures from the guidelines on such a basis were permissible only if the court found that the negative effects on the defendant's family were "present to an exceptional degree or in some other way makes the case different from the ordinary case where the factor is present."[101] That said, federal courts did make exceptions in a number of cases and even across a wide range of crimes.[102]

Courts extending such departures usually did so after determining that the offender provided an irreplaceable (or at least critical) role as caregiver to family dependents.[103] Moreover, the exceptions were typically supposed to be made only if the downward departure contemplated by the judge would suffice to "cure" the harm that would otherwise be visited upon the family member.[104] Thus, the more severe the criminal offense level of a particular offender, the less likely it would be that a departure based on family responsibilities would be granted—because, as the USSC stated in its commentary on the relevant provision,[105] the departure should be capable of resolving the problem of the irreplaceable caregiver.[106] That said, the fact that a defendant was an "irreplaceable caregiver" was not always a necessary or a sufficient explanation for federal court practice. Some courts authorized departures if a defendant was not the sole caretaker because the court recognized the extraordinary nature of the family situation and wanted to minimize disruption to the children's lives.[107] Other courts refused to extend departures even if the defendant was an irreplaceable caregiver.[108]

These family ties departures had the capacity to cause wide disparities between otherwise similarly situated offenders, as shown by the description of the *Johnson* case above. The *Johnson* case dramatizes the disparity because the offenders were codefendants in the same case—but the disparity that resulted there is at least as likely to arise across cases as within them. Moreover, some judges recognized that departures motivated by a desire to minimize the harms inflicted on innocent third-party family members conferred a windfall benefit on the defendant.[109] Those courts typically justified their decisions by reference to a cost-benefit analysis under which the costs to the innocent children were weighed against the public benefit of incarcerating the defendant; the reasoning under such analyses, however, was usually conclusory.[110]

Finally, although departures on the basis of family responsibilities in the federal context had been discouraged pre-*Booker*, district court judges retained discretion to sentence within the range prescribed by the federal Sentencing Guidelines, and in that area of discretion, judges may have considered the influence of the factor of family ties and responsibilities, although it is difficult to determine just how much influence that factor had.[111]

2. Federal Practice in the Post-*Booker* Landscape

With the Guidelines now advisory in a post-*Booker* world, federal courts have a wider berth to impose sentences outside of the ranges established by the USSC.[112] As a result, courts are awarding more downward departures than were awarded under the old regime.[113] In the post-*Booker* world, as the Ninth Circuit observed, "[c]onsideration of family responsibilities" may now be viewed as part of a defendant's "history and characteristics,"[114] and judges can assess those traits as reasons to mitigate the length of sentences.[115] Whereas various federal district court judges felt, prior to *Booker*, that the Guidelines were too harsh because they failed to give significant weight to family ties and responsibilities,[116] these judges can now invoke family ties and responsibilities as a basis for departure from the Guidelines with greater frequency and flexibility.[117] Indeed, given the US Supreme Court's recent decisions in *Gall v. United States*[118] and *Kimbrough v. United States*,[119] which affirmed the wide discretion available to district court judges, we should not be surprised to see more trial judges invoke those authorities as a basis for disagreeing with the USSC's policy decision that family ties and responsibilities should be generally discouraged as a basis for downward departures.

3. State Practices

The flexibility that now exists in the federal sentencing system regarding consideration of family ties and responsibilities also prevails in many states, especially those that endow sentencing judges with wide discretion to determine the length of a sentence. Approximately thirty-two of the nation's jurisdictions have retained an indeterminate sentencing scheme, with the remainder having some form of sentencing guidelines in place.[120] These eighteen sentencing schemes may have voluntary guidelines, presumptive guidelines, or fixed guidelines, depending on the jurisdiction, as well as variations on these themes. By contrast, the other states have traditional indeterminate sentencing schemes that extend virtually unfettered discretion to sentencing judges (or, in some cases, sentencing juries) to sentence within the statutory limits set by the legislature. In some jurisdictions, determinations about release on parole are also made under wide discretion. Generally speaking, the decision makers in those indeterminate sentencing states may consider the nature and extent of family ties or responsibilities (along with a wide range of other reasons for leniency) in setting a sentence or releasing an offender.[121] And, for the most part, they are not required to explain that a particular sentence was enhanced or reduced on account of family ties or responsibilities. Iowa's sentencing scheme, for example, simply makes "clear that sentencing is a matter of [a] trial court's broad discretion," and trial courts will be reversed there only for "abuse of that discretion,"[122] though what counts as an abuse of discretion is substantially unpredictable to the outside observer.

The multiplicity of sentencing structures in the states is mirrored by the various approaches states take in setting sentences in relation to the family ties or responsibilities of an offender. In some jurisdictions, the presence or absence of family ties and responsibilities will do little to affect one's sentence.[123] For instance, in Oklahoma's noncapital sentencing proceedings that occur before a jury, a defendant may not introduce evidence solely designed to mitigate the sentence, such as information about family ties and responsibilities.[124] Florida's sentencing scheme is somewhat similar in that it does not articulate any express exception for defendants with family ties and responsibilities; the relevant statute states that sentencing "should be neutral with respect to race, gender, and social and economic status,"[125] but it is unclear whether social status includes familial ties and responsibilities.

By contrast, in Massachusetts, the state legislature authorized the courts to consider an offender's family ties and responsibilities in setting an offender's sentence.[126] Consideration of family ties and responsibilities has also been expressly permitted in Louisiana,[127] Pennsylvania,[128] Utah,[129] Wisconsin,[130] Tennessee,[131] Arizona,[132] and North Carolina.[133] Indeed, in Louisiana, the legislature has said that a court, when deciding to suspend a sentence, should consider whether "[t]he imprisonment of the defendant would entail excessive hardship to himself or his dependents."[134] Perhaps the most unusual feature of some courts' family ties sentencing jurisprudence is that some judges will consider the absence of family ties to an area as a reason to not extend any leniency in a sentence.[135]

F. Prison Policies

Our punitive practices regularly require governments to make choices about how to address family ties and responsibilities. For example, should offenders with families be entitled to special visitation rights? Should offenders get special dispensations (like furloughs) to see family members outside of prison? Should offenders with families have priority in terms of prison placement decisions? While there is still empirical work to be done regarding how these issues are resolved among the fifty states, we examine below how these questions are resolved in the context of the federal criminal justice system. Our descriptive discussion focuses primarily on the facial family ties benefits, but we also briefly explore a few of the "informal" family ties benefits.

1. Federal Prison Visitation Policies

The Federal Bureau of Prisons' policy statement announces that "visits [by family] are an important factor in maintaining the morale of the individual offender and motivating [him] toward positive goals."[136] Although some advocates have gone so far as to argue that family visitation in prison is a "fundamental" right protected by the United States Constitution,[137] courts have not, generally, found such a "right" to exist,[138] though some courts have shown solicitude for family visitation if privileges are withheld unreasonably.[139]

In the final analysis, however, courts rarely intrude on the wide discretion afforded prison administrators in devising visitation policies.[140]

That said, most prisons make some provision for family visitation, though such policies routinely give prisoners access to visitors who are not members of the offender's family as well.[141] Accordingly, although families do not necessarily get privileged status in the realm of visitation policies (because inmates can also be visited by friends and business associates),[142] it is likely that family visitation would be greeted with greater deference than nonfamily visitors at the prison administration level, given the Federal Bureau of Prisons' general embrace of family ties as especially important for rehabilitative purposes.[143] Some jurisdictions may view furnishing families with special opportunities for visitation as important to ensure family reunification after incarceration and to avoid the termination of parental rights.[144] Indeed, some states *require* reunification services for incarcerated parents.[145]

2. Federal Prison Furlough Policies

An offender's family ties are directly implicated in prison furlough policy. Furloughs are authorized unaccompanied absences from a corrections facility during a term of incarceration and are privileges (not rights); they are explicitly sanctioned by federal law at 18 USC §§ 3622 and 4082 and are available to eligible inmates based on the severity of the crime and sentence, the inmate's release date, and other factors. According to the federal guidelines, there are many reasons that might justify furloughs, including: needing to appear in court, participation in job training, participation in "educational, social, civic, religious, and recreational activities which will facilitate release transition,"[146] and participation in the "development of release plans."[147] Moreover, furloughs are often used to facilitate the provision of healthcare, mental health, or dental services not available on site at a correctional institution.

Nevertheless, according to the Federal Bureau of Prisons' Program Statement about furloughs, "[d]ay furloughs are generally used to strengthen family ties."[148] And the policies that govern furloughs make clear that furloughs may be given so that an inmate may be "present during a crisis in the immediate family"[149] and may request a furlough "[t]o reestablish family . . . ties."[150] Families get special consideration in the distribution of furloughs—and, all else being equal, those eligible inmates with families will likely get more furloughs than those without.

3. Federal Prison Placement Policies

Notwithstanding the general preference of Congress and the USSC to discourage sentencing departures based on family ties and responsibilities, there are various ways in which the federal criminal justice system is sensitive to family ties and responsibilities when dealing with "the nature, extent, place of service, or other incidents of an appropriate sentence."[151] In this respect, a judge could, in consideration of a family's location, recommend that the Federal Bureau of Prisons place an offender closer to his family.[152] Indeed, as Judge Posner wrote in *Froehlich v. Wisconsin Department of Corrections*,[153] concerning the transfer of a female state prisoner whose children sued to keep her in Wisconsin, although such an accommodation is not constitutionally imposed on prison officials, "it may be a moral duty."[154]

Additionally, a series of programs to accommodate families in placement decisions have emerged, though often in very short supply.[155] For example, the Federal Bureau of Prisons instituted a program called Mothers and Infants Nurturing Together (MINT). Under this program, "[e]ligible women who have been sentenced to incarceration reside in a community correction setting with their infants for up to 18 months after delivery."[156] Myrna Raeder elaborates upon other similar programs put in place at the state level:

> California funded its Pregnant and Parenting Women's Alternative Sentencing Program Act and has opened two long-term community correctional facilities pursuant to California Penal Code 1174, to which women are sentenced directly, without serving time in prison, where they can reside with their minor children under six years of age for up to three years. The focus is not only on treatment of the mother, but emphasizes the development of the mother-child bond. In addition, for the last 20 years, California also has operated a Community Prison Mother Program, where inmates with less than six years remaining on their sentences may reside with their children in a residential facility where they receive comprehensive programming to enable them to better reintegrate into their communities. Small programs exist in a number of states, but currently there is no groundswell to make such programs the norm rather than the exception.[157]

4. Other Intersections of Family Status and Prison Practices

There are still other punitive policies and practices involving family status. For example, in the event of an inmate's death, the federal prison system notifies family members and allows federal chaplains to be involved with the inmate's family during the initial periods of grief.[158] The Bureau has also developed parenting programs with the objectives of promoting "family values," counteracting "negative family consequences resulting from . . . incarceration," and intending for the "institutional social environment [to] be improved through opportunities for inmates to maintain positive and sustaining contacts with their families."[159] These programs spend substantial governmental resources on developing family ties between offenders and their families.[160]

*****

As this Chapter has made clear, the criminal justice system in this country—at both the federal and state levels—provides a number of important family ties benefits.[161] Members of state-recognized families fare better throughout the system, which is designed quite self-consciously to make sure defendants with families will get benefits that others will not. In the next Chapter, we try to build a normative framework to help analyze these family ties benefits.

TWO

A Normative Framework for Family Ties Benefits

A. Some Prefatory Remarks

Our survey in chapter 1 shows how there are various areas in which the criminal justice system explicitly distributes benefits to defendants based on their family status, benefits they would not enjoy in the absence of those family ties and responsibilities. Some important issues warrant discussion as a result of this phenomenon.

First, in making any benefits available solely on the basis of a defendant's family status, the state necessarily is making express normative judgments regarding who counts as family and who does not.[1] Thus, large numbers of persons who might justifiably, in our view, see themselves as entitled to family ties benefits are excluded. Perhaps the most obvious example is families of same-sex couples, who are routinely denied treatment as equals in the provision of family ties benefits, such as the evidentiary privileges.[2] The same sense of exclusion applies to those individuals in polyamorous unions. If the state makes choices regarding families, it risks marginalizing persons who consider themselves family members but are not recognized as such by the state. In this sense, the use of the family to distribute benefits may be underinclusive.[3]

Second, even assuming one could agree on which people count as a family, reliance on that category may be overinclusive. One might have a terrible relationship with one's spouse and be eager to testify against him, but the spouse still might reap the benefits of an intrafamilial testimonial privilege.[4] To be sure, the obvious advantage of using state-recognized family lines is ease of administration. But, as we describe later on, one possible solution to the administrability challenge would be for each eligible person to designate a discrete number of persons for privileges through a registry.[5] As a general matter, because of the way in which these benefits might stand in the way of criminal justice, we are more eager to see them abolished than expanded to include more relationships. Yet if the government is committed to handing out benefits, we do not think it should do so in a way that discriminates against those in family units unrecognized by the state.

Third, the government does not always demonstrate a consistent pattern when choosing who counts as family for each of these benefits. In the federal sentencing context, for example, if the courts look to determine whether the defendant is an irreplaceable caregiver, the concept of family for determining extraordinary family ties and responsibilities appears rather broad.[6] Thus, if a grandparent or an aunt can take care of the children, then the single-parent defendant is unlikely to get a substantial departure, if at all.[7] By contrast, in other areas in which the government distributes family ties benefits, the range of relevant family members may be very narrow—for example, evidentiary privileges that do not recognize same-sex partners or much family beyond the opposite-sex spouse.[8] What this means is that family status in the criminal justice system is inconsistently defined.

Fourth, we recognize that a number of practices that confer benefits on defendants on account of their family status may also serve other purposes that in fact directly benefit the state. For example, pretrial release determinations that examine the presence of a defendant's family ties in the area may be viewed as a benefit both for the family and for the defendant lucky enough to possess meaningful family ties. Nonetheless, familial considerations may also serve as an imperfect proxy for assessing a defendant's flight risk, an issue in which the state has a clear and appropriate interest. Moreover, if a parent or caregiver is being detained, dependents may find themselves needing the state to perform care functions that would be more cheaply and more carefully executed by defendants while they await trial. Similarly, the various accommodations of the family in the context of prison administration may reflect (imperfect or indirect) choices of decision makers in the criminal justice system to advance goals such as strengthening precarious families or, alternatively, reducing recidivism or facilitating offender rehabilitation and reintegration into society.

Although we therefore acknowledge the difficulty of identifying what counts as a genuine benefit to the family (either as an institution or in particular cases), we think it remains necessary to examine more specifically those laws that benefit defendants directly on the basis of their family status. Thus, our analysis in this book focuses on those sites and not the ones in which the criminal justice system may be said to be accommodating or promoting family interests as such. Consequently, we train our attention on those sites discussed in Chapter 1 in which the criminal justice system actively chooses policies that distinctively benefit those offenders with families. This chapter shifts from the descriptive to the normative, as we consider what factors should help determine whether a particular accommodation of family interests by the criminal justice system is an appropriate policy choice.

B. The Family and the Modern State: An Ambivalent Relationship

The modern defense of using the state, its institutions, its laws, and its coercive force to support the family often rings in communitarian tones. The argument usually proceeds by drawing upon the "historical,"[9] "constitutive,"[10] or "situated"[11] selves that constitute a polity.[12] Such selves are composed of loyalties, role-responsibilities, and personal ties that are, in some very basic sense, logically and morally prior to the individual. The self, it is sometimes argued, is linked so inextricably to these group and relational affiliations that any moral system embodied by a state and its laws must appreciate, respect, and facilitate the self's authentic expression of that which creates its very identity. States must either find a way to acknowledge special associative duties flowing to family members that may conflict with and trump more general duties to people as such,[13] or risk irrelevance and illegitimacy.

Accordingly, it can be argued that states ought not to ignore the individual self's derivation from and debt to the family.[14] If the family helps define the individual, a state's administration of justice must serve its citizens by appreciating the very sources of their individuality. Privileging and giving priority to family status may be one way to have the state connect with the individuals to whom it must dispense justice. Moreover, without extending benefits and immunities that might assist the family, the state risks losing compliance from its citizens; perhaps some family ties benefits are necessary to establish and maintain the state's legitimacy. Indeed, even if the benefits seem inappropriate in the context of the criminal justice system, they might be viewed as a net benefit for inducing general compliance with a legal regime.[15]

There is yet another available justification for the state's support of the family—one that is potentially more practical and less philosophical. One could argue that because the state either cannot or will not live in accordance with what Plato's *Republic* idealizes for the Guardian class—no private families with all children being held in common[16]—the state needs to keep families together and solvent. The state can draw from the rich panoply of resources naturally furnished and expended by the family in creating good citizens. By giving families special support through family ties benefits, the state may be able to economize on expenditures that it would otherwise be forced to bear in educating its citizenry and preparing its members to contribute to the stability and flourishing of the regime. This is a crude way of thinking about the matter, to be sure. But it is one that must have a grain of truth: the state simply cannot afford or perform on its own all the services families routinely provide; consequently, such work is, in effect, subcontracted to the family—which is paid accordingly. Families will not be able to provide care services completely for free—and can rightfully demand that the state (which is parasitically living off of its successes) subsidize the hard work of helping children "take their place as responsible, self-governing members of society."[17] The state helps itself when it subcontracts cheaply the "formative project of fostering the capacities for democratic and personal self-government"[18]—and leaves it in generally reliable hands.

There is a third argument available to those wishing that the state continue to furnish families with special treatment. Some argue for an ethic of care in political and moral life more generally—and think the state can facilitate this ethic by supporting families in the right way.[19] As Deborah Stone puts it,

> Caring for each other is the most basic form of civic participation. We learn to care in families, and we enlarge our communities of concern as we mature. Caring is the essential democratic act, the prerequisite to voting, joining associations, attending meetings, holding office and all the other ways we sustain democracy. Care, the noun, requires families and workers who care, the verb. Caring, the activity, breeds caring, the attitude, and caring, the attitude, seeds caring, the politics.[20]

Accordingly, making sure the state cares for the family ensures that citizens can care for one another, the state, and politics.[21] A less "political" version of this notion states that families are instrumentally required for individuals to flourish, and states should help secure the conditions for human flourishing by facilitating the emergence and maintenance of family life.

These arguments have much to recommend them. Together, they seem persuasive and suggest that the law's recognition of family ties might be more than just irrational sentimentalism or a knee-jerk instantiation of "family values."[22] These arguments go beyond the oft-heard notion that strong families lead to a strong nation and the contention that families help furnish "civic virtue" and "social capital."[23] Although many have tried to connect familial self-government with democratic self-government,[24] the scholars we draw upon here put meat on the bones of the mottos and creeds routinely invoked. Obviously, we have not exhausted the field or comprehensively explained how these ideas cash out in particular legal contexts; instead, we have aimed only to summarize very briefly the arguments of those who grapple with the role of the family in the state's endeavor to secure the political conditions for human flourishing.

Ultimately, we find little to quarrel with when these arguments are considered at the most general level. All things being equal, we do not think states can succeed without being attentive to the way in which selves are constructed through families—and we agree that if states are going to feed on the capacity-generating benefits families confer, it is not inappropriate for families to demand some subsidization in return. Families may be labors of love, but they are full of real undercompensated labor all the same.

Nevertheless, we do not think that the arguments to support family benefits at a general level of political theory can succeed in every area of the law. For the reasons we sketch in the remainder of this Chapter, we think that the criminal justice system needs to be especially leery about distributing benefits to defendants based on the state-drawn lines of who counts as family.[25] Put briefly, the consequences of wrongly or unfairly distributing criminal penalties or causing more crime trump the reason for granting family status special force in this legal venue.

We advance four normative cost considerations; together, we think they justify a presumption—albeit a rebuttable one—against family ties benefits in the criminal justice system. The structure of the presumption we have in mind is borrowed from philosopher Sam Scheffler: "To say that these [arguments] are seen as [creating a] presumption is not to say that they can never, in the end, be outweighed by other considerations. It is merely to say that, in the first instance, they present themselves as considerations upon which one must" render judgment.[26] The normative costs we identify can be summarized briefly. Benefits based on a defendant's family ties or status historically facilitate gender hierarchy; undermine the pursuit of accuracy in the effective prosecution of the guilty and the exoneration of the innocent (thus, possibly leading to unwarranted harshness or leniency in the administration of justice); disrupt our egalitarian political commitments to treat similarly situated persons with equal concern and discriminate against those without families recognized by the state; and can tend to incentivize more crime and more *successful* crime. For these reasons, we are generally skeptical of using the criminal justice system to distribute family ties benefits absent a substantial reason and no feasible alternative means.

C. Some Normative Costs of Family Ties Benefits

1. Patriarchy and Power: Historical Perspectives

The historical context in which family ties benefits evolved reveals that many family ties benefits often served (and, in some cases, continue to serve) to perpetuate patriarchy, gender hierarchy, or domestic violence.[27] A few examples serve to make the point. In the context of evidentiary privileges, their patriarchal origins are clear: women could not testify against their husbands because they lost their claim to any separate legal existence upon entering into marriage.[28] Defendants have long enjoyed a sanctuary from the reach of the criminal law in the context of crimes against children, specifically through the parental discipline defense. The cultural assumption here has been that the "natural bonds of affection" between parent and child will protect children, an assumption sometimes validated by members of the US Supreme Court.[29] But this assumption has entailed a perverse result, namely, a culture of relative indifference toward violence in the family, particularly against children.[30] To be sure, many family ties benefits have "liberalized" over the years and now operate to prevent family members from using their special immunities to subvert prosecution for domestic violence and child abuse. Still, there can be no question that some of the policies canvassed in Chapter 1 have ignoble origins and serve to facilitate domination in the private sphere. We think that places the burden of justification on those seeking such benefits.

As recounted in Wayne Logan's illuminating article, "Criminal Law Sanctuaries," the family has long been understood as an untouchable site for criminal justice.[31] Under Roman law, the doctrine of *patria potestas* empowered fathers and husbands to dominate family life without fear of the state's interference; thus, adulterous wives could be killed without public retribution, and wives could be beaten with impunity.[32] In colonial America, Puritan courts squarely "placed family preservation ahead of physical protection of victims,"[33] allowing men to use force against wives and children for "legitimate" reasons, a limit rarely tested out of reluctance to disturb the privacy of family life.[34] Law enforcement interest in family violence then waxed and waned over the generations, with periods of activism butting up against a deep-rooted tradition of noninterference in the affairs of a family.[35]

Over time, wife beating was officially banned,[36] but like so much else, the law on the books eclipsed life on the streets, as the act of wife beating was often viewed as a nonevent from the eyes of the state—it was, as one scholar perhaps cynically called it, the "rule of love."[37] Unsurprisingly, children also suffered under the *de facto* sanctuary from the reach of criminal law.[38] Needless to say, there was still great difficulty in prosecuting and punishing marital rape.[39]

In the 1970s, matters improved at least in part as a result of greater sensitivity to the concerns raised by feminists. Police officers, for instance, were no longer urged or instructed to play the role of "mediator" or "peacemaker" when called to a domestic disturbance; they could play their normal role of enforcer of the criminal law.[40] Those developments, of course, led to an expansion of the debate about how the criminal justice system can best serve the individual members of a family—for example, some scholars contest whether that "normal" role is a desirable role in the family context for fear that the implementation of "no-drop" or "shall-arrest" policies[41] might end up alienating victims from a criminal justice system that is indifferent to or dismissive of their particular interests.[42]

But the underlying problem remains. Notwithstanding some advances in prosecution norms for domestic violence, the criminal law system still exhibits a great reluctance to interfere in the private life of the family. Scholars, such as Logan, point to several examples of this ongoing phenomenon: elder abuse,[43] tolerance of domestic violence in homosexual relationships,[44] the continued difficulty of prosecuting marital rape,[45] and the free use of corporal punishment against children.[46] Moreover, the scourge of domestic violence continues at astonishingly high levels.[47] The effects of these willful silences and deferential nods to defendants using violence in the family context have been, in Logan's words, an unrelenting "form of criminal predations, perpetrated in the shadow of public law."[48]

The historical context briefly sketched above only partly underwrites our presumption of skepticism.[49] Our argument reaches well beyond the fear that family ties benefits facilitate the perpetuation of gender hierarchy and domestic violence—though these reasons alone might suffice to reorient our doctrines and practices.

2. Accuracy and Justice

Family ties benefits in the criminal justice system also endanger the accurate and just imposition of punishment. As we described earlier, various jurisdictions afford defendants special privileges that allow them to bar others from testifying at trial or from providing other assistance to law enforcement, even though the latter have information critical to the accurate prosecution of the defendants or the exoneration of others.[50] At bottom, there are places where truth and family loyalty conflict, and the state should not knowingly afford defendants family ties benefits or exemptions from duties borne by other members of society simply because of familial status. If innocent people mistakenly sit in prison (or guilty people escape prosecution altogether) as a result of these benefits, then our commitment to the accurate distribution of justice is undermined at an intolerable cost.

To be sure, we recognize that our concern about family ties benefits also has an empirical component. For one thing, in defense of the testimonial privileges, the state can argue that it will be effectively inviting perjury without them—and that no "truth" benefit can be conferred by forcing people to testify against their better judgment to maintain the secrets of a loved one against state intrusion.[51] Although we have found no empirical evidence to support the thesis that family members would lie under oath if forced to testify against a loved one (in sufficient numbers to undermine the quest for truth in criminal trials), there is some plausible appeal to the suggestion. Additionally, it may turn out that having the privilege deters future crime because the communication of the information to the spouse may have the salutary effect of prompting the spouse to encourage the defendant to forbear from further crime. (Of course, if it turns out that this is empirically grounded, then the privilege or immunity should be limited to communications regarding future conduct, not past conduct.)

Similarly, a necessary assumption at work in the exemption for family members' harboring fugitives is that the temptation to commit the crime of harboring is overwhelming in certain contexts. A parent would have a very difficult time turning away a child at the door precisely at a moment of extreme vulnerability. Some might think that prudence demands that we exempt those family members who are, in this situation, undeterrable.[52] Others might think leniency is appropriate for those unwilling to turn their closest relatives away in a time of desperate need. Indeed, some jurisdictions seem to acknowledge that family members have reduced culpability; accordingly, some states do not immunize family members but charge them with a lesser crime.

Our reaction to these efforts to excuse family members' commission of a crime (perjury and harboring) is the same: the criminal law is a separate sphere of justice, with its own primary values, among which are the protection of citizens and the accurate and fair prosecution of those who have endangered public safety and contravened the laws passed to protect that interest in security.[53] Although it cannot be denied that humans are frail and fallible—particularly when it comes to family loyalty—the state simply cannot legitimize its acceptance of perjury and obstruction by refusing to prosecute individuals who engage in these practices. Moreover, those who think it is unattractive to make a parent testify against a child should undertake a thought experiment: imagine that, because of a parent's failure to testify against her child, another person sits wrongfully on death row, a person who would otherwise be exonerated. That wrongfully convicted person may also have a family whose interests in their child's life should be protected. The fact that it appears to be only a distant and disembodied government that loses access to evidence should not obscure the fact that the state is acting on behalf of potential future victims, past victims, and family members of those who stand wrongfully accused. The state must fairly and effectively balance its solicitousness of the defendant and his or her family against its need to protect others in society.

There are certainly other aspects of the criminal justice system that similarly undermine the quest for accuracy, such as the exclusionary rule associated with evidence procured in violation of the Fourth Amendment.[54] But we do not believe the existence of such practices necessarily undermines our argument here. The exclusionary rule, for example, vindicates another critical interest of our system of criminal justice—the constitutional prohibition against unreasonable searches and seizures by state actors .[55] In contrast, we do not think the interest typically invoked in defending those family ties benefits that impede accurate punishment or exoneration—encouraging close familial relationships—constitutes sufficient reason for the state to deny our commitment to the truth-seeking function of the criminal justice system.

3. Equality

Family ties benefits not only impede the accurate and just administration of criminal penalties, but also threaten basic commitments to equality under law. Thus, our third difficulty with family ties benefits is that they can disrupt norms of equality.[56] Criminal law investigation and prosecution should treat citizens' interests with equal concern, without fear or favor based on morally arbitrary characteristics like family status. The extension of special privileges to persons simply because of their family situation (if that proxy bears no real relationship to a legitimate criminal justice goal) bears an onus of justification, especially because any benefits that accrue to those who have specially recognized family ties will be unavailable to those who lack such family ties. Whether this constitutes pernicious or permissible discrimination may be subject to some debate, but, for reasons we elaborate on in Chapter 3, we think it is the former in all but the rarest of circumstances.

We do not think it especially controversial to draw upon a principle of equality under the law. This basic egalitarian commitment underwrites not only our governing documents and institutions, but it is a prerequisite for a legitimate system of criminal justice as well. Accordingly, benefits and special treatment that emerge from leniency on account of family status are, generally speaking, unattractive.[57] Why should this be?

At one level of abstraction, if a criminal derogates from the democratically derived codes of proper conduct, he indicates a superiority that claims he is not bound by the rules that bind others. Society builds credible criminal justice systems to diminish the plausibility of those claims of superiority, and by its attempt to punish offenses, the criminal justice system endeavors to make clear that no one is superior to the law or to any other member of society. Family ties benefits can threaten the very basic equality principle undergirding our constitutional democracy, because, in some instances, they allow the offender to maintain a claim of superiority and to point to that unanswered wrongdoing as evidence of that superiority.[58] This is especially problematic when the judiciary confers this family ties benefit on defendants without legislative imprimatur. Because at least part of the justification for the state's administration of criminal justice is that it must—under the principle of equality—try to diminish the offender's claim of superiority, the state fails part of its essential purpose in having a criminal justice system when it distributes benefits to some offenders merely because of their family status.[59] Having a family, while "constitutively" relevant to an individual's identity, is typically morally unrelated to the offender's claim of superiority represented by the crime. Accordingly, allowing leniency based on family ties subverts the institutional task of recalibrating the messages of equal worth undergirding the legitimate institutions of criminal justice.[60]

The principle of equality also has a more straightforward valence. Unjustified disparities in sentence disposition or duration contribute to the perception of the *illegitimacy* of the criminal justice system. To illustrate, imagine that one physically attacks one's neighbor and that such attacks are illegal. If the state, in its ordinary course of business, knowingly did nothing in the face of this crime, its inaction could be read to express two social facts. The first fact is an indifference to the legal rights of its citizens, particularly to the security of their persons and property; and the second is the condescending assertion to the offender that his actions will not be taken seriously by the state. If the state makes an effort to investigate, prosecute, and punish the crime, by contrast, the message is that one will be held accountable for one's unlawful actions. It also sends a signal to one's fellow citizens that their legal rights are being vindicated by the state.[61]

These various expressions and communications of care and concern are significantly more difficult to articulate if the state must address many offenders, many victims, and many citizens. These difficulties are best alleviated if institutions exhibit fidelity to rule of law values, under which like cases are treated alike, in accordance with legal norms that are known or knowable to the offender. In a situation in which we address two similarly situated offenders and an unjustified disparity results, these departures from rule of law values will invariably trigger demoralization, resentment, and, perhaps in some cases, outrage and violence. Thus, in light of the risks associated with disparity—and the cuts in the moral fabric of impartial justice such disparities create—the principle of equality should be a lodestar guiding our collective actions in the criminal justice system.

It goes without saying that invoking the principle of equality does not mean mindlessly giving every offender the same punitive response. Some level of granular analysis is required to sort cases appropriately—only the "like" should be treated alike. But once we have devised reasonable bases for distinguishing among classes of offenses and offenders, only compelling reasons and narrow options should suffice to displace the outcome that would have been otherwise obtained in light of the classification scheme that has been established through democratic institutions.[62]

That said, we recognize that incarceration may wreak havoc on innocent third parties, many of whom are wholly innocent family members.[63] But our concern for minimizing harms to innocent third parties should not necessarily be tethered to the proof of a family relationship; it is both over- and underinclusive to limit benefits only to those individuals in a state-sanctioned family unit. Moreover, as we explain later, there may be more broad-based ways to minimize these harms without actually extending unfair sentencing discounts to someone simply because that person is a father or mother, or son or daughter. Still, to the extent that rehabilitative aims are pursued through our corrections systems, we can imagine sites within the criminal justice system in which the presumption is overcome by distributing benefits in a manner that is neutral to family status but still pays close attention to the obligations of those with unique caregiving roles.

4. Do Family Ties Benefits Incentivize More Crime?

Finally, we note that some family ties benefits can have the unwanted effect of incentivizing more criminal activity—and more successful criminal activity to boot. To the extent that the law effectively signals to the public that family membership confers special benefits, some family ties benefits will encourage family members to keep their criminal enterprises in the family or to actively solicit help from other family members because, after all, they can assist without fear of punishment. Jeremy Bentham disfavored the notion of spousal privilege precisely because "it secures, to every man, one safe and unquestionable and ever ready accomplice for every imaginable crime"[64]—and facilitates criminals converting their own castles into "a den of thieves."[65] Today, many jurisdictions have acknowledged the need for a joint spousal criminal activity exception, precisely to reduce the likelihood of the den of thieves arising in the castle. Moreover, if sentencing policies serve to create a nonincarcerable (or less carcerable) class of persons because these persons are "irreplaceable caregivers," then those persons will seek out criminal endeavor or be, other things being equal, more sought after by others to serve in criminal enterprises.

In short, we fear that family ties benefits will help fortify a sanctuary from criminal law, and thus encourage the enlistment of family members into criminal enterprises of all sorts, whether fraud or murder, embezzlement, or racketeering.[66] With respect to sentencing, we should be especially anxious, for as Judge Kleinfeld noted, "[n]o class of persons can be immunized from imprisonment without assisting recruitment for criminal enterprises by providing an incarceration-proof labor force."[67] This point has been reiterated by other appellate courts construing sentencing departures based on family responsibilities,[68] as well as by members of other branches of government.[69] We note that we have, thus far, found little empirical research examining this hypothesis; it remains fertile ground for future research.[70]

D. Scrutiny of Family Ties Benefits: A Normative Framework for the Presumption

In light of these four distinct normative concerns, we think a presumption against family ties benefits is warranted when considering a potential policy in the criminal justice system that affects family life, even though not every family ties benefit triggers all of these concerns.[71] Thus, the bare proposal of a benefit should not be categorically rejected under this framework—it just means the benefit should undergo scrutiny.

This scrutiny requires inquiry into several matters. First, to what extent does the particular family ties benefit contribute to patriarchy, inaccuracy, inequality, or risk of heightened crime, collusion, or complicity? If the family ties benefit does not incur one of these normative costs, then it may be appropriate to extend it, especially if the interest underlying the family ties benefit is substantially beneficial (and substantially achievable through the benefit). Usually, though, we find that the bare use of family status as a basis to distribute a benefit to the defendant is one that triggers equality and discrimination concerns. Typically, these concerns can be resolved by more careful drafting such that the distribution of the benefit occurs in a way that is neutral to family status while still achieving its underlying goal. When that is the case, there is good reason to distribute the benefit more broadly than would be done under the rubric of *family status* currently recognized by most states.

On the other hand, if the family ties benefit triggers normative costs that cannot be ameliorated through mere redrafting into family-neutral terms, then, at that point, we think the state must have a compelling or heightened interest that vindicates the use of the family ties benefit (the purpose test) and the state must have adopted narrowly tailored means to achieve that purpose. A good example might be something like sentencing discounts for defendants with young children. This is a rather typical family ties benefit, but we think the policy associated with such benefits can be more granularly administered, as we discuss in the context of time-deferred sentencing, such that it might apply to more people who could benefit from it but in a way that does not create the same normative costs. By contrast, if the benefit in question affirmatively *impedes* the state's interest in ensuring the safety of vulnerable persons, such as the continued vitality of the parental discipline defense, which has been used to legitimate what would otherwise be criminal assaults upon one's children, it should be soundly rejected.

In other words, an especially weighty public interest would be needed to justify the family ties benefit, along with an inquiry into whether alternative measures were available to promote that interest without triggering or increasing the normative costs we identify. Moreover, we would still want to ensure that the underlying public interest that is being vindicated is distributed in a way that is not predicated on family status alone, but rather on voluntarily assumed obligations of caregiving. To be sure, our proposed method of scrutiny will not resolve all questions; we will inevitably have disputes about the strength of competing claims. But this method will help us think more clearly about the challenge of family ties in criminal justice.

THREE

Applying the Framework to Family Ties Benefits

IN THIS CHAPTER, we apply the normative framework to a number of the family ties benefits discussed in Chapter 1. Using the framework developed in Chapter 2, we examine how some of the benefits from Chapter 1 fare under our normative approach. Thus, we briefly explore how evidentiary privileges, harboring fugitive exemptions, violence within the family, pretrial release, sentencing, and prison practices should be analyzed in light of our normative framework. In most cases, our framework adds new insights into how policymakers, judges, and citizens should think about family ties benefits. In the case of any benefit, there are multiple considerations that will be relevant to policymakers beyond our presumptions and analyses. But we are hopeful that our framework can shed new light on these benefits, some of which are very much contested while others have escaped any substantial analysis. As we will show, in many cases, our analysis recommends eliminating the benefit.

Other benefits, by contrast, such as sensitivity in assigning prisoners to specific prison locations, survive scrutiny because there are compelling state interests that are properly vindicated or because the benefits trigger such minimal normative costs that the presumption against family ties benefits should be rebutted. However, even in these situations, we think there should be some effort to distribute the benefits in terms that are neutral to family status when possible. Doing so, at the very least, can remove some of the inherent gender and heteronormative biases that the benefits display. We also discuss how some benefits can succeed by being retailored through alternative means. In the section addressing sentencing, for instance, we discuss the case of the irreplaceable caregiver who is asking for a sentencing discount. In this connection, we discuss the use of "time-deferred sentencing,"[1] as well as the use of programs that redound to the benefit of family members, but not exclusively to them and not on account of their status as family members. This final insight paves the way for the second part of the book, in which we are able to see protecting voluntary caregiving relationships as the center of the family ties burdens we discover; we are also able to start the project of redesigning all family ties intersections with the criminal justice system in family-neutral terms, focusing more on function than status. But that effort, which preoccupies us much more pointedly in the second part of the book, is also very useful in some of the cases of family ties benefits that we explore here. Ultimately, however, because inaccuracy, crime creation, inequality, and patriarchy are such severe costs of family ties benefits in the bulk of cases, we can only support, promote, and vindicate privileging family status in the rarest of cases of family ties benefits.

A. Evidentiary Privileges

1. Competing Assessments of Familial Privileges

Views about the marital privileges are, unsurprisingly, mixed. These privileges are ostensibly justified not only because they are rooted in the common law but because they are presumed to have a persuasive rationale. For instance, the spousal immunity "provides social benefits by preventing marital discord,"[2] and the marital-communications privilege is said to "foster[] openness between spouses by ensuring that none of their confidences will be revealed in court."[3] In short, "[t]he basic reason the law has refused to pit wife against husband or husband against wife in a trial where life or liberty is at stake [is] a belief that such a policy [is] necessary to foster family peace, not only for the benefit of husband, wife and children, but for the benefit of the public as well."[4]

But not all agree that the spousal privileges are proper exceptions to the hoary rule that every man's evidence should be available in the administration of justice. In recent years, the spousal immunity has come under more serious fire from commentators than the marital-communication privilege, which on its face just looks like other confidential communication privileges, such as the attorney-client and psychotherapist-patient privileges.[5] Still others think that spousal immunity makes sense if we really care about protecting family harmony—and that we do not need the marital-communication privilege because people will trust their spouses naturally and are usually indifferent to legal entitlements to privileges. Moreover, once the marriage dissolves, the justification of "keeping the family together" dissolves with it—and a marital-communications privilege certainly should not outlive the marriage (as it currently does in some of the jurisdictions that recognize it).[6] Finally, some oppose the immunity because, in practice, it operates in a gendered manner: "[t]he plain fact is that . . . the adverse testimony privilege operates largely to prevent wives from testifying against their husbands . . . [and] reinforce[s] a traditional ethic of self-sacrifice for women within marriage."[7] The detractors aside, the marital privileges enjoy widespread support in the nation's courts and state legislatures.[8]

With respect to broader intrafamilial privileges, there are several arguments offered by their proponents. Proponents argue that "[f]orced disclosure of confidential communications between children and parents not only destroys the trust between parent and child necessary to foster open communication, it pits a parent against a child in a court of law."[9] As the *In re Agosto* court put it, "[t]o damage the parent-child relationship would result in damage to the child's relationship to society as a whole."[10] Advocates routinely cite the United States Supreme Court's decision in *Wisconsin v. Yoder*, which stressed that "[t]he history and culture of Western civilization reflect a strong tradition of parental concern for the nurture and upbringing of their children."[11] The importance of this relationship is the reason that society seeks to foster open communication between parents and children.[12] In short, the "arguments in favor of adoption of the parent-child privilege center around the importance of loyalty . . . inherent to the [] relationship."[13] This is generally known as the "preservation of the family" argument.[14]

Another related argument relies upon the "cruel trilemma" presumably imposed upon subpoenaed family members who must "either (1) testify truthfully and condemn the accused relative, (2) testify falsely and commit perjury, or (3) refuse to testify and risk contempt."[15] As *In re Agosto* found, in putting witnesses in this position, "the law would not merely be inviting perjury, but perhaps even forcing it."[16] This argument emphasizes not only that we put family members in an awkward position but that the search for truth itself will be hampered because in our zealous pursuit of it, we are inviting falsified testimony that will adulterate the system more than it will foster the system's integrity. There is also the possibility, as mentioned earlier, that the extension of these privileges works in favor of reducing crime; a spouse with an adverse testimonial immunity may decide to talk to his wife (because he knows she cannot testify against him), and during that talk, she may persuade him to desist from future crimes.

More generally, advocates of the expansion of intrafamilial privileges beyond the spousal privileges argue, by analogy, to other privileges already recognized in the courts and by legislatures. The professional privileges are generally thought to encourage the free flow of information in socially valuable relationships in which trust is required for the success of the relationship.[17] Similarly, the marital privilege supposedly serves the function of preserving harmony and fostering openness in socially valuable relationships. Proponents of other intrafamilial privileges argue by analogy to other relationships of trust to reinforce their case.[18] A final strategy proponents (and adopting courts) have drawn upon is basing the extended privilege in the constitutionally recognized right to privacy.[19]

In response to those who favor extending intrafamilial privileges, critics (including judges on many federal and state courts) argue that there is no case law to support such a new privilege; that privileges are meant to be granted very sparingly and narrowly for they are in derogation of the search for truth; that further intrafamilial privileges do not pass the Wigmore Test[20]; and that Congress may, if it wishes, furnish such a privilege if there is a true need for it.[21] More basically, critics "commonly assert that people typically know little or nothing about their privilege[s] and that, even if they did, the knowledge would rarely alter their communicative behavior."[22] In short, intrafamilial privileges are very unlikely to incentivize people to talk with their families if they are not otherwise inclined to do so. As unseemly as it may be to force people to testify against their family members, it may just be the cost of doing justice.

2. The Framework's Application to Evidentiary Privileges

We think our normative framework offers a different perspective on intrafamilial privileges, one that has heretofore often been overlooked: that family ties generally ought not to be exalted or privileged in the administration of criminal justice. Accordingly, not only should courts and legislatures reject the parent-child and more attenuated intrafamilial testimonial privileges, but they should also revisit the marital privileges, which enjoy widespread support. In short, it is our view that the family neither needs nor deserves any special protection when the smooth and fair administration of criminal justice is at stake. Just as our society values friendship as a very beneficial social relationship of trust but fails to entrust friends with testimonial privileges,[23] we believe that the family can sustain itself without special immunity from the criminal justice system. We take no position here, however, on the ongoing debates about whether there should be intrafamilial privileges in the civil context.[24] But because the intrafamilial evidentiary privileges implicate our four normative considerations—and all four of them, no less—we think such benefits are inappropriate and should therefore be abandoned.

As we have already recounted, the testimonial privileges have an undeniably patriarchal lineage. Based on an old English common law rule of complete disqualification in which a wife was not allowed to testify against her husband,[25] the testimonial privileges have roots that would offend our first normative consideration. Indeed, at common law, women were not considered to be competent witnesses at all. Even those who contest the disqualification theory of the derivation of the privileges and assume that the privileges developed from a theory of "petit treason" against the head of a household could not deny that the protection of the "head of a household" traditionally protected men.[26] And although the testimonial privileges have been modernized in most places to defang their patriarchal origins,[27] they continue to operate in a male-friendly manner: men commit more crime, so it will benefit men more often if their spouses (or mothers or sisters) are prevented from testifying against them. As Wayne Logan writes, "[e]videntiary law . . . continues to betray an age-old reluctance to interfere; the spousal privilege, for instance, prohibits the government from compelling the testimony of a battered spouse, should prosecution ensue."[28] This is especially disconcerting in the wake of *Crawford v. Washington*, which will only further exacerbate the use of spousal privileges to protect male domination in the household.[29]

Even bracketing the gendered roots and effects of the intrafamilial testimonial privileges that give us pause, our second normative consideration is also implicated. Testimonial privileges are very much exceptions to the common law principle that "the public has a right to every man's evidence."[30] Because the public has a compelling interest in the efficient and correct administration of its criminal justice system, the law should not lightly create exceptions to the rule that people must testify truthfully before legal tribunals. Even the few privileges recognized by the law are not to be "expansively construed" because they "are in derogation of the search for truth."[31] Privileges that facilitate the exclusion of relevant evidence from a fact finder seriously impede the truth-seeking function of the trials, which hampers both the effective prosecution of the guilty and the exoneration of the innocent. These privileges matter not only at trial, but also beforehand, because their availability at trial casts a shadow over plea-bargaining between the state and the defense lawyer. Without other independent evidence, a prosecutor will be more likely to drop a case against a potential defendant if the prosecutor knows a husband can block the testimony of, or revelations about communications to, his wife.

We acknowledge, of course, the speculative concern that the privileges may help prevent perjured testimony from polluting the trial. Perhaps the privileges function to prevent family members from lying on the stand—a result that may, after all, serve the truth. To the extent that any credible empirical evidence would bear out such a claim, we would reconsider our conclusions about the benefit's implication for the normative consideration of accuracy. We also recognize the empirical possibility that the privileges may have a deterrent effect on crime if spouses communicate intentions to commit future crime and are subsequently able to dissuade each other from committing that future crime.[32] We have not seen empirical evidence to support this possibility, however, and we suspect such instances are rare.

Third, there is a basic inequity built into intrafamilial testimonial privileges. Although this inequity is not as obvious as the central case in which an offender gets differential treatment in a sentence on account of his family ties, the normative consideration of equality is implicated nevertheless; those with spouses (rather than friends or same-sex partners) get to share the details of their crimes with a loved one without consequence. This may have a cathartic effect for offenders, rendering an ultimate confession to the police less likely. And it may enable more intimacy to flourish in state-sanctioned families in a way that will be discouraged in less traditional family structures, though as we suggested earlier, we are uncertain about how responsive many people are to the signals or incentives created by these laws in particular.

More importantly, this particular benefit creates a class of persons, who might otherwise have extremely useful information about an offender, immune from questioning at trial. This allows the offender to maintain a sense of superiority—both over his household and over the polity, whose interests in vindicating justice play second fiddle to the protection of the sanctity of his family. This is unfair to the state and unfair to victims whose rights can be vindicated only if the police and prosecution can do their jobs effectively. Creating rules that prevent the police and the prosecution from learning the truth are counterproductive to the tasks of criminal justice. Although one can sympathize with the difficulty of testifying against a family member, we suspect that thoughtful citizens would not want to live in a regime with such privileges for family members when they realize that a perpetrator of crimes is being shielded from justice by family members who are immune from questioning on the witness stand.

Finally, our last normative consideration is also implicated by the testimonial privileges. To the extent that defendants receive signals from the evidentiary privileges,[33] the privileges furnish incentives to keep criminal conspiracies within the family. Spouses are more likely to recruit each other into criminal activity because they know they can shield their communications with their spouse later on. The law needs tools to disrupt conspiracy and make it less efficacious, not more so. A better system would realize that the law should aim at "help[ing to] destabilize trust within the conspiracy, cue the defection of conspirators, and permit law enforcement to extract more information from them."[34] Unsurprisingly, some jurisdictions have adopted a joint-spousal-criminal-activity exception to the marital-communications privileges.[35] Obviously, in lieu of a full-scale abandonment of the privileges, we welcome at least this development.

But in light of the troublesome normative costs in the context of evidentiary privileges, we think there is a good basis to eliminate these privileges. We do not see any compelling state interests that could render these privileges appropriate or acceptable, unless our empirical concerns regarding perjury and deterrence were proven demonstrably.[36] Moreover, although we recognize that some argue that familial interests are prepolitical or prelegal in some sense, such that the law needs to step aside in the face of family loyalties (rendering family interests to be sufficient to override the maxim that the public is entitled to every man's evidence), we are not persuaded. At least as a matter of fit with other aspects of the legal landscape, we note the state's extensive regulation of family law; thus, it is hard to take this argument seriously. Marriage itself is an undeniably legal relation—and it betrays common sense to think a general respect for the private sphere of the family should be sufficient to overcome our normative framework, which itself derives from the task of trying to assess whether family ties benefits are appropriate in the criminal justice system. In this case, to say that family ties should override our normative framework is only to disagree that our normative framework establishes a presumption against family ties benefits in the criminal justice context in the first place. When the benefits are disbursed to reinforce inequality, gender bias, patriarchy, and inaccuracy in the criminal justice system, the costs are too great to bear.

Moreover, those who wish to support this family ties benefit (and others like it) as a way of generally supporting an important social institution of caregiving have an extra step of justificatory work to do that we think cannot be done successfully—one must defend not only the general idea that it would be nice for the law to protect the family from some legal incursions but also the more specific proposition that the law must protect families *in the context of criminal justice*, a site where we think the law cannot afford this type of benefit. Too much is at stake when the lives and liberties of men and women are held in the balance.

That said, we can imagine that jurisdictions might be interested in narrower options than the ones we endorse. For instance, Maryland has a two-strikes policy regarding the invocation of the privileges in courts.[37] Alternatively, jurisdictions might want to limit the application of the privilege to cases involving a discrete set of crimes, leaving violent or more serious felonies outside the scope of the privilege (or even other benefits, such as the exemptions and defenses that are based on family status). A third strategy might be to limit the privilege to cover communications regarding only future conduct, not past conduct.

We cannot, of course, deny that our catalogue of normative considerations might seem to condemn other testimonial privileges. For example, the attorney-client and psychotherapist-patient privileges might result in prosecutors and police having less information to pursue justice. Although these privileges have no especially ignoble histories, they are, at a general level, in derogation of the search for truth and have the potential to implicate an equality norm.

Still, we think the normative considerations we have highlighted condemn intrafamilial privileges in ways different and more substantial. In the first place, we think other testimonial privileges do not fare as badly through our normative framework: they neither offend our first consideration, nor do they reasonably trigger substantial concerns under the fourth consideration. On the contrary, the lawyer-client privilege, for example, can help *prevent* crime by facilitating communications with potential offenders to steer them away from unlawful conduct. Moreover, even our second normative consideration—accuracy—does not clearly disfavor the lawyer-client privilege. The lawyer-client privilege substantially contributes to the vindication of our adversarial system of justice. By giving the defendant a true and zealous advocate who is bound by a duty of confidentiality to him, we give the defendant a fighting chance to use the criminal justice system to prove his innocence; this ultimately contributes to the project of accuracy. We do not often worry that psychotherapists and lawyers are actually going to become co-conspirators (though, of course, such results are not unheard of). Moreover, our "crime-creation" prong fares better with the lawyer-client privilege and the psychotherapist-patient privilege than it does with the marital privilege: some professionals in some jurisdictions might be required to reveal when their client threatens a third party with substantial harm or a crime. Not so with the marital privilege.

Finally, while one can make the claim that other testimonial privileges also fail our normative framework, we would not be the first to notice that some of the privileges rest on less-than-firm footing: a number of scholars have argued that, to the extent the privileges have value, the value extends only to advice regarding prospective behavior—not past behavior.[38] In any case, to the extent that the other privileges pursue compelling state interests that *are* appropriate in the criminal justice sphere, we acknowledge that our normative framework is not the final word on whether a benefit is acceptable. Other testimonial privileges may be justifiable by countervailing interests that override the considerations outlined above.

B. Exemptions for Family Members Harboring Fugitives

As discussed in Chapter 1, another way in which states favor family relationships in a facial manner is by exempting family members from prosecution. Eighteen states currently exempt immediate family members from prosecution for harboring a fugitive or reduce their potential liability.[39] What are the rationales offered for these family exemptions? First, perhaps, "it is unrealistic to expect persons to be deterred [by the possibility of criminal prosecution] from giving aid to their close relatives."[40] Criminal punishment is therefore unwarranted as a deterrent because it would be ineffective in any event. Second, perhaps such statutes are "an acknowledgement of human frailty."[41] Under this view, legislatures have simply recognized that the bonds of familial love will inevitably trump any perceived obligation to the state. A third rationale suggests the exemption vindicates "society's interest in safeguarding the family unit from unnecessary fractional pressures."[42]

Analyzing these statutes under the framework of our four normative considerations, we conclude that the family exemption is misguided and should therefore be soundly rejected by state legislatures. The exemptions obviously contribute to a fundamental inequity: close friends who provide assistance face prosecution, while family members do not. Further, like the evidentiary privileges, these exemptions have patriarchal origins and may serve to shield from prosecution those who commit crimes in the home. The focus of these exemptions at common law was to exempt wives from liability for following their "duty" by shielding their husbands. To be sure, these statutes have now become gender neutral by extending their protection to other immediate family members, so perhaps they should not be invalidated on the basis of their patriarchal roots alone. But these are not our strongest normative arguments; we therefore turn to our two remaining considerations.

In terms of accuracy, these exemptions do a different kind of mischief than threatening our ability to sort the guilty from the innocent; they facilitate a guilty person's escape from punishment entirely. Allowing an individual to obstruct justice by hiding a family member obviously frustrates "the essential government functions of locating and apprehending criminals."[43] Moreover, this immunity is granted without regard to the heinousness of the underlying crime—the exemption is granted whether the fugitive is a forger or a murderer. The statutes sweep with too broad a brush in another regard as well—they protect those family members who might never have previously enjoyed a meaningful relationship with the primary offender, but simply came to the aid of a relative when asked for assistance after the commission of a crime.[44] Moreover, the laws are written only to protect those in traditional state-sanctioned familial units. It is also difficult to accept that it is the government's decision to prosecute that creates significant stresses upon the family; rather, the responsibility for that would seem to lie squarely on the shoulders of the family member who decided to enlist his relatives to assist him in his illegal activities.

Finally, like the testimonial privileges, these statutory exemptions create perverse incentives. In a state with a family exemption, there is no reason for a defendant to commit a crime unilaterally; he has every incentive to enlist close family members to help him conceal evidence and hide from the authorities because those family members face no criminal consequences for their actions. Why should we create an incentive for a defendant to recruit accomplices and thereby increase the chances of success for his criminal venture? As the Supreme Court recognized forty years ago:

> [C]ollective criminal agreement—partnership in crime—presents a greater potential threat to the public than individual delicts. Concerted action both increases the likelihood that the criminal object will be successfully attained and decreases the probability that the individuals involved will depart from their path of criminality. Group association for criminal purposes often, if not normally, makes possible the attainment of ends more complex than those which one criminal could accomplish.[45]

Because family exemptions pose such significant costs in terms of preventing the government from punishing criminal activity and creating incentives for conspiratorial activity, we believe our presumption against such benefits is clearly triggered. Further, these benefits provide no substantial benefit to the criminal justice system. We reject the notion that allowing siblings to dispose of murder weapons for one another is an essential component of family harmony. Even if we were to concede the point that not every brother would be deterred by the threat of criminal punishment from hiding a murder weapon for his beloved sibling, it might still be the case that the possibility of punishment would deter the killer from making the request in the first instance.

C. Violence Within the Family

In demonstrating how our normative framework would apply in the context of familial status defenses, we have chosen to focus here on the example of the parental discipline defense as it is used in child abuse prosecutions. Parents have employed corporal punishment to discipline children and mold their characters for centuries with minimal interference from the state.[46] The historical origins of the tradition of noninterference in matters of family violence, and its obviously troubling patriarchal origins, have been well documented.[47] We choose here to focus on the less obvious concerns this defense raises in terms of equality and incentivizing more criminal activity.

In terms of equality, the parental discipline defense elevates the right of the parent to discipline his child over the right of the child not to be subjected to physical force. We would never allow an adult to exercise comparable physical force against another adult or against someone else's child; any adult who took a belt to the backside of an unrelated adult or child would be eligible for swift and condign punishment.[48] Why is a child's relative entitled to escape punishment within the criminal justice system when an unrelated adult is not? The nature of the defendant's conduct and the physical harm suffered by the victim is the same under both scenarios. Critics, of course, respond that the *motive* underlying the conduct is different, that the parent wishes to discipline and the non-parent wishes to harm. But non-parents may also have "altruistic" motivations. And we shouldn't uncritically embrace the rose-colored view of parenthood that so often permeates the practice of criminal law. We as a society desperately want to believe that all parents are altruistic and loving individuals who always act in their children's best interest.[49] But the prevalence of child abuse and neglect in America shows this assumption is too often untrue.[50]

In terms of the negative incentives created by the use of corporal punishment, spanking is often a precursor to more serious parental violence.[51] Deanna Pollard argues that "the defense of 'discipline' is raised in forty-one percent of homicide prosecutions against parents who 'accidentally' killed their child."[52] Pollard further suggests that spanking increases the chances that the child victim of a parent's violence will himself be more likely to engage in aggression and other antisocial behavior later in life, including engaging in domestic violence in his own family.[53]

Because of the normative costs associated with these family status defenses, we believe it triggers our presumption. We recognize that critics of our position will argue that the utilities of this "family ties benefit" are indeed substantial. Many believe spanking is in fact beneficial to children; others simply believe that parents should be allowed to make their own disciplinary choices without undue interference by the state. For the reasons stated above, we are unpersuaded that these interests are sufficient to override our normative considerations. Far from promoting the safety of vulnerable persons, this particular benefit exposes children to state-sanctioned physical harm, and thus cannot survive scrutiny under our framework.

D. Pretrial Release

As we described in Chapter 1, many jurisdictions expressly direct judges or magistrates to consider a defendant's family ties and responsibilities when deciding whether or not to release him pending trial. Thus, it is not difficult to imagine a scenario in which a defendant who is a father to minor children is able to secure his release pretrial, while a single, childless defendant charged with an equivalent crime is not. Equality and discrimination concerns are therefore clearly implicated under our normative framework. These disparate decisions can have very real consequences. For example, it is undoubtedly easier to mount a successful defense from outside the correctional system than it is from the inside, because incarcerated defendants have much more constrained access to lawyers, witnesses, and other investigative resources. As a result, there is some statistical evidence showing that pretrial release is correlated with higher acquittal rates and even stronger evidence regarding sentencing. Detained defendants are more likely to receive a sentence including incarceration than those who are released.[54] Accordingly, distributing the pretrial release benefit only to family members risks creating a two-track criminal justice system with the "haves" (with children and dependents) coming out ahead of the "have-nots." That seems an odd and unfair result.

Our concerns about patriarchal origins do not seem to be implicated here. But we do worry that heteronormativity could rear its head if persons with ties or responsibilities to non-traditional family units (whether homosexual or polyamorous) were being denied pretrial release while those in such state-recognized units were granted such release. Moreover, marginal increases in crime-creation may very well be an issue worth considering. During the period of release, a defendant with children might be especially prone to flee if he can take his family with him, because he knows that possible incarceration would have a terrible effect not only on him but also on his dependents. The same concern might especially motivate the defendant to attempt to obstruct justice in order to increase his chances for an eventual acquittal.

Our concern about accuracy may be relevant as well. As suggested above, a defendant who is released pretrial may be able to interfere with potential witnesses, evidence, and the like, such that the accuracy of the ultimate adjudication of his guilt is called into question. This problem may be particularly acute for defendants who are charged with committing a crime against a family member, because they will potentially have easier access to their victim and potential witnesses than defendants who committed a crime against a random stranger, for example.

In the end, if detention is being proposed because the defendant poses a danger to the community generally or an individual within it, then one's family ties and responsibilities should not be enough to afford a defendant preferential treatment—the need to ensure the safety of the community must be the primary consideration. If the issue is whether a defendant poses a flight risk, then it would seem that responsibility for minor children, for example, could be considered as one of a myriad of factors that would lead to a conclusion that a defendant will not flee—but it is one of many possible relevant factors and not a dispositive one. Indeed, for reasons we mentioned before, the fact of responsibility for minor children might enhance the risk of flight. Thus, judges should try to reduce flight risk without reference to family ties and responsibilities; indeed, there are ways of reducing the risk through other means, such as GPS devices or other location tracking devices. And if such alternatives are not available, then we are ultimately more comfortable with judges focusing on whether the risk is attenuated by reference to *all relationships* of caregiving, rather than merely focusing on traditional family relationships, which may not reflect any particular defendant's actual circle of affection. Indeed, to look only at traditional family ties or responsibilities would often entrench heterosexist conceptions of the family, which have no proper place in the criminal justice system.

One other aspect of pretrial treatment of defendants warrants mention. A child-sensitive arrest policy is a good example of a situation where our normative cost structure is not implicated.[55] Arranging to arrest an individual outside the presence of his minor children, while ensuring that the children have safe and comfortable living arrangements after the arrest, can be a family ties benefit or accommodation in the sense that it might be more administratively burdensome for police or prosecutors and might be disbursed now only to those that meet a certain definition of status. But the four costs we identified in Chapter 2 are of only attenuated relevance. Therefore, the presumption against such a benefit can be rebutted, and we believe the policy is an appropriate one for the criminal justice system to pursue. However, because we ultimately worry that this respect for certain relationships of caregiving can still be carried out in a manner that is heterosexist and insensitive to those outside traditionally recognized familial organizations, we are hopeful that these policies can be revised to extend their protections outside the limited confines of the solely biological and heterosexual family. For instance, in the context of the arrest of a caregiver, and in the absence of exigent circumstances, we think it is not too much to ask the police to apprehend the caregiver in a manner sensitive to the responsible care of any vulnerable persons under the care of the arrestee.

E. Sentencing

As discussed earlier, until the recent *Booker* decision by the Supreme Court, which rendered the federal sentencing guidelines advisory,[56] the federal government's position on family ties discounts at sentencing has probably been the most restrictive compared to the policies guiding sentencing in the states. Even in the federal context, of course, courts found ways to extend discounts to offenders with extraordinary "family ties and responsibilities." Now, with the imprimatur from the Supreme Court in *Booker*, federal courts are more likely to award discounts out of compassion for the defendant's family responsibilities. Moreover, to the extent that the federal courts conform to the pre-*Booker* guidance from the United States Sentencing Commission (USSC), it bears emphasis that the federal courts address only a small fraction of the cases in the national criminal justice system. And as we saw earlier in Chapter 1, many states expressly tell judges to calibrate a sentence based, in part, on one's family ties and responsibilities in sentencing offenders.

Thus, offenders who are parents or caregivers to spouses or elders may, depending on the jurisdiction, be in a position to receive a sharp discount from the punishment they might otherwise receive. Not only does this facilitate ad hoc disparities between offenders who are otherwise similarly situated across cases, it also creates inequalities between persons involved in the very same offense.[57] These disparities require justification.

An offender—so long as he satisfies the competence criterion for punishment[58]—anticipates (or should reasonably be expected to anticipate) a risk that he will be punished in accordance with extant sentencing norms. If we make that presumption, which is not an unreasonable one, there is nothing unfair—putting aside proportionality issues—about the offender seeing that risk of punishment materialize. No unfairness to the defendant attaches to punishing persons for conduct they could, by hypothesis, control with consequences they can reasonably anticipate.[59] The resulting disparities in sentences across otherwise similarly situated defendants at least shift the burden of justification for discounts onto their proponents. A person who commits a crime can reasonably foresee that, if prosecuted and punished, his punishment will affect not only himself but also his family. Extending a discount to an offender for a reason unrelated to his crime constitutes an undeserved windfall. In addition, as we adverted to earlier, giving benefits to defendants with family ties in the currency of sentencing discounts will also, on the margin, incentivize this class of defendants to seek out greater criminal opportunities, or they will be recruited or pressed into action by others.

Of course, the fact that offenders do not "deserve" sentencing discounts in an abstract sense does not mean that accommodations should never be made—there may be compelling, non-desert-related reasons to extend such accommodations. Incarcerating a defendant with significant family responsibilities unquestionably imposes tremendous costs on innocent family members, and those costs are most severe when the defendant is an irreplaceable caregiver to vulnerable family members. Therefore, although we advance the unusual position—taken primarily and unpopularly by the federal government's sentencing guidelines—that, ordinarily, a defendant's family ties and responsibilities should not serve as a basis for a lighter sentence, we are sensitive to the serious arguments made by proponents of sentencing departures for those with significant caregiving responsibilities.[60] These arguments merit attention and amplification.

Primarily, the proponents of these departures can point to the anticipated harms to innocent third parties as a reasonable basis to distinguish the sentences caregivers should get from those who do not have those responsibilities.[61] In other words, they can reject the claim that offenders with urgent family responsibilities are similarly situated to those offenders without pressing family responsibilities. Insisting on such a distinction is reasonable, they might add, because, in a particular case or class of cases, the private harm of removing a caregiver's support to an innocent third party outweighs the public gain from continuous incarceration.[62] In this respect, the judge need not be expressing any claim about the diminished moral culpability of the offender who receives the sentencing discount. Rather, the claim is simply that, although this offender deserves no breaks, the weight of these harms to innocent third parties should trump the need for a lengthy incarceration. To the extent that this departure disrupts equality norms, the proponents say, such departures are justifiable.

The justification may take several forms. First, it can be argued that depriving children of parents in order to incarcerate the parents for the purpose of punishment is itself a criminogenic (crime-creating) policy.[63] Second, notwithstanding the culpability of the offenders and the harm suffered by the victims of their crimes, it can be argued that the harm is already done; the state should not inflict its own harms on the offender's children or other persons benefiting from the offender's caregiving. Indeed, if we urge offenders to bear responsibility for the reasonably foreseeable consequences of their actions, so too must the social planners who create institutions of punishment bear such responsibility.

By that logic, our compassion and concern should properly extend to the harm imposed on innocent third parties by the state's punishments.[64] We are therefore willing to agree that compelling circumstances arise when an offender is the sole and irreplaceable caregiver for minors or for aged or ailing persons with whom the defendant has an established relationship of caregiving. However, we abjure any reason to privilege *only* the traditional familial relationship in the context of any accommodations made to "irreplaceable caregivers." What matters from our vantage point is that the defendant is serving a critical social role as an irreplaceable caregiver. We recognize our approach may incur slightly higher "information costs" by abandoning the simple proxy of family status, but this approach in practice is not apt to be more costly than the extant costs of verifying the reality of familial caregiving responsibilities.

Ordinarily, however, we think that harms to innocent third parties should be ameliorated through the institutions of distributive justice, not criminal justice. In an attractive polity, a child without a parent should receive state and communal aid regardless of whether the parent is not around due to sickness, death, or imprisonment. But where the state has persistently failed its obligations of distributive justice, it would not be unreasonable to tailor the punishment of caregiver offenders in a way that mitigates third-party harms without simultaneously elevating the offender's status in violation of the principle of equal justice under law.

For that reason, we think, assuming the crime was severe enough that some form of incarceration is deemed necessary, it may be appropriate for legislatures to authorize greater use of time-delayed sentencing to offenders with irreplaceable caregiving responsibilities.[65] For example, if an offender is the irreplaceable caregiver for children, the offender in a time-delayed sentencing scheme would defer the incarcerative aspect of his punishment until after the children reach the age of majority or until alternative and feasible care can be arranged.[66] In the case of caring for aging parents or ill spouses, the sentence may be delayed until the person receiving the care is deceased, improves in health, or is able to obtain care from another person or entity. During the period that the sentence is deferred, the offender's freedom of movement would be dramatically limited so that only work and necessary chores (*i.e.*, taking one's child to the doctor) would be permitted. Electronic bracelets or other tracking devices could be used to ensure compliance. Additionally, during the time of deferral, the state could attach extensive community service obligations or other release conditions, such as drug testing. Failure to abide by the conditions would lead to more severe punishment than would be experienced absent the deferral of the sentence to minimize possible exploitation by the defendant.

Of course, this option should not be restricted to only those with a blood relationship or marriage. If there is an established relationship of caregiving, then that should be the critical issue. On the other hand, this option should not be available when the defendant has already committed a crime either with or against the recipient of the care, or has exhibited a propensity to harm his family (*e.g.*, prior convictions for reckless endangerment of a child), or is such a dangerous criminal that it would be foolish for society to let him remain free. Simply put, there might be some crimes whose nature would render an offender ineligible for this kind of differentiated-sentencing scheme. But generally speaking, there are ways of implementing punishments that still, by their coercion or deprivation, communicate to the offender the norms of equal liberty under law without wreaking (as much) havoc on the lives of innocent third parties.

As should be clear from the foregoing, we are very sympathetic to the concerns of innocent third parties affected by draconian sentencing policies. Myrna Raeder, for example, has forcefully illustrated that our current sentencing regime has particularly harsh consequences for incarcerated mothers and their children.[67] But recognizing the consequences of a sentencing regime is not the same as effectively condemning it in whole cloth. For one thing, a caregiver who is also a serial killer should not receive a sentencing discount simply because of the caregiver's status as a mother. Rather, the critical issue here seems to be that many of the crimes for which women are convicted (providing low-level assistance to a drug trafficking ring, for example) do not deserve the extremely harsh sentences that are currently imposed for such activity. Thus, many of Raeder's very legitimate concerns about the "gendered differences in criminality"[68] could be taken into account if we properly consider factors such as the nature of the criminal conduct, the criminal history of the defendant, and so on, in making a sentencing decision for an individual defendant or a class of defendants similarly situated. Further, many of the harms to innocent third parties can be addressed by reducing across the board the sentences imposed for nonviolent crimes, which are the crimes, some suggest, that women are more likely to commit in any event. But this analysis and the prescriptions that flow from it do not require an uncritical extension of sentencing discounts simply because of family ties or responsibilities. Instead, we need to focus on whether a defendant has irreplaceable caregiving responsibilities and how we can best accommodate that caregiving role. It bears emphasis that for us it is the voluntary caregiving and not the familial status that justifies greater sensitivity.

In sum, we recognize that punishment (especially in the form of incarceration) affects innocent third parties. Those innocent third parties, however, are not connected to the defendant through family status alone. Thus, to the extent legal officials *should* tailor a punishment in recognition of its deleterious impact on innocent third parties, the law should reject a categorical effort to accommodate only those innocent third parties who are family members.[69] Second, we doubt that the criminal justice system should be the first resort to resolve the social needs of families in distress. But in those situations in which distressed-family problems arise with no alternative resources available to ameliorate the situation, it is preferable to establish more options, including time-deferred sentencing or, for example, custodial options where the sole caregiver and the cared-for individuals can live together, assuming that the offender's offense was not directed against his children (or other's children) in the first instance.[70]

F. Prison Policies

Our normative framework requires a fairly nuanced approach to the evaluation of prison policies. That is because each individual policy we mentioned in Chapter 1 implicates different normative considerations. Accordingly, we cannot present a unified approach to prison policies as such. At some very basic level, it is understandable that our punitive practices aim to take account of family ties; we often harm entire families for one member's wrongdoing by punishing and removing the wrongdoer from the home. Still, our normative framework furnishes some reasons to think that there is an unfairness and inequality associated with state promotion of family ties in the penal context. Moreover, we think many of the policies can be recrafted in terms that are neutral to family status.

We think there is one central difference, however, between most of the other family ties benefits discussed and the set of practices we group together as prison policies: the state's legitimate interest in successful offender reentry. In the context of corrections, we cannot ignore that one's family can play a central role in facilitating successful prisoner reentry, one of the most important, if often overlooked, functions of our penal system. The criminal justice system's interest in offenders prior to the service of a sentence must focus on the inculpation of the guilty and the exculpation of the innocent—a task routinely undermined by the provision of benefits for family ties. Nevertheless, once an offender is sentenced and responsibility for a crime is placed on the right shoulders, our penal system can rightfully draw upon the resources of the family to help reintegrate an offender back into society and encourage rehabilitation during periods of incarceration. It is the penal context that the interests in rehabilitation and reintegration might trump the considerations within our normative framework—and where family networks might warrant benefits precisely because they are doing work that is subcontracted out by the state. As we discussed in our introductory remarks to Chapter 2, one of the strong arguments for having the state benefit the family arises when the family is doing work the state very much wants done—but the task can be accomplished more cheaply and effectively by drawing upon the natural resources within the family. Nonetheless, our normative framework remains useful in analyzing a host of prison policies.

For example, in trying to assess the furlough policies we recounted in Chapter 1, our normative framework demands an inquiry into how such policies could potentially implicate an ideal of fairness or equality. Why should those with family members get more days off from their prison sentences than those without family? Although our other normative considerations do not seem applicable to furloughs, our norm of equality seems offended by policies that favor those with family members.

Similarly, visitation policies that bar visitors who are not within the state's definition of family are very unfair to those without a family recognized by the state.[71] Because courts give prison officials substantial discretion in devising visitation policies,[72] there can be inequities that escape notice. Accordingly, the normative framework we offer here indicates that prisons ought to devise such policies with care. It offends a sense of justice when inmates with families receive preferential treatment via certain prison policies as compared to those inmates without families. To the extent that discrimination against those without families implicates our third normative consideration, our presumption against family ties benefits has some—albeit limited—force.

Yet, in the post-sentence phase of the criminal justice system, we cannot help but conclude that certain substantial interests of the state may counteract our worries about family ties benefits. First, only one of our four normative considerations is implicated here—the equality prong. Moreover, we acknowledge the role that relations of caregiving can play in the corrections system. The policy statements of the Federal Bureau of Prisons embrace family ties because they can be especially rehabilitative.[73] We acknowledge that family reunification after incarceration may serve as an appropriate predicate to favor the family in certain prison policies. Accordingly, our sympathy for some of the "pro-family" arguments we adumbrated at the beginning of Chapter 2 are given effect in this context. In particular, the state interest in successful offender reentry informs our assessment of how family ties should be addressed by the criminal justice system.

Still, as with child-sensitive arrest practices, we are mindful that there are ways to administer these benefits that do not reinforce a heterosexist and overly traditional conception of the family. Our preferred strategy would be to look at function instead of status. If it is possible to craft the relevant policies in ways that satisfy the goals of prisoner reentry without reliance on family status—because family status may be both under- and overinclusive—then we should look at those possibilities rather than using the imperfect proxy of "family" to achieve these goals.

An additional way in which we think the state can satisfy the imperatives of punishment while exhibiting concern for innocent third parties and successful prisoner reentry is to realize that the coercion the state metes out as part of its punishment need not be done in temporally contiguous ways. If we think of punishment in terms of units, and we assume, arguendo, that some period of incarceration is required, it might be better to ensure that offenders spend five days a week working at home and the remaining two days in a carceral facility. That might lengthen the period in which the punishment occurs, but it might also serve society's interest by ameliorating innocent third-party harms and achieving successful prisoner reentry. If courts or prison officials are given the guided discretion to decide whether a punishment-units approach should be embraced, then the offender is still being coerced—and for the public's purposes, not for the sole benefit of the offender. Moreover, the condemnatory social message of this punishment can still be expressed clearly by limiting the offender's movements when not serving time in prison.

A related issue requiring sensitive application connects to the placement of inmates within the correctional system.[74] If prisons are built in remote rural areas, or if prisoners are sent to prisons far from their families, then it will be harder for the families of most prisoners to visit. Equally difficult may be access to the programs we want to make available to offenders as part of the coercive punishment they endure at the hands of the state.[75] Family ties are routinely considered when establishing an inmate's "place of service."[76] Although this effort to use prison placement to help families might be seen as a family ties benefit—and might also implicate the inequality/discrimination aspect of our normative considerations (like furlough and visitation policies)—we think the heightened state interest in successful reentry works to rebut the presumption against such benefits. It seems perfectly appropriate for states to consider ease of access for those who may facilitate reentry (whether family or friends) when making decisions regarding prison construction or prison assignment after conviction. A location-sensitive policy does not offend our four normative considerations and simply prevents the intimates of inmates from paying extra costs and forcing offenders to serve "harder" time.[77] Still, our normative consideration of nondiscrimination against those without family counsels for sensitivity in designing such benefits: those with other good and rehabilitative reasons for visits, furloughs, and specific placement needs should be heeded so as to minimize favoritism toward those with families recognized by the state.

There is yet another potential state interest that also counsels for more toleration of family ties benefits in the penal system, namely, the interests of extremely vulnerable third parties and their need for care. Just as irreplaceable caregivers can, under certain conditions, get some reconfigured sentencing, they may appropriately be given special consideration in their incarceration as well. As we mentioned in Chapter 1, a number of innovative programs have been created to help mothers and their children stay together, notwithstanding a prison sentence that would otherwise seperate a mother from her children.[78] To be sure, the focus on providing only women with these alternatives could be said to implicate our first normative consideration insofar as such programs reinforce traditional gender roles and stereotypes (*i.e.*, that parenting is primarily a woman's responsibility, and that men are entitled to less consideration for their status as fathers). Moreover, our third normative consideration is potentially offended because women who are not pregnant or mothers do not get the same "discount" in their prison terms; and men are almost completely excluded from such programs as the federal Mothers and Infants Nurturing Together (MINT) Program and California's Pregnant and Parenting Women's Alternative Sentencing Program Act.[79] Finally, our fourth normative consideration is implicated because such programs could set up incentives for mothers to be targeted for criminal recruitment because they may be afforded especially light sentences.

Nevertheless, we think these programs may yet be defensible in service of the potential irreplaceability of a caregiver, something we discussed at length above, in connection with sentencing. We would recommend, however, that such programs become non-gendered, in that they be made available to men who, for example, have sole custody of infants.

G. Conclusion

We think it bears emphasis that the accommodations to caregiving that we endorse or tolerate in this Chapter might better be viewed as doing away with a burden on all offenders than affording a real benefit to those with family ties recognized by the state. For instance, time-deferred sentencing for irreplaceable caregivers may benefit those with families more often than others, but we would not want to see the benefit of time-deferred sentencing restricted only to those who give care for their children. This is a perfect example of how helping families need not offend our normative considerations—and we have no trouble signing on to policies that help families in this benign way, affording a benefit in a nondiscriminatory fashion. Although we are generally skeptical toward distributing family ties benefits prior to and in determinations of criminal liability, and in many instances of sentencing, when it comes to sentencing of irreplaceable caregivers and matters affecting the incarceration of an offender, we are more inclined to reengineer the current panoply of family ties benefits in terms that are neutral to family status. In those contexts, we prefer to allocate benefits in a manner sensitive to promoting established relationships of caregiving.

We hope we have demonstrated how privileging individuals because of their membership in a state-denominated family unit potentially threatens some core functions of the criminal justice system. When we excuse certain classes of individuals from prosecution entirely, solely on account of a family relationship, we both allow potentially dangerous individuals to escape punishment and create a more attractive class of accomplices. When we allow a husband to prevent his wife from offering relevant testimony on the witness stand that may exculpate someone else, we inhibit the truth-seeking function of a criminal trial. When we allow a wife to claim a privilege but not a partner in a same-sex relationship, we subtly but inevitably convey our disapprobation of that relationship. Although this seemingly simple story can get more complicated, we have argued that it rarely gets so complicated as to sanction the privileging of family ties over our commitment to doing justice in a sphere in which the liberty and lives of women and men are at stake.

To be sure, the troubling normative costs we associate with these family ties benefits require verification; and we hope other scholars will participate in assessing the empirical costs of these family ties benefits.[80] It is possible that comparing crime rates in jurisdictions that have these benefits with those that do not (both domestically and abroad) will yield interesting results. Some family ties benefits for instance, may prove to be self-defeating.[81] Other family ties benefits might demonstrate tangible public advantages, such as securing greater compliance with the legal system.[82] And still others are less susceptible to empirical "verification" because the benefits involve tradeoffs between competing normative values, such as the family ties benefits that pose risks to relevant equality norms.[83]

Although we are open-minded about the possible empirical effects these various benefits cause, we are, at least right now, doubtful that the family needs systematic support through the use of criminal justice benefits in order to enable and ensure its flourishing.[84] We recognize that the tension between loyalty to the family and loyalty to the state is real, and that the choices faced by families like the Sheinbeins and Madoffs are agonizing. But when conflicts between family and the criminal justice system arise, especially prior to the determination of the sentence, the state's and the public's interests should generally prevail over the need to promote the comparatively private interest of family preservation and "harmony." Indeed, if family relationships involve criminal complicity, those families are already in disrepair and are likely undeserving of state protection.

Although our presumption against family ties benefits can be rebutted, we believe the scrutiny called for under our presumption is warranted—and entails curtailing some of the family ties benefits we have already and being cautious in the creation of new ones.

But, thus far, we have addressed only part of the story. It is certainly true that the criminal justice system extends a number of privileges and benefits to those with state-recognized family relationships. There are, however, a number of instances in which offenders are treated worse than other offenders by virtue of their family relationships. We turn to that part of the story in the next half of the book.

PART TWO

Punishing Family Status
A Roadmap

In 2005, Christina Madison watched while her new husband repeatedly punched her four-year-old son in the stomach after the child refused to get dressed for school. Madison did nothing to stop her husband from hitting the child. The child eventually died from internal bleeding as a result of a tear in his intestine. Prosecutors charged Madison for her failure to act; she was sentenced to twelve years in prison.[1]

Stories like Christina Madison's abound. In the absence of her family status, Christina's omission or failure to rescue a child would trigger no criminal liability. But because of it, she faces a very significant sentence. In this part of the book, we examine the various places in the American criminal justice system in which the law imposes burdens on defendants on account of their familial status or familial connection to the crime. Where do these burdens exist? Why do we have them? What, if anything, is wrong with them? How can they be reformed? Thus, this part of the book analyzes various "family ties burdens" and asks whether they are justifiable—or whether they could be justified if redesigned. Although scholars have considered these burdens individually, part of our contribution here is viewing these burdens synthetically and explaining what, if any, sense can be made of them once taken as a whole.

Our research uncovers the following family ties burdens: parental responsibility laws imposing liability on parents because of crimes or misdeeds committed by their children, omissions liability for failing to prevent harm to family members, and criminal liability for nonpayment of child or parental support. Defendants are also burdened on account of their family status when they face prosecutions for incest, adultery, and bigamy.[2] We survey these family ties burdens in Chapter 4. In all seven of these instances, in the absence of the particular familial status of the defendant, the actions or omissions at issue would largely be ignored by the criminal justice system or, in some cases, treated more leniently.

We begin Chapter 5 by explaining why we have generally taken a defendant-centered perspective in thinking about the sites of family ties burdens, since many burdens on defendants based on family status may, conversely, have been established in order to advantage the family members of such defendants (and potential defendants).[3] Focusing on family ties burdens from the defendant's perspective helps raise awareness about why such burdens are normative yellow flags. As we explain, most centrally, they have tremendous potential to discriminate.

Consider the example of omissions liability. When the state charges an individual because of his or her failure to protect another human being from harm, the state is signaling that the relationship at issue is one worthy of special treatment from the state. But in the context of family ties burdens, large numbers of persons who might justifiably, in our view, see themselves as entitled to benefit from omissions liabilities are excluded. Absent a contract or other special circumstances, a hypothetical Jill cannot rely upon the state to signal to her life partner Denise that Denise is obligated by law to reasonably prevent harm to Jill. When the state makes choices regarding families and uses the criminal justice system to send normative signals about those choices, it risks marginalizing persons who consider themselves family members but are not recognized as such by the state or other institutions. In this sense, targeting persons with unusual treatment on account of familial status is an underinclusive (and, at times, overinclusive) mechanism to distribute both the tangible and expressive benefits conferred by the criminal law.

The rest of Chapter 5 constructs a normative framework to explain the circumstances under which burdening family status might be justified. We highlight that the vast majority of the burdens implicate the caregiving function of families. For example, society imposes liability on parents for their omissions to reinforce the notion of a special obligation, one worthy of enforcement through the criminal justice system, to care for their children by protecting them from harm. The same logic of promoting caregiving plausibly motivates criminalization of nonpayment of child and parental support and some of the other family ties burdens we discuss. The problem is that the ways the promotion of caregiving is expressed in these family ties burdens are at times illiberal and insufficient.

This conclusion is underwritten by an underappreciated point about how the criminal justice system allocates family ties burdens. Our research shows that the criminal justice system tends to enforce family ties burdens against those who have *voluntarily chosen* their caregiving role.[4] In other words, state-imposed burdens tend to fall chiefly on those persons who have voluntarily entered into a status relationship and enjoyed the privileges associated with that relationship, thus making it seem more just to be required to carry some burdens in return. Building upon this internal coherence, we argue that a voluntary caregiving orientation to burden allocation in the criminal justice system is much more attractive than allocation on formal familial status alone. Regardless of what one thinks about relational obligations within the family that are divorced from ideas about consent or voluntarism, when it comes to criminal justice design, liberal principles recommend focusing on voluntary caregiving rather than an arbitrary status-based allocation of duties.

Indeed, a voluntarist approach to family ties burdens is expressive of and consistent with our *liberal minimalist* orientation to criminal law legislation more generally. That orientation, in other words, is *liberal* in that it justifies additional interference into interpersonal relationships through criminal sanction only through a showing that individuals have roughly consented to these extra obligations by their antecedent conduct to join or start particular relationships. And it is also liberal in a second sense, in that it tries to carve out a large space for personal freedom to operate in a way compatible with the personal freedom and security of others. It is only with respect to these two notions (voluntarism and respect for robust individual liberties) that we use the term liberal or liberalism.

Our orientation is *minimalist* in two ways too: first, we seek a narrow tailoring between government objectives and the means used to advance those objectives, and second, we seek to constrain the use of the criminal law sanction when non-criminal measures are available and equally or nearly as effective in realizing the substantial interest the public has in reducing the prohibited conduct. Thus, even when the promotion of voluntary caregiving motivates the establishment of a family ties burden, that is not sufficient justification if there are alternative and equally effective means of achieving the goal without resort to the criminal justice system and its particular power to infringe upon citizens' liberties.

With these principles in mind, Chapter 6 rethinks the family ties burdens we identified earlier. We hope to show why some burdens do not pass muster and how others can be preserved in some form, as long as they are reconstructed to avoid the substantial costs of using family status alone to distribute burdens. Although we do not make the constitutional claim that family status should be a suspect classification worthy of strict scrutiny when the criminal justice system discriminatorily burdens individuals on the basis of family status, we do believe that, as a policy matter, the government should view skeptically the use of family status. In other words, to use the language of equal protection, without making the constitutional claim, the objective of the government should be at least "important" and perhaps "compelling," and the means adopted to pursue that objective should be "narrowly tailored," looking especially to see whether alternative non-criminal measures might be equally effective. We also believe that the impairment of liberties (including those associated with sexual autonomy) by pain of criminal sanction on the basis of family status needs to survive heightened (if not strict) scrutiny as a matter of policy.[5]

As we discussed in the book's Introduction, there are many important studies of the ways various criminal justice policies unintentionally wreak devastating harm on families and their communities. Our focus here is different and has yet to be sufficiently addressed by the community of scholars interested in how the criminal justice system affects families. Here, we examine those distinctively purposeful practices that consciously target defendants for special burdens on account of their familial status. Scholars have been successful in analyzing the *effects* of certain criminal justice policies and practices on the family. But most scholars have not recognized the panoply of laws expressly written to disadvantage persons based on family status alone. This part begins that inquiry.

In defining our focus this way, we do not intend to suggest that the particular liabilities addressed in this part of the book are necessarily guided by the intent of hurting or burdening family life as such. Indeed, it may be that many burdens on family status are "remedial" or intended to benefit family life even though they penalize particular defendants on account of their familial status. But in this context, it is worth remembering that many laws disadvantaged women, for example, in the name of "protecting" them.[6] Our purpose here is to excavate the family ties burdens currently imposed by the criminal justice system and to assess their desirability both now and as they could be.

FOUR

A Survey of Family Ties Burdens

CERTAIN CRIMES PERMIT THE PROSECUTION OF A DEFENDANT for conduct that would otherwise be lawful in the absence of a defendant's familial connection to the crime. For instance, incest statutes generally proscribe sexual conduct otherwise permitted between mature and consenting individuals. The examples of this phenomenon on which we focus include certain omissions and parental responsibility laws; incest, bigamy, and adultery statutes; and statutes criminalizing the nonpayment of child and parental support.[1] In all of these examples, state-determined familial status alters the blameworthiness that the criminal justice system assigns to the underlying conduct.[2] Although these examples are not necessarily exhaustive, we believe they are the most frequently found examples of the criminal justice system's decision to criminalize certain conduct on the basis of family status.[3] In what follows, we provide an overview of the doctrine associated with these family ties burdens.

A. Omissions Liability for Failure to Rescue

In June 2002, prosecutors charged Shavon Greene, a twenty-one-year-old mother, with aggravated manslaughter after her boyfriend allegedly beat her twenty-one-month-old daughter to death. The prosecutor did not allege Greene was even present during the beating; instead, the prosecutor alleged she had disregarded warnings from a social services investigator not to leave the child alone with her boyfriend. Greene eventually pled guilty to culpable negligence.[4]

At a high level of generality, the dominant rule in American criminal justice (as well as tort law) systems remains that citizens are under no obligation to rescue each other.[5] In other words, even though the failure to help another person in distress can constitute a moral failing, the criminal justice system does not generally impose liability on those who simply keep on walking.[6]

The exceptions to the general rule are well-known. As the D.C. Circuit stated in *Jones v. United States*:

> There are at least four situations in which the failure to act may constitute breach of a legal duty. One can be held criminally liable: first, where a statute imposes a duty to care for another; second, where one stands in a certain status relationship to another; third, where one has assumed a contractual duty to care for another; and fourth, where one has voluntary assumed the care of another and so secluded the helpless person as to prevent others from rendering aid.[7]

In addition, one bears liability if one directly created the conditions of the victim's peril or if one bears responsibility for the cause of the conditions of peril to the victim (*e.g.*, parents of children who pose peril to the victim). There are limits to when liability will be imposed, however. First, liability will not be imposed if rescue requires the defendant to make an undue sacrifice or if the defendant cannot physically perform the rescue.[8] Second, "the defendant's failure to act must be accompanied by whatever *mens rea* the crime requires for its commission."[9]

Of special interest here are the triggering conditions for liability based on family status. The relationship of spouse to spouse and parent to child are paradigmatic, even if not exclusive, examples of status relationships in which one owes a duty to rescue sufficient to trigger *criminal* responsibility (rather than mere tort liability).[10] Thus, if a defendant "realizes (or culpably fails to realize) his wife is in danger, realizes (or culpably fails to realize) that he can rescue her with minimal risk and/or sacrifice, and realizes (or culpably fails to realize) that she is his wife," then he can be liable for homicide "if he is aware of the existence of the three elements (wife's peril, his ability to rescue with low risk/effort, and wife's identity)."[11] In the parent-child context, parents have been held criminally liable for neglect for failing to protect a child who was being sexually abused by another individual,[12] and held criminally liable for manslaughter for failing to protect a child from fatal physical abuse inflicted by another.[13] These prosecutions exemplify the family ties burden phenomenon by which persons in certain family relationships are held accountable for harms to others even when those harms are inflicted by another independent actor.

Trying to understand who precisely faces omissions liability based on the status of spouse or parent can be a bit tricky since these categories are sometimes defined by courts with sensitivity to differing circumstances. With respect to spouses or spouse-like relationships, courts have been leery of recognizing the obligation to rescue outside of a state-sanctioned marriage. It is generally not enough to simply be dating or be paramours to trigger the duty to rescue,[14] but some courts have recognized obligations between unmarried couples. Where that has happened, however, it can often be explained on alternative grounds, such as situations in which the long-term girlfriend caused the peril to the boyfriend and thus is assigned a duty to rescue for having created the peril.[15] But drawing the line can be difficult in other places too. Why should couples who married within days of meeting each other have more legal obligations to each other than couples who have lived together for ten years but never married? Why should the heterosexual married couple have duties to rescue each other but not the long-term homosexual couple who are legally prevented from marrying in most states? What should happen when there is a married couple who have lived apart for years but are not formally divorced?[16]

The murkiness is worse in the context of duties to rescue children. To be sure, biological parental linkage is not required to create a duty and thus the law places the same package of burdens on adoptive parents. But courts are divided over whether to extend duties to rescue to people who have not expressly consented to assuming legal responsibility for a custodial role over the children.[17] Further, just as biology may not be necessary to impose a duty to rescue, there are certain circumstances in which it is not sufficient: what should happen if biological parents have renounced or terminated their parental rights prior to or after conception or birth of the child, *e.g.*, sperm or egg donors, or surrogate mothers and the resulting children?

Importantly, consider the status relationships associated with grandparents, cousins, uncles, and aunts: none of these individuals is ever under a legal duty to rescue their reciprocal relations—nor are siblings, regardless of whether the relationship is biological, adoptive, or step-sibling in nature. That said, it is possible that any one of these people might be under a duty toward the victim for other reasons: perhaps they have induced detrimental reliance, agreed to care for the victim, created the perils, etc.[18] But in the common law and around the country, it is exceptionally rare to find duties to rescue based on familial status relationships outside the context of spousal and parental relations.

B. Parental Responsibility Laws

In St. Clair Shores, Michigan, prosecutors charged Susan and Anthony Provenzino with a misdemeanor for failing to "exercise reasonable control" over their sixteen-year-old son, Alex Provenzino.[19] *Alex had committed a number of crimes, including burglarizing churches and homes and attacking his father with a golf club. Despite knowledge of some of his burglaries, the Provenzinos supported Alex's release from juvenile custody, after which he continued to commit crimes. The jury convicted the Provenzinos after fifteen minutes of deliberation. The parents were each fined $100 and ordered to pay $2,000 in court costs.*[20]

Parental responsibility laws command widespread attention among politicians, courts, and academics.[21] To provide an avenue of restitution for victims and a stronger dose of deterrence to reduce the incidence of juvenile crime, some jurisdictions permit criminal liability for parents whose children misbehave.[22] Statutes criminalizing the parenting of those like the Provenzinos have an extended history,[23] and their popularity seems to ebb and flow.[24] This section provides a short overview of the nature and scope of parental responsibility laws in recent years and how courts have evaluated them.

To begin with, it's worth mentioning that most states have laws that specifically prohibit *any* adult from endangering the welfare of a minor or contributing to the delinquency of minors through specific affirmative actions, such as knowingly providing guns or alcohol to them, which can be viewed as proximate causes of the child's wrongdoing.[25] These kinds of statutes are not only ubiquitous but longstanding, beginning at the latest in 1903.[26] In some instances, these statutes may also target any person's omission that arises under special circumstances, as opposed to affirmative acts, and sometimes these statutes create liability resulting in fines or imprisonment without any specific showing of fault required by the government.[27]

In truth, parental responsibility laws might reasonably be seen to encompass civil liability statutes or laws criminalizing the knowing contribution of an adult to the minor's violation of truancy and curfew laws, or laws creating liability for parents who provide a weapon to a child.[28] However, for our purposes here, we want to restrict what we refer to hereafter as parental responsibility laws to the category *of criminal liability imposed upon family members based on a theory of failure to supervise.* This category is controversial in large measure because, under a generalized failure to supervise theory, the wrongdoing of the defendant's child is enough to trigger liability, subject, in most cases, to certain affirmative defenses the parent may raise.[29]

In a number of cases, these laws require the government to show a lower level of *mens rea*—usually criminal negligence, but in others strict liability. In other situations, these improper parenting statutes differ from the general delinquency statutes by defining the child's misconduct with greater sweep (beyond actual criminality). And in some cases, the parental responsibility statute both lowers the *mens rea* and broadens the scope of a child's misconduct (beyond actual criminality) that together expands potential liability for parents.[30] These parental responsibility statutes are different in that they have to do with *parents and legal guardians of the children*—the scope does not extend to *any* adult, unlike most of the statutes that address endangering the welfare or contributing to delinquency of a child.[31]

These parental responsibility laws are exemplified by an Oregon statute that holds parents criminally liable of a misdemeanor if their children violate a curfew law, violate a truancy requirement, or commit an act that brings the child within juvenile court jurisdiction.[32] There does not need to be a showing that the parent specifically knew about or contributed to the violation or criminal wrong by the child. Similarly, a Cleveland suburb not long ago passed an ordinance under which parents can be charged with a crime based on the misdeeds of their children; a third conviction under the statute could result in parents serving 180 days in jail.[33] Although parents would be permitted to raise as a defense that they had taken reasonable steps to control the child, an Ohio court recently struck down the Cleveland ordinance because it was inconsistent with a state statute requiring the person charged to commit an act or omission as a predicate for culpability.[34] The ordinance, however, was modeled on a similar and widely reported law in Silverton, Oregon.[35] And according to the Mayor of Silverton, the law was very successful at reducing crime committed by juveniles in part because "[w]hen their parents are being dragged into it, most kids see things a little differently. They realize they're not the only ones who pay the price for their actions, and kids begin to take stock of themselves."[36]

Because many of the failing to supervise laws are created at the municipal level,[37] they are more difficult to survey, and no accurate scholarly estimates exist so far as we know.[38] At the state level, only a few states appear to have created parental responsibility statutes that go beyond the general delinquency statutes discussed above.[39] But various cities or towns have similar laws around the country.[40] And some have created unique hybrid laws that both lower the *mens rea* required for the parent and define as evidence of improper parenting conduct by a minor that would not be separately subject to criminal sanction.[41] Moreover, proposals to create such liability regimes are regularly considered around the country.[42]

Jurisdictions vary with respect to how courts greet these legislative efforts. To be sure, there are relatively few reported cases considering the constitutionality of these parental responsibility statutes. In addition to the court that struck down the local Maple Heights ordinance, two state appellate courts have also struck down parental responsibility statutes that rested upon strict liability.[43] In *State v. Akers*, the New Hampshire Supreme Court struck down a statute that imposed criminal liability on parents for a child's violation of a statute concerning recreational vehicle usage. The court concluded that the statute violated the due process clause of the state constitution because it did not impose liability on the basis of any act or omission committed by a parent but instead imposed liability solely because of an individual's status as a parent.[44] Similarly, an appellate court in New Jersey struck down a town's parental responsibility ordinance under the United States Constitution's Due Process Clauses, concluding that its presumption that repeated juvenile misconduct "was the result of parental action or inaction" could not be sustained based on the information about the root causes of juvenile delinquency presented to the court.[45]

But not all courts have reached the same conclusions. The California Supreme Court has upheld a parental responsibility statute with criminal penalties.[46] On its face, the statute seemed like a relatively straightforward attempt to criminalize contributing to the delinquency of a minor, but a 1988 amendment to the statute provoked the constitutional challenge at issue. According to the statute, "a parent or legal guardian to any person under the age of 18 years shall have the duty to exercise reasonable care, supervision, protection, and control over their minor child."[47] The court rejected the complainants' challenge that the statute was "unconstitutionally vague, overbroad, and an impingement on the right to privacy."[48] The court rejected the vagueness challenge on the basis that requiring parents to exercise "reasonable care" provided "sufficiently certain" guidance because it "incorporates the definitions and the limits of parental duties that have long been a part of California dependency law and tort law."[49] The court acknowledged that "neither the amendment nor prior case law sets forth specific acts that a parent must perform or avoid in order to fulfill the duty of supervision and control" over minor children, but the court shrugged off that obvious difficulty, stating that a statutory definition of perfect parenting would be "inflexible." Instead, "law-abiding parents" should simply understand that "the concept of reasonableness" should serve as their guide for complying with the statute.[50]

Notwithstanding some courts' disapproval of parental responsibility statutes, we anticipate that state and local legislatures will continue to explore regulatory strategies to reduce juvenile misconduct that will invariably burden those of a particular state-sanctioned family status.[51] And burdens they are. One of the most interesting features of these parental responsibility laws is the way they frequently create liability for parents based on their status as a parent and the misconduct of their child alone, leaving the intentionally responsible parent to plead their good parenting skills as an affirmative defense instead of making the prosecution show the absence of good parenting as part of its case-in-chief against the parent.[52] We say more about the rationales and problems associated with these laws in Chapter 6.

C. Incest

In 1997, Allen and Patricia Muth were convicted of incest after they entered into a sexual relationship and had four children. Allen and Patricia were biological brother and sister, although they did not meet until Patricia was eighteen because she had been in foster care since she was a baby. At the time of their convictions, Allen was 45 and Patricia was 30. At the time of sentencing, the judge stated "I believe severe punishment is warranted in this case. . . . I think they have to be separated. It's the only way to prevent them from having intercourse in the future."[53] *The judge then sentenced Allen to five years in prison and Patricia to five years. Their parental rights to at least one of their children were also terminated because of the incestuous relationship.*[54]

Incest laws, which prohibit both sexual relations and marriage within certain kinship relations, reflect one of the enduring sexual taboos.[55] Perhaps surprisingly, incest was not a crime at English common law,[56] and it is not even today a punishable offense in all jurisdictions.[57] It is also yet another complicated example of a situation in which criminal liability may attach to a person only on account of some familial status (though as we suggested in Part I, it can sometimes be "beneficial" for a defendant to be prosecuted under incest laws rather than generally applicable sexual misconduct laws, because the penalties and collateral consequences may actually be less severe).[58] The elements of incest are usually (1) sexual relations between two persons within a particular prohibited level of consanguinity (or affinity through adoption or marriage); and (2) the defendant's awareness of that relationship.[59]

While prohibitions of incest are usually general, in theory they can be grouped into three different categories: regulation of sex between adults, regulation of sex between an adult and a minor, and regulation of sex between minors. Most jurisdictions are unlikely to make these distinctions; indeed, under most incest statutes, it is irrelevant whether the participants jointly consent to the sexual activity.[60] The issue of consent bears further mention. As alluded to above, in most states, lack of consent is not an articulated element of the incest charge, which, in theory, renders victims vulnerable to prosecution under statutes that are lacking specificity. In cases in which joint consent exists, both parties may still be criminally liable, as in the case of the Muths, whose parental rights were terminated and who were both convicted and incarcerated. This crudeness in drafting raises a series of normative questions we address in Chapter 6.

In the United States, all states but Rhode Island have criminal prohibitions on at least some consanguineous relations between family members who are not a so-called conjugal couple, although there is some variation between the states in terms of what relationships are prohibited.[61] For example, all states having criminal incest statutes ban sexual relationships between (biological) parents and their children, regardless of the child's age,[62] but not all incest statutes prohibit sex between adult stepchildren and the stepparent.[63] All states with incest statutes also ban sexual relationships between consanguineous siblings and most ban relationships between aunts and uncles and their nephews and nieces.[64] There is more divergence on the question of cousins; only eight states criminalize sexual contact between first cousins,[65] but twenty-five states do not permit first cousins to marry. Some states also extend their prohibitions beyond blood relationships: "twenty-two states criminalize sex between stepparents and stepchildren," and some states treat adopted children the same as biological children for purposes of incest prohibitions.[66]

D. Bigamy

In 1953, Marlyne Hammon's father and dozens of other men in her community were arrested and sent to jail on charges of polygamy. Although her father was released shortly thereafter, the family corresponded in secret and continued to live apart because they feared further prosecution. Now an adult, Hammon is involved in a polygamous relationship and advocates for the decriminalization of polygamy.[67]

Bigamy laws in the United States, broadly stated, prohibit an individual from entering into multiple and simultaneous marriages when the first spouse is still alive and the initial marriage relationship has not been terminated.[68] Although there is some variation around the country regarding incest prohibitions or the scope of omissions liability and parental responsibility laws, no such ambivalence exists regarding criminal laws prohibiting polygamy in the United States. Indeed, these bigamy laws are universal around the country,[69] and, with a few exceptions in certain geographic communities, they are often enforced.[70] As we discuss in Chapter 6, these prohibitions raise substantial questions about the proper scope of the criminal law and its relationship to issues of family status.

E. Adultery

In 2004, John R. Bushey Jr., the former town attorney of Luray, Virginia, was charged with adultery after his paramour reported the misconduct to the police when the affair terminated. Bushey eventually pled guilty and was sentenced to twenty hours of community service. Along with twenty-three other states, Virginia can prosecute a husband or wife for having consensual sex outside marriage.[71]

Adultery laws, at least as crafted in some jurisdictions without fornication statutes,[72] prohibit a married individual from engaging in extramarital sex, notwithstanding that such sexual relations would not otherwise be subjected to legal sanction.[73] Perhaps because of the pervasiveness of adultery,[74] a bare majority of states no longer regulate extramarital relations,[75] even though large majorities of Americans continue to view adultery as immoral.[76] Regardless of the cause of adultery's relative demise as a crime, we recognize that most jurisdictions do not actively prosecute or punish this misconduct anymore, even though twenty-three states and the District of Columbia still have statutes criminalizing this conduct.[77]

Although one might be tempted to dismiss the significance of adultery laws today, we are loathe to do so in light of the continued enforcement of such laws in some jurisdictions,[78] especially in the military.[79] Indeed, although civilian courts have generally seen a decrease in adultery prosecutions, there is a steady flow of such prosecutions in the military courts.[80] And during the Clinton-Lewinsky scandal, many members of the armed forces were especially critical of their Commander-in-Chief, who could have faced a court-martial on adultery-related charges if he had been a mere service member.[81] Additionally, even though someone might not get prosecuted for the crime of adultery in a jurisdiction forbidding such misconduct, it bears mention that the fact that the criminal laws remain on the books has real consequences in civil contexts other than the military, such as child custody, adoption, and employment.[82] Moreover, there is an odd discrimination resulting from adultery laws that only apply to heterosexual couples,[83] which we think needs some articulation and evaluation. It goes without saying that, as applied to the defendant who is married, adultery laws are a clear and conventional family ties burden.

F. Nonpayment of Child Support

In 1997, an Anchorage, Alaska father was sentenced to five days in prison and five years probation for failing to pay almost $98,000 in child support.[84] *A government official stated: "Our job is to collect money for children. Parents need to realize there are penalties for ignoring their children."*[85]

Ordinarily, the failure to pay a debt to a non-governmental entity (like one's cable TV provider) is not a criminal act.[86] An aggrieved party is forced to pursue civil remedies to obtain redress.[87] In contrast, failure to pay child support is a crime. For example, the Child Support Recovery Act,[88] amended in 1998 as the Deadbeat Parents Punishment Act,[89] makes it a federal crime to owe more than $5,000 in child support or to be in arrears for longer than one year if the child owed the support lives in a different state than the delinquent parent. In addition, many states have statutes criminalizing a parent's failure to pay child support.[90] This statutory regime demonstrates yet another way family status can turn an act that ordinarily would be non-criminal into a criminal one.

G. Nonpayment of Parental Support

The last area we explore here is a variant of the preceding family ties burden. It has to do with what are sometimes called filial responsibility laws.[91]

These laws, as their name suggests, require adult children to provide care or support to their indigent parents if the adult children have the financial means. But filial responsibility is actually a bit of a misnomer; many of the very statutes that establish these obligations to parents also encompass the obligation to materially support spouses and children as well. Most of the thirty states that have filial responsibility statutes authorize only civil actions. Nonetheless, twelve states currently authorize courts to levy a criminal sanction upon adult children who fail to provide adequate care for their parents.[92] When applied to the situation of adult children with elderly and indigent parents, it bears mention that, in contrast to the period prior to the 1970s, the vast majority of these state statutes are not enforced at all, or very rarely, especially in the criminal context.[93]

As to the mechanics of these statutes, California's language is typical: "every adult child who, having the ability so to do, fails to provide necessary food, clothing, shelter, or medical attendance for an indigent parent, is guilty of a misdemeanor."[94] Massachusetts, like some other states, adds a proviso that such liability will not attach to a person who was not supported by parents as a minor or to a person who, "being one of two or more children, has made proper and reasonable contribution toward the support of such parent."[95] Our analysis in Chapter 6 will focus on the requirement to support parents under these laws.

Having canvassed some of the ways that a defendant's family status is burdened in the criminal justice system, we now turn to develop a normative framework to assess these various family ties burdens.

FIVE

A Normative Framework for Family Ties Burdens

IN THE PREVIOUS CHAPTER, we identified some practices we characterize as family ties burdens. Here, we present a normative framework for analyzing whether and how such burdens can be justified. First, we explain why we adopt a defendant-centered perspective despite the fact that when other perspectives are introduced, family ties burdens could be thought of as bringing benefits to the family as an institution or to particular family members other than the defendant. Then, we revisit some of the normative costs of *family ties benefits* that we explored earlier in the book to ascertain whether any retain applicability in the context of *family ties burdens*. Finally, we highlight the voluntary caregiving feature we see in the structure of many family ties burdens. We think this feature of voluntary caregiving can serve as a guide for scrutinizing burdens more generally, especially within a criminal law framework informed by what we call a "liberal minimalist" approach. Informed by these various principles, we offer a potential structure of normative analysis for laws creating criminal liability predicated on the defendant's family status.

A. A Defendant-Centered Perspective, Among Others

In looking at family ties burdens, we have been making a claim that the defendant is being treated differently, on account of some action or inaction, because of his family status. In this Section, we explain why we make the choice to use a defendant-centered perspective but we also try to contextualize that choice among the other perspectives one could adopt when looking at the laws that create family ties burdens in the criminal justice system.

1. The Defendant as the Object of Punitive Coercion

In examining family ties burdens the way we have examined family ties benefits in Part I, we are clearly looking at the nature of the wrongdoing from the defendant's perspective. We think this perspective is important because it is, after all, the defendant whose liberty the state seeks to place in peril. The conduct-guiding rules at the core of this book are aimed at defendants—and it seems necessary to analyze those conduct-guiding rules on their own terms. Ultimately, it is the defendants who are coerced in the name of state punishment; and the criminal justice system's coercive nature is its most important feature demanding justification.

But there is, of course, much more to say on the matter. Although family ties burdens might be thought of as burdens on the defendant, they might also be viewed as burdens on or benefits to others, such as victims, other family members, the state, or society at large. Let us explain how these other perspectives might operate.

2. Family Members as the Object of Harm

In a number of cases, the burden imposed on the defendant is also a burden on those whom it is allegedly supposed to help. Thus, for example, a woman whose ex-spouse is jailed for failure to pay child support may object on the ground that this burden imposes a terrible hardship on her family as well as on the defendant, in that it reduces the ability of her children's father to play any kind of meaningful role in their lives. Thus, many of the practices we have described in Chapter 4 powerfully affect family interests beyond those of the defendant. Consider how the punishment of someone for failing to supervise, rescue, or support a family member might impair that person's future ability or willingness to supervise, rescue, or support a family member. The nature and intensity of the punishment for the offender may have serious detrimental effects on the very family members who were initially harmed by the defendant's antecedent failure to satisfy his duty. The same is true, at least in certain conditions, when we punish offenders for bigamy, incest, or adultery. Incarceration or fines for violation of these laws may impair the capacity of the offenders to care for and support their families. In other words, the children in the Muth family felt the weight of that family ties burden too.

Undoubtedly, no legislator enacts these family ties burdens with the intention of inflicting harm on innocent family members. But because the harms to innocent third parties are often foreseeable, it is the legislators' obligation to weigh these costs in the balance of deciding whether and how to insert family ties burdens in the criminal justice system.

3. Burdens as Devices for Promoting "Family Life and Values"

Another prism arises when we view these laws from the *ex ante* rather than the *ex post* perspective. In other words, we might consider whether *the family* as a social institution could be described as benefiting from the law creating the family ties burden. On this view, what appears to be a penalty on familial status in an individual case could have been created as part of a strategy designed to confer benefits to the social institution of the family as a whole. So, even if some individual families lose out because of the penalty imposed on the defendant enduring the family ties burden, the goal is that many more families will ultimately benefit from having these laws.

For instance, the recent criminalization of nonpayment of child support looks like a family ties burden in the sense we defined it earlier. That is because, as a general matter, the failure to pay a debt is not a reason for criminal punishment. Indeed, other legal mechanisms exist to help debtors, most prominently bankruptcy. But now, the failure to pay child support, which is a form of debt, is a basis for criminal punishment. Indeed, family support obligations may not generally be discharged during bankruptcy. Thus, failures to meet some kinds of intrafamilial financial obligations are now penalized much more harshly than the failure to meet other financial obligations. That definitely creates a burden on a defendant, at least as we defined it earlier.

Characterizing these practices as burdens on the particular defendant might be mistaken if we alter the lens through which we are looking at the problem. If we move from an *ex post* perspective focused on the defendant to an *ex ante* perspective focused on the institution of the family, the offender in question might have agreed with having these family ties burdens as laws if he assessed them impartially, that is, without anticipating that he would end up being the target of these laws. He might approve of these laws in the belief that the family ties burdens were important to promote a certain vision of family life within society. Thus, from the *ex ante* position, criminalizing failures to rescue, failures to supervise, or failures to support, and banning incest, adultery, or bigamy are all aimed at keeping certain kinds of families together to perform the work associated with a certain kind of idealized family life. If this is the purpose, the policy of criminalizing nonpayment of child support might provide a benefit to both the offender and the institution of the family overall. Imposing a penalty on the offender for his violation of these laws is simply a way to ensure that people do not defect from what they themselves, as reasonable and rational persons working in concert with each other, would otherwise agree is needed to secure the conditions for human flourishing.[1]

4. Burdens as Devices to Serve Goals Beyond Family Promotion

Family ties burdens might have other rationales too—aside from simply promoting a particular vision of family life. First, the various burdens placed on offenders may reflect the imperfect or indirect choices of decision makers in the criminal justice system to enhance distinctive criminal justice goals such as deterrence or retribution. For example, the state legislature may be using the criminal justice system to communicate to offenders that when one wrongs certain family members, one is more worthy of reproach and condemnation.[2] In this respect, the burdens might be thought to advance the criminal justice system's norm-projection purposes by reflecting society's deep values. Thus, certain burdens based on failures to care for one's family members entail a breach of a trust relationship, which certain persons created when opting into a caregiving relationship.[3] If heightened penalties attach in the context of crimes against victims with whom one has opted into a relationship of caregiving, then those burdens might be justifiable: when one hurts or fails to protect someone whom one has already signaled to society that one will care for, then one might plausibly say there is an extra wrong (a breach of trust based on implicit or explicit promise) that has been committed. That wrong is not only a wrong against a particular victim, remediable by compensation. Rather, the wrong has a different texture because the wrongdoer has lulled others in the public into a false sense of security, leading the public to fail to help or monitor the vulnerable person in question.

A distinct but related idea is that these burdens serve other legitimate goals of the state that have little to do with deterrence or norm projection or even the vitality of family life. On this view, it might be that family ties burdens stand to serve other purposes that, in fact, directly benefit the state. For instance, the legislature might believe that imposing impediments to even consensual incest between adult siblings is important for reducing the prospects of increased social expenditures on food stamps and medical care, because the legislature assumes that incestuous relationships will produce offspring who are more likely to require subsidized medical support.[4] Again, here, we will have to weigh very carefully these purported benefits in any one instance; if they serve compelling or important interests, perhaps discrimination on the basis of family status is justifiable. But these compelling interests cannot be assessed in the abstract and must be pursued in the specific context of each burden, an analysis we begin undertaking in the next chapter.

5. Burdens in Relation to Family Ties Benefits

As shown in the preceding discussion, we obviously do not deny that the laws creating what we call family ties burdens lend themselves to examination from a variety of perspectives. We do think, however, that there is something about these family ties burdens that requires more caution than typically extended in discussions of any one of these laws in isolation from one another and in isolation from the benefits the criminal justice system extends to defendants based on family status. Indeed, in light of the fact that our work in the first half of the book examines the *benefits* the criminal justice system extends to defendants based on family status, we don't think there is something inherently biased when we look at the *burdens* placed on family ties here. To our minds, then, the inquiry at the core of this part of the book is important—when should family ties become the basis of distinctively criminal liability?

One answer to this question would be to look at these burdens in relation to the various family ties benefits. It might be thought that the burdens "balance out" this discriminatory treatment pervasive within the criminal justice system, just as, perhaps, family ties benefits may be a form of compensation for the havoc the criminal justice system indirectly wreaks upon families. But balance itself requires further justification to explain why there is a need to have any family ties benefits or burdens at all. After all, there would be reciprocity or balance in the absence of both family ties benefits and family ties burdens.

The better approach, we think, sees family ties benefits or burdens or both as serving some "protective" role of a particular notion of family and its associated caregiving responsibilities. But this protective role itself needs further elaboration. Consider the following: how exactly do sentencing discounts for those with family ties and responsibilities rest consistently with criminalizing polygamy, adultery, or incest? At first glance, the benefit and burden seem to be in tension—why would we make allowances based on family ties in one place and then punish based on family ties in the other situation?

But there may be an identifiable logic here. The former—sentencing discounts based on familial obligations—is arguably protective of family caregiving functions *ex post*. The others can be deemed "protective" of such caregiving functions from an *ex ante* perspective. That's because some might plausibly view incest, adultery, or polygamy (or the conduct giving rise to any of the other family ties burdens) as endangering the caregiving functions associated with the traditional family unit. On this view, these family ties burdens and benefits work in tandem to signal that society cares deeply about promoting particular conceptions of family even when they interfere with other norms informing the construction of an attractive and effective criminal justice system.

While this explanation sounds plausible, it suffers from the randomness of choice as to when to adopt an *ex ante* perspective and when to adopt an *ex post* perspective. It is arbitrary because it chooses to justify the practices by selecting an *ex post* focus on benefits and an *ex ante* focus on burdens without any further explanation of why such a choice is justifiable. The problem is that the protective function could arguably be promoted by selecting an *ex ante* view of benefits and an *ex post* view of burdens. But that would require a radical reorientation of the rules we have.

To illustrate: when taking an *ex ante* perspective on family ties benefits, one might think that if a state decided it will not give sentencing discounts based on family ties and responsibilities, then that would create extra deterrence with those parents sensitive to the signals the criminal law is emitting. The same rationale attaches to spousal testimonial immunities or exemptions from prosecution for harboring fugitives. In those situations, *ex ante*, people might think that they will forbear from crime so as not to put their loved ones in jeopardy of having to testify against them or to house them when they are fugitives. Forbearing from wrongdoing could be a way to demonstrate how they care about each other because it avoids putting the family members in a tough spot later on, a spot where they will have to choose between the obligations of kinship and citizenship. Moreover, because the *ex ante* view means that persons will consider themselves from the perspective of the victim's family at least as much as the perspective of the accused's family, they will have a more impartial and multifaceted view about what the better rules are here. Examined *ex ante*, most of the family ties benefits should be jettisoned when they interfere with particular criminal justice objectives they otherwise value. All this would be an argument for getting rid of at least those family ties benefits that impede criminal justice objectives.

By contrast, when examining family ties burdens from the defendant's *ex post* point of view, the defendant will strenuously argue that punishment for the family ties burdens will actually serve to interfere with caregiving roles served (or potentially served) by the defendant—especially when they strip resources (time, liberty, and money) from the defendant that might otherwise be allocated toward caregiving functions.

The preceding discussion shows only that legislators need not have necessarily adopted an *ex post* view of benefits and an *ex ante* view of family ties burdens. Moreover, since legislatures and scholars have likely not looked at these benefits and burdens systematically and as designed to be offsetting, critical and independent analysis is warranted.

B. Revisiting the Costs of Family Ties Benefits

When we analyzed family ties benefits in the first half of the book, we scrutinized the plausible justifications for getting the state to help the family in Chapter 2. There, we highlighted how critical it is to appreciate how the family both molds the individual and reduces the states' burdens. Indeed, without repeating our views unnecessarily, we recognize that the institution of the family helps create and fashion our individual identities, our "historical,"[5] "constitutive,"[6] or "situated"[7] selves that depend heavily on our families and our familial associations for survival and sustenance.[8] And by giving families special support, the state can economize on expenditures that it would otherwise be forced to bear in educating its citizenry and preparing its members to contribute to the stability and flourishing of the regime.

Notwithstanding the recognition that the family's role properly warrants, and the risk that states incur of irrelevance and illegitimacy when they fail to treat persons as constituted selves, we ultimately concluded in Chapter 2 that general arguments rooted in communitarian political theory were insufficient to underwrite the special treatment of the family in the *criminal justice system.* In particular, we noted how these family ties benefits create the risks of inequality, gender bias, inaccuracy, and more crime. Consequently, we expressed hesitation and skepticism toward many of the family ties benefits distributed throughout the criminal justice system.

The reasons for our skepticism toward the distribution of family ties benefits inform our approach to thinking about family ties burdens. First, we must address whether, and to what degree, the normative considerations we identified earlier in connection with family ties benefits—patriarchal domination and gender bias, inaccuracy, inequality, and crime-creation—apply in the context of family ties burdens. But because we are also looking at the creation of criminal liability (as opposed to exemptions or benefits), we must also say a bit more about the liberal minimalism that informs our view of the proper basis of criminal liability in a liberal democracy.

Let's begin with the framework used for assessing family ties benefits and how it translates to the context of burdens. One can see relatively quickly that two of these considerations—crime creation and inaccuracy—are mostly inapplicable in the context of family ties burdens. In other words, unlike family ties benefits, family ties burdens rarely trigger concerns that they will create more misconduct or impede the accurate prosecution of the guilty and the exoneration of the innocent.[9] Although it may be possible that these two costs are implicated in a hypothetical burden that we have not identified, we do not see them as generally applicable in the case of family ties burdens and do not think it would be appropriate to criticize family ties burdens along these lines.

But two of the normative considerations that we identified earlier do seem generally relevant when analyzing family ties burdens: inequality (and its relationship to morally arbitrary discrimination) and the related issue of gender bias. Notice that although inequality and gendered *effects* of a neutrally drawn criminal justice regulation would not come within the ambit of our discussion—for family ties burdens, as we define them, must facially discriminate against family status—they are normatively relevant in judging the viability of any particular burden drawn on the basis of family status.

So, even though omissions liability, bigamy, and nonpayment of child support law are, for example, written in gender-neutral terms, once they are identified as facially discriminatory against family members, it is appropriate to ask under our model whether they have effects that reinforce gender stereotypes.

1. Inequality and Discrimination

In many contexts, family ties burdens risk treating similar conduct unequally—and affirmative discrimination against the family is hard to justify. For example, incest prohibitions affecting consensual sexual relations among adults restrict liberties that would otherwise be unregulated and generally protected. The nonpayment of a debt becomes a criminal offense in one context (child support) while it remains a civil action in most others. Although it is obvious through the exaction of burdens that we are often seeking to have family members take special precautionary measures to protect vulnerable potential victims, the tool of punishing otherwise non-criminal conduct on the basis of familial status alone is surely worth scrutinizing more carefully, since it does implicate norms of equality and nondiscrimination that a criminal justice system within a constitutional democracy should embrace.[10]

Indeed, as a general matter—and in ways we will expand upon presently—we tend to think that targeting familial status is generally both an overinclusive and underinclusive approach to achieving sound policy objectives. It may make sense for the criminal justice system to try to protect our most vulnerable members of society. But many types of citizens are vulnerable, and targeting the state-defined family is not a sufficiently narrowly tailored means to achieving that objective. Nothing about estranged family members, for example, necessarily renders them especially vulnerable to one another to justify the imposition of special burdens upon offenders and potential offenders. Thus, family ties burdens could be overbroad if they penalized, say, estranged siblings with duties to rescue, support, or supervise. By contrast, many vulnerable citizens warrant protections that the criminal law currently renders unavailable. The families of same-sex couples, for example, experience the same vulnerabilities as the idealized traditional family does—but get few or none of the criminal law protections. Thus, family ties burdens that do not protect people who would agree to such protection and such burdens *ex ante* should be reconfigured to promote the underlying value of voluntary caregiving relationships. We say more about this below.

2. Gender Bias, Heteronormativity, and Repronormativity

Imposing a burden or penalty on an individual in the criminal justice system solely on the basis of family ties enmeshes the state in an expressly normative dispute over who counts as family and who does not—and in what the family should be doing, namely, procreating.

And the position the state takes is one that is not merely conventional; it also threatens to promote a discriminatory and gendered set of policies. Thus, as noted above, in the context of family ties burdens, large numbers of persons who might (justifiably, in our view) see themselves as entitled to benefit from the imposition of family ties burdens are excluded. In this sense, the use of the family as traditionally delineated is an underinclusive (and at times, overinclusive) mechanism to distribute the tangible and expressive benefits conferred by the criminal law when it targets persons with unusual treatment on account of familial status. Although the exclusion of same-sex coupling is the most obvious example of the criminal law's heteronormativity bias,[11] grandparents and other relatives routinely create homes that fall outside the criminal law's design for family ties burdens as well.[12]

Additionally, as we will argue, several of the family ties burdens express a clear policy to promote procreation—an orientation some scholars have called *repronormativity*.[13] To the extent that the criminal justice system is engaged in penalizing citizens criminally to further its repronormative agenda, we think that calls for special justification. On the other hand, we think that some family ties burdens are a useful counterbalance to repronormativity bias. That is, although the state promotes having children, some of the family ties burdens serve as a way to mitigate the effects of subsidizing procreation through tax and welfare policies.

Finally, in certain circumstances, family ties burdens are used in ways that reinforce gender stereotypes. Although routinely drafted today in gender-neutral terms, many family ties burdens raise substantial questions about gender relations more broadly—and once a family ties burden is identified, it seems fair game to analyze whether the burden is contributing to gender bias more systematically. As we explain in Chapter 6, we think that some of the family ties burdens raise this concern.

C. Uncovering a Structure of Family Ties Burdens: Voluntary Caregiving

Five of the seven family ties burdens we find in the law—omissions liability (for failure to rescue), parental responsibility laws, bigamy, adultery, and nonpayment of child support—reflect a pattern that, to our mind, has not been sufficiently emphasized. This pattern suggests an internal structure that we find helpful in rethinking family ties burdens in our criminal justice system.

Specifically, these five burdens occur in the context of relationships that have a voluntary or opt-in nature, meaning that the individual who faces the burden has voluntarily entered into the relationship that serves as the basis of potential subsequent liability for doing or forbearing from actions that would otherwise be lawful. This is not the case with most incest statutes, which prohibit sexual conduct in relationships that are both voluntarily and involuntarily created. Nor is it the case with filial responsibility statutes, which attach liability to persons who did not consent to the relationship—though there is, perhaps, some reason to marginalize this example in light of the relatively trivial level of enforcement. But if one looks at the dominant practices with respect to family ties burdens, they are imposed on defendants in two kinds of relationships: spouse to spouse and parent to child.

Although we do not see this pattern as itself authoritative, we do think it is illuminating in various ways. First, when family ties burdens are limited to relationships reflecting this voluntary nature, we find the imposition of these burdens more attractive. The voluntary nature at the heart of these obligations takes at least some of the bite out of the charge of discrimination: if parties freely choose relationships that themselves trigger liability after fair notice, liability on the basis of family status seems more defensible, at least up to a point at which the penalty is proportionate to the wrongdoing and the reason for imposing the burden can withstand some critical scrutiny of the sort we describe below.[14]

While voluntarism matters, there's also a basic trade-off going on: if one wishes to benefit from the ways in which society privileges building family relationships through institutions of distributive justice, then one needs to be aware that greater burdens may be imposed to ensure the discharge of one's caregiving responsibilities. Moreover, in light of the fact that society confers so much leeway to persons regarding how they treat children, there is a strong reason to create a floor of obligations to rescue, support, and supervise in that context. By contrast, extending family ties *benefits* only to those who have opted in to relationships of caregiving seems to discriminate more against those who are deprived of the opportunity to develop legally recognized caregiving relationships in the first place. In other words, not everyone can choose (or wants to choose) to marry or procreate—and those who do not make this choice should generally not be treated disfavorably by the criminal justice system.

To be sure, voluntary relations can be fuzzy at the margins: Have we really chosen our in-laws even though they have not chosen us? Have we really chosen to have children when a pregnancy is the result of failed birth control methods? Still, we think the relatively easy cases of spousal and parent-child relationships help expose an important insight about appropriate burden distribution; that is, family ties burdens generally seem more palatable in the context of voluntary relationships of caregiving.

Why should voluntariness matter? For one thing, restricting the imposition of family ties burdens to those who choose to bear them is a way of respecting one's autonomy; if we forced all sorts of obligations on family members who did not choose to enter a relationship of care with someone, we would be impinging on their reasonable liberty interests. This is why we think the filial responsibility statutes have been improperly adopted—they are basically illiberal, as we explain in Chapter 6, because their basis is established through reciprocity and "required" gratitude, rather than consent. Incest laws that do not track consent suffer from similar problems.

Additionally, the special obligations some family ties burdens impose can be understood in terms of signaling theory.[15] On this view, family ties burdens are appropriately imposed on someone who has voluntarily entered into and maintained a relationship because by their consent to that relationship they are signaling to others that they are going to be "first responders;" society can then trust them to look after the people with whom they have created a covenant of caregiving. The germ of this idea appears in duty to rescue law.

As we discussed earlier, one does not generally labor under a duty to rescue other people.[16] But as we explained, there are widely acknowledged exceptions to this no-duty principle. For instance, if Alice is walking by the beach and sees Charlie drowning, and she then waves away Bob, who was also on his way to rescue Charlie, Alice is now under a special obligation to rescue Charlie. She cannot just walk away at that point, absent special justification (such as a new threat to her life). The actions of marrying or parenting can be interpreted to be creating similar statements about responsibility.

When a person enters into a covenant of care in the form of marriage or parenting, one message that decision signals to society is that she will be a "first responder" to the person with whom she is covenanting when that person is in danger.

Beyond signaling a willingness to be a first responder, those whose actions exhibit a willingness to take on the obligations of spouse or parent have also signaled their willingness to create a relationship of trust to care and support the other spouse or child. When someone fails to rescue, support, or supervise (in the case of minors), there is a breach of that trust relationship, a breach which the state has an especial interest in since the state has been effectively waved away by the person opting into the caregiving relationship.[17]

It follows, we believe, that if voluntariness matters, then a family ties burden should not be placed on someone who has had a familial status *imposed* upon him. Consider siblings. Almost no child freely chooses whether or not to have a sibling; that decision is generally made by parents. Unsurprisingly, the law ordinarily does not impose special obligations upon an individual to take or face risks on a sibling's behalf. Other family relations fall into the same category: no one freely chooses whether to have an aunt, uncle, or cousin.

By this logic, it seems clear that some family relationships are involuntary in the sense that they were not deliberately entered into by the relevant parties. The filial responsibility laws, which place burdens on adult children to support their parents in their dotage, are an example of a family ties burden that is at odds with the general vein of promoting voluntary caregiving relationships. The children never consented to the relationship they have with their parents. Indeed, maybe that explains why there is so little enforcement in the case of this family ties burden.

The more difficult question is whether there are family relationships that are, in fact, truly voluntary. At first blush, the most obvious example of a voluntary relationship would seem to be that of spouses—it is certainly true for most cultures in this country that no one is forced to marry and individuals may freely choose their own partner.[18] To be sure, some human trafficking victims are coerced into marriage, but that marriage results from legal wrongdoing; it does not instantiate or exemplify what we think to be marriage's modern nature.[19] Although some have argued that social and economic forces render marriage compulsory,[20] we think such conclusions are generally unpersuasive. The strong social and economic pressure to marry does not vitiate the voluntariness that renders people's decisions their own for the purposes of being responsible to take on family ties burdens and benefits. Of course, current government policies and social norms undoubtedly reward an individual's decision to marry, and make that choice more attractive, but these rewards nonetheless stop short of compelling an individual to marry. By the same token, some government policies also prevent an individual from marrying a person of his or her choice and that, to our mind, is an undue intrusion of the state, since it denies opportunities and expressive benefits on grounds we find morally irrelevant.

As to the parent-child relationship, we see this relationship as generally voluntary (although there might be some social pressures in some communities to reproduce).[21] A mother who does not wish to parent is legally free to use very reliable birth control methods—and she may terminate her pregnancy or place a child up for adoption. To be sure, there are complications with this general observation of voluntariness.[22] For example, fathers have long been held by courts to be forced to parent against their will in the sense that they are subject to child support obligations even if they take affirmative steps to avoid fatherhood.[23] Still, for the most part, these complications are indicative of the exceptions, not the general case. Most parents want and choose their children. This is not to say that the laws that attach to parents as family ties burdens are always justified. Rather, the fact that these relationships are usually voluntary helps us understand the underlying structure of burden allocation by the criminal justice system.

Let us reiterate some features of this analysis, for we have earlier left prior commentators on this aspect of our argument confused. Professor Michael O'Hear suggests, in his thinking on our work, that we embrace the view that "the voluntary assumption of a duty . . . adds substantial support for the criminal enforcement of that duty."[24] Professor Rick Hills likewise worries that we "root" criminal liability in "consent" to provide care.[25] Although we think that voluntariness is relevant in analyzing family ties burdens, we think the use of the phrase *substantial support* overstates our position because we believe that voluntariness is not in and of itself a sufficient reason to bring the criminal law to bear. Similarly, we resist the idea that we root liability in consent, since it is not itself the reason for liability; it is only a necessary, not a sufficient condition for criminal law liability. In the omissions context, for example, it is the failure to perform some underlying caregiving duty that remains the basis for the liability; voluntariness with respect to the assumption of that duty only plays a role in delineating whose acts or omissions may properly serve as a basis for criminal liability in a liberal state.

So what is our account of voluntariness and how is it different from the voluntariness associated with criminal acts that the criminal law routinely focuses upon? In deriving our voluntariness test we examined the way in which criminal justice systems picked out familial relationships for burdening. In five out of the seven family ties burdens that we explore here—adultery, bigamy, parental responsibility, omissions, nonpayment of child support—the liability only attached to a person who could plausibly be said to have voluntarily created the relationship of caregiving. Moreover, with respect to filial responsibility laws, we noticed the near complete lack of enforcement today.

To be sure, this casual empiricism does not decide the matter for us. But it does illuminate it for us because voluntariness must clearly play a central role in assessing the fairness of allocating criminal law liability in these contexts. That is, the pattern of voluntariness evidenced by the family ties burdens we uncover here is consistent with what we think a liberal state should do: namely, give people some autonomy about entering relationships before using the relationship status as an element of a crime. This autonomy principle is in some sense being stifled by the use of traditional family status, since the laws in question often exclude from coverage many people who should be covered because of the nature of their caregiving roles in others' lives, whether they are persons in homosexual relationships, polyamorous unions, siblings, or some other form of committed un-married persons.

Although this conception of voluntariness does not have a large explicit role in most areas of the criminal law, if the criminal law seeks to burden a relationship with the use of a status-oriented approach, we think liberalism requires that the burdens created have been voluntarily assumed. If the law requires that public officials provide the public their "honest services,"[26] that is, to act as quasi-fiduciaries to the public, it is fair, in part, because they have not been forced into these jobs. In the world of family status liabilities that we have found, most of which are predicated on a relationship, we think that being able to choose or reject the relationship is a necessary requirement to have the law comply with our basic commitments to autonomy specifically and liberalism generally.[27]

Of course, that we are voluntarists in criminal law design does not commit us to any voluntarist vision of the constitution of moral life and the source of moral norms. We simply take a position about the institutional design of criminal justice practices in a liberal state. It may well be the case that our parents or siblings have legitimate moral claims on us that stem from their relationships to us, independent of choice. But the liberal state should avoid enforcing those claims through the criminal law for all the reasons we have specified here. In short, voluntariness of the sort we have identified is a reasonable test for legislators to surmount if they are designing the enforcement mechanisms of the criminal law to target relational obligations.

D. Overcoming Family Status Through a Focus on Voluntary Caregiving

Notwithstanding the ambiguities that might attach in particular situations regarding whether a familial relationship is voluntary, using voluntariness rather than familial status as a basis for distributing these kinds of obligations is initially quite attractive. Indeed, using voluntariness as a criterion helps us solve the problems of underinclusiveness and overinclusiveness that arise when using family status alone. Importantly, it allows us to encompass those who view themselves as obligated to others through their own choices and actions regardless of the state-established delineations of an "acceptable" family. Thus, same-sex partners, unmarried heterosexual partners, grandparents caring for extended family members, even platonic or polyamorous friends living together in a committed caregiving relationship—all of these people are engaged in voluntary relationships. They may both *want* and *warrant* the protections and expressive benefits of burdens solely allocated on the basis of family ties in our current policy environment.

Yet, how can one go about limiting the extension of such burdens that the state is expected to prosecute with its criminal justice resources? Can a teenager choose his third closest friend as the person to whom he owes a special obligation of protection? If he does, should scarce criminal justice resources be used to reinforce that obligation? We need to know, in other words, both *who decides* and *by what criteria* a particular relationship should be deemed a voluntary relationship in which the party is willing to assume obligations toward another and for which the law is willing to intervene.

In our view, voluntariness as a stand-alone criterion is insufficient for assessing whether it is just and attractive to impose or enhance criminal penalties on the basis of a particular relationship. When assessing criminal liability, we suggest that voluntariness be used in conjunction with whether a component of the relationship includes an obligation of some form of *caregiving*. Our sense is that many sorts of people assume these caregiving roles and not all of them are familial in nature. Roommates, for example, might choose to adopt an ethos of mutual care over a period of time. If that relationship is freely entered into and maintained by individuals capable of informed and intelligent consent,[28] we do not see why they should not be able to enter into the covenants of care similar to the ones that presumptively characterize spousal or parental relationships.[29] But they should not necessarily be required to adopt all of the obligations that the law ascribes to parents either. Although this scenario may be unlikely, one roommate might only choose to undertake a duty to perform easy rescues, while the other might undertake obligations of financial support and a duty to rescue. Friends or roommates should be able and encouraged to create obligations that are both capable of being scaled in size or intensity and enforced through threat of criminal sanction. That is, if we are going to recognize caregiving responsibilities through the criminal law, they should not be restricted to ones that are familial.

That said, we do think there are meaningful differences between a spousal or parental duty of care and the additional covenants of care that we are prepared to recognize. For example, we believe that one's familial status qua spouse or parent may be presumptively used to establish that the relationship involves voluntarism, whereas such a presumption would not be justifiable in the case of roommates. After all, the act of marriage in our society is, absent any contrary evidence in particular cases, the product of individuals choosing to marry each other; and the same goes for the choice to raise children, generally speaking. In contrast, the presumption in other relationships would not automatically attach. Thus, familial status as such would be neither necessary nor sufficient to justify a family ties burden.

There is also the related question of whether voluntary assumptions of responsibility can be terminated. We think they ought to be terminable under certain conditions, depending on the context. In the context of married couples, legal separation would be the appropriate way to signal an opting out of the marital family ties burdens. And in the context of a parent giving up his or her child to friends across the country, the termination of parental rights is the way to opt out of the special duties of parenthood. But it is not obvious to us that these potentially costly signaling mechanisms should be the only ways to break the covenants that trigger the special responsibilities of voluntary caregiving.

Although for the average dyad (whether parent-child or spouse-spouse), the legal opt out might not be unduly burdensome, there might be cases when it seems unfair to require divorce or termination. Perhaps, in exceptional circumstances, parties to these special relationships ought to be able to show that they should be deemed "equitably" divorced or terminated for the purposes of the family ties burdens. One way to determine the bona fides of these parties is to ascertain whether they have tried to capture family ties benefits through either the criminal or the civil system (say, by claiming a dependent for tax purposes); in situations in which the parties have not claimed those benefits, we can envision the very rare case when parties should be saved the pain and cost of an official divorce and termination.

Spousal relationships, however, should not be treated the same as parents' obligations toward their children. After all, minor children cannot avoid their own vulnerability.[30] Thus, although letting spouses opt out does not generally offend a sense of fair play, letting parents ditch their vulnerable children without their consent (for minors cannot really consent by law) quite centrally violates the most basic tenets of what many think parents owe their children.[31] But that is just another way of specifying why allowing parental opt out without termination should be even rarer than allowing spousal opt out without divorce.

Nevertheless, just because it should be rare does not mean it must be categorically proscribed. Indeed, if we are right that voluntary caregiving underwrites and furnishes justificatory principles for some status-based burdens in the criminal justice system, we should seek ways to narrowly tailor the family ties burdens to capture only the right kinds of offenders. If we had to give up our children to good friends for several years because of illness or incapacitation, for example, the scope of criminally enforceable parental duties would have to be adjusted, though not necessarily eliminated. If a child visits her parent in prison, it is not wrong to continue to assign that parent an obligation to perform an easy rescue just because the parent is not the primary caregiver anymore. On the other hand, the fact that the parent is in prison may be a good basis for not assigning criminal liability on the basis of nonpayment of support if there is no income or wealth for the parent to tap for the child's support.

For most other relationships outside of childrearing and spouses, however, we think a registry could be created in which people opt in and opt out of relationships of caregiving as long as they provide notice to the affected parties.[32] This strategy would allow adults to select a number of additional persons eligible for receiving the adult's responsibility. If unrelated roommates wanted to sign up (or create such covenants as a prerequisite for living with another adult), they could do so, signaling commitments of care *for* each other, *to* each other, *and* to those around them. And if adult children wanted to signal their willingness to shoulder burdens to care for their parents, then that would be an *option*, rather than the *requirement* it is under a few states' rules.

To be sure, there is something cheaply administrable when the law selects simply a few family status relationships instead of creating a registry for relationships of voluntary caregiving. But it does not seem that much more difficult to use a registry of the sort we describe, especially when it lends promise to the prospect of all sorts of people pledging their hearts and sense of obligation to others around them. Moreover, as alluded to above, the administrability of this system can be rather cheaply achieved by requiring that spouses and children occupy a special role with respect to family ties burdens—*i.e.*, certain duties can be imposed on parents and spouses to ensure they meet the responsibilities they agree to when they volunteer to be a spouse or parent. Our registry network, in other words, would supplement the core relationships of spousal and parental obligation, not supplant it.

In short, adopting a voluntarist approach to burden distribution in the criminal justice system harmonizes well with what we think the system appears to seek for itself, albeit imperfectly. Moreover, it might provide for a better intellectual fit with the competing interests in promoting freedom and autonomy, which is thought by many to undergird the no-duty-to-rescue pattern of law.[33] Additionally, the difficulties associated with the under- and over-inclusive nature of family status can be remedied in large measure by use of a registry where one can declare who counts within one's sphere of accepted responsibility for the purpose of some of the crimes discussed here. This would strengthen voluntary assumptions of caregiving responsibilities (of which the family is sometimes a great example) rather than rely upon inflexible categories based upon antiquarian notions of status.

Spurning our embrace of a voluntariness requirement, Professor O'Hear, in his published comments on earlier versions of these arguments, offers an alternative basis of liability premised upon *vulnerability* and *proximity*.[34] Presumably, this would entail an obligation of an older sibling to rescue a younger sibling when possible, not to mention neighbors and co-workers.[35] We certainly believe there is a moral basis for rescue in these scenarios, but the question upon which we focus is whether the *criminal* law ought to be used to punish a failure to satisfy that moral obligation. To our mind, vulnerability and proximity are aspects that matter insofar as they are parts of a voluntarily created relationship of caregiving.[36] But insofar as they serve to create liability where no one consented to that caregiving obligation, we find such status-based obligations problematic.[37] Under our view of these duties to rescue, without one party agreeing to perform some degree of caregiving, no criminal liability ought to attach.[38] So we do not disagree that Professor O'Hear's normative foundations for these liabilities should also play a role in thinking about when to exact them and from whom; it is just that we remain convinced that the liberal state needs to assess some baseline voluntariness of the relationship in the first instance.[39]

Instead of voluntariness or proximate vulnerability, Professor Hills, in his published comments on a previous version of this argument, offers a different principle that, on his account, both fits and justifies a number of the family ties burdens we reveal here. Hills would reorganize family ties burdens to promote child-rearing. We find that alternative deeply troublesome for the liberal state.

Professor Hills makes a good case for the child-rearing value as a good fit with some of the family ties burdens we discovered in the law. Each burden in its own way can be part of a story in which the criminal justice system brings itself to bear on families because families are subcontracted the task—without much oversight—of raising children for the state.

Yet it does not suffice to say, as Professor Hills does, that our society would "be deprived of the future value of humanity" without "properly raised children."[40] That may or may not be true. Indeed, if children are a positive good, why do they become less valuable to society once they are less vulnerable as adults? Presumably what makes children valuable is also what makes adults valuable, in which case Professor Hills has a hard time explaining why we would not extend the reach of these family liabilities to all, or at least to those who still have procreative (and caregiving?) capacity. In sum, we think a liberal state may not use its criminal law to reinforce a very particular version of the right way to organize the institution of the family through the use of status-based liabilities that citizens have never had the opportunity to reject. We are also mindful that child-rearing values are often used in service of discriminating against non-traditional groups.

Thus, at least two central differences with Hills' focus on child-rearing are worth highlighting. First, we see family ties burdens as efforts to cope with and oversee relationships in which people often find themselves vulnerable in intimate contexts in which the state can perform comparatively little oversight. So we would not have criminal liabilities contingent on whether anyone had children, something that—the future of humanity, notwithstanding—seems morally arbitrary to us, at least as far as the criminal law is concerned. Second, while we might concede the view that the perpetuation of our species and the acculturation of our citizens through private resources are central goods that the state should pursue by propping up the family and subsidizing its activities,[41] we are still committed to the view that there are certain liberal norms that constrain *how* the state may choose to pursue such ends in the criminal law. Our normative framework highlights that point through both our voluntariness inquiry as well as our minimalism. Without some compelling proof that the state needs to use the criminal law to forward its agenda of only allowing one man and/or one woman to raise a child, we remain convinced that our account is more consistent with basic liberal commitments, requiring only a focus on whether the obligation of care was voluntarily assumed. It still might be a bad use of resources to criminalize this world of intimacy and inaction; but that is a separate question from our threshold inquiry into whether a liberal state should create such crimes in the first place.

E. Bringing It Together: How to Scrutinize a Family Ties Burden

In light of all these various considerations, we propose that family ties burdens—whether the ones we described in Chapter 4 or some others that might be contemplated—undergo scrutiny, using a set of normative speed bumps designed to track our discussion here. Our general approach in light of the foregoing is that special criminal justice burdens based on familial status alone require justification. Perhaps unsurprisingly, just as we exhibited a tendency to be skeptical toward most family ties benefits in the first part of the book, we are also inclined to protect individuals from penalties or burdens based simply on traditional familial status. However, because we are sensitive to the caregiving contributions that might stand in need of special protection from the state, we believe that some of the concerns people might have about abandoning family ties burdens can be addressed instead through careful drafting that substitutes attentiveness to voluntary relationships of caregiving in the place of familial status alone. Thus, our skepticism toward family ties burdens does not entail eliminating all such burdens. Instead, we propose that such burdens undergo a searching inquiry framed by a liberal minimalist paradigm.

What is liberal minimalism? A liberal minimalist approach to criminal liability is reflective of two basic, though not uncontested, values. With respect to the word liberal, we are relying on its roots to connect to a particular notion of when it is appropriate to use family status as an element of a criminal law. To our mind, the family relationship that is an element of criminal liability must be one that is the product of freely chosen behavior. Specifically, we deem a burden to pass muster under our first "liberalism" concern if the relationship which serves as the basis for a family ties burden is one that the defendant freely created through her choice. The consent is not always explicitly extended, but it may, in some cases, be reasonably inferred in light of the other available options available to the offender. Beyond this first basic liberal concern is also a need for some showing that the relationship is one of caregiving. Without this additional element, we risk allowing the criminal justice system's apparatus to be co-opted by mere contract.[42]

A second and more general liberal concern we deem important is that a justice system must allocate liberty to citizens consistent with other persons' liberty, putting the burden of justification on those who would limit individual liberty.[43] For this reason, in designing laws that target family status, one must assess the liberty interest at stake—and how important it is.

With respect to minimalism in criminal law, we ask whether the government has an important or compelling objective it is trying to achieve through the use of the family ties burden. This purpose analysis is obviously fraught with controversy and so, in many situations, we usually stipulate to the objective's importance in order to assess the means used to pursue the ends. This means analysis involves two kinds of questions. First, has the government narrowly tailored the criminal sanction to its putative objectives to avoid overinclusiveness or underinclusiveness? Second, is there good reason to believe that the use of a family ties burden via criminal sanction is justified if and when other alternatives (education, advertising, regulation, tort, or contract) could be equally effective in achieving the state's objective?[44] These questions are important because criminal sanctions use coercion to limit liberty; are especially costly to both the state and to the offender; and are subject to error and abuse. For those reasons, we support a principle of pragmatic frugality both in the drafting of criminal legislation and the amount of punishment imposed. Punishment should be no more severe than necessary to achieve the legislature's reasonable interests, and the legislature should forbear from coercion through criminal sanction when possible. At a relatively high level of abstraction, this is a principle (also connected to proportionality) that theorists of many stripes can embrace.[45] Although there is much more that can be said about both these notions of liberalism and minimalism,[46] we do not wish to stray too far from the subject at hand.

As applied to our project on the use of family status to create criminal liability, we think the liberal minimalist agenda, coupled with the concerns about discrimination and gender bias alluded to earlier, trigger a set of questions for the normative review of the family ties burdens we discussed in Chapter 4. These questions are similar (though not identical) to the ones asked by courts in liberal democracies like the United States and Canada when they review legislation alleged to impair a fundamental liberty or alleged to rely on a suspect classification.

Of course, we must determine as a threshold matter whether the state is in fact targeting a defendant for prosecution (or enhanced punishment) based on his family status.[47] But in the case of the seven burdens we have discussed in Chapter 4, we can readily conclude that family status is relevant and necessary for the liability the defendant faces, so when it comes to the application of the framework in Chapter 6, we will dispense with this threshold question and instead focus on the rest of the framework develop here, as follows.

First, does the burden fall only on persons who have voluntarily created a relationship of care? Second, does the burden impinge on some liberty that should be recognized as deserving of protection in a liberal society? Third, are the laws drafted in such a way as to be narrowly tailored to the governmental objectives? Fourth, are there non-criminal measures that could be equally effective in achieving these government objectives, assuming these government objectives were sufficiently compelling or important to vindicate through law? Last, in what ways do the existing family ties burdens contribute to concerns about gender, inequality, and discrimination?

As before, this kind of scrutiny will not resolve all questions. Inevitably, disputes about the strength of competing claims will persist – and means testing will implicate empirical evidence, which is too often indeterminate or simply non-existent. But, as we hope we achieved in our systematic inquiry into family ties benefits in Part I, we hope to do some important work in helping clarify the problems under consideration and alerting lawyers, policymakers, and judges to some of the potentially hidden costs of family ties burdens in the criminal justice system.

SIX

Applying the Framework to Family Ties Burdens

IN THIS CHAPTER, we undertake some analysis of the various family ties burdens we identified in Chapter 4. In what follows, we do not exhaustively analyze each family ties burden—even from within our own framework. As we acknowledged at the very beginning, each of the burdens we have identified requires its own long-form analysis, taking account of its particularized context and its systemic effects on the justice system and relevant family members. Accordingly, all we endeavor to do in this Chapter is furnish a basis for how our framework contributes to a more comprehensive accounting when analyzing each family ties burden. We think our framework recommends caution about the bulk of the family ties burdens we have identified and urges creativity in redesigning these burdens to make them less discriminatory.

A. Omissions Liability For Failure to Rescue

The question of omissions liability for failure to rescue is a difficult one, and the analysis seems to vary according to the kind of family status relationship at issue.

1. Parental Duties to Rescue Children

Let us begin with the most common scenario where we see liability imposed: the prosecution of parents who fail to protect their children. What are the rationales used to describe why we impose criminally sanctioned obligations on parents to rescue their children when they are imperiled and when parents have an easy rescue to make?

Imposing liability on parents for failing to protect their children seems to vindicate a compelling state interest—the need to protect children from harm.[1] It is in this scenario that our concerns about fostering the caregiving capacity of individuals reach their zenith. But the concern for protecting children from harm would seem to require that anyone with the chance to make an easy rescue should be under such an obligation. After all, young children are often helpless to protect themselves from harm; responsibility must seem to fall on the shoulders of those adults in the position to be a child's only lifeline. But this is not how the laws of rescue are drafted as a general matter.

Thus, the objective of restricting the duty to rescue a child to its custodial figure has to do, at least in part, with an expressive function about the kind of commitment made by a parent to the world regarding the child. The law seems to be saying that parents who have voluntarily chosen to retain the benefits conferred by the parent-child relationship should endure some burdens in return, and ensuring the safety of a child entrusted to the parent's care represents the most fundamental of reasonable burdens. When a person opts to have children, the parent is, as we suggested earlier, signaling to others that the parent will be a first responder.

In this respect, imposing a duty to rescue here is analogous to the imposition of liability on those people who have "waved away" others. The goal, of course, is not to tie an albatross around the neck of every parent. Omissions liability does not create a responsibility to rescue against unreasonable risks. It operates only to ensure that when a parent is in a position of protecting the child from imminent harm, the parent takes reasonable measures to do so.

a. Voluntary Caregiving and Its Limits

We think it is fair to conclude, in most circumstances, that imposing obligations to rescue one's children (defined as minors for whom one has legal custody) is consistent with voluntarist caregiving. That said, the question of what justifies a status-based duty to rescue is a bit more complicated than the one that grounds a spouse-like relation. To be sure, the vast majority of parents eagerly assume the obligations associated with parenting—and, therefore, the law's placing a burden to rescue may be unnecessary. But whether it is necessary or not as a policy matter is not our primary concern here: we are first concerned about how consistent the policy is with a general commitment to voluntarist caregiving.

Some parents might resist the ascription of voluntariness to their actions or to the results of their actions. First, one might say that he volunteered to have sex, but he didn't consent to have a child that resulted from sex. Or one may claim, under the circumstances of rape or stolen sperm, that one didn't even volunteer to have procreative sex.[2] As a general matter, however, we view the risk of pregnancy as a risk people voluntarily assume when they engage in sexual relations, even when using birth control. The question is whether the risk of pregnancy should also be conflated with the risk of being conscripted into parental obligations that are vindicated through the criminal law.

If women have exclusive control over the decision to abort and primary, albeit not necessarily exclusive, control over the adoption decision, then that makes more compelling the inference that mothers who have ultimately acquiesced to or embraced the task of raising children should bear responsibility for caring for the child, at least as far as the criminal law is concerned. To be sure, the absence of either of these alternatives would undermine the moral basis for ascribing a burden of care to a person. So, too, would it be inappropriate to establish omissions liability on sperm or egg donors who make clear that they are renouncing future interests to those accepting the sperm or eggs.

As to men: if men who have taken reasonable precautions in terms of birth control—or who reasonably relied on express precautions taken by the woman—lack control over the choice to abort or give the baby up for adoption, then it is inaccurate to say that they are consenting to the obligations associated with parenting unless there is some other way to categorically renounce their parental rights and obligations. Thus, if one biological parent objects to becoming a parent over the wishes of the other parent, and secures a pre-conception waiver from the other person, then, at least according to two of us (Markel and Leib), that might be a basis for releasing the objecting parent from the family ties burden.[3] But in the absence of such evidence, it is not unreasonable to place a burden on parents who, through biology or adoption, assume this caregiving role. Indeed, to the extent that there are borderline cases, we might highlight that the burden (on the potential defendant) may operate to help the vulnerable child, so questionable cases of consent should default to burdening the parent.

Might these consent or voluntarism arguments founder if we ask whether parents specifically consented to taking care of a child with X, where X is illness or a behavioral problem? The consent still exists so long as there is a procedure by which parents can terminate their parental rights to the state through voluntary relinquishment, a relatively widespread practice.

Still, because not all children live with their biological parents,[4] we believe that the use of traditional family status to limit omissions liability is a problem. A child could reside with another relative, such as a grandparent, a family friend, or a foster family, to name just a few possible permutations.[5] Alternatively, as we explain below, there may be homosexual couples or gay and straight persons involved in polyamorous contexts who care for the child, but their parenting status may not be recognized by the state. There is also the difficult question about the caregiving responsibilities that occur outside the home: schools, religious institutions, Girl Scouts, sports leagues—in all these sites, adults and adolescents with supervisory roles play an increasingly important role in the rearing of children.[6] Therefore, limiting omissions liability to biological parents and their children has the potential to be underinclusive, in that it does not recognize non-traditional relationships of caregiving.

Using only an opt-in registry system (of the sort described in Chapter 5) seems unsatisfactory when it comes to duties to rescue children. Parents who bring children into the world should be presumptively required to rescue and care for their children, who are, after all, without resources to avoid their own vulnerability and cannot sufficiently protect themselves from harm through other means. However, the underinclusiveness (and, in certain circumstances, overinclusiveness) of biological parentage necessitates a test that focuses on something other than only biological parenthood in the context of duties to rescue children: *does the individual in question stand in the position of a primary caregiver to the child?* If the answer to this multi-factored question is yes,[7] then that individual should face liability for failure to rescue on an omissions liability theory, absent any relevant and compelling excuse or justification.[8] It is important to note that more than one individual could fall into this category—for example, both the mother and the father of the child, assuming they both live with the child, and a grandparent who also lives in the home. This test would avoid the overinclusiveness problem of relying on biology too. There might be situations in which a biological parent has parental rights terminated, and in those situations, we think (and the law concurs) there should be no duty to rescue under the criminal law.

Several options exist for dealing with underinclusiveness and overinclusiveness and the use of presumptions or registries. First, one could entirely decouple omissions liability in this context from parental status. Although we do not embrace this position, we recognize that if we abolished the established linkage between parental status and omissions liability, then that would serve as a default rule that might spur the use of the registry and at the same time decenter the role of parents in our quest to ensure the safety of children. Under this rule, family units may choose to require opting in as a precondition for hiring nannies and babysitters; additionally, private associations such as neighborhood groups or churches might require opt-ins of members to signal that this is an especially caring community. (The registry would effectively create an easier method than exists now to facilitate a private ordering regime that the state could monitor for purposes of prosecuting omissions cases.)

Alternatively, one could abolish the link between omissions liability and status and instead simply require all primary caregivers (and discard special references to parents altogether) to face omissions liability.[9] This second option creates a baseline in which liability for all *primary caregivers* is created (as opposed to a baseline of no liability for anyone in the first situation); it would also preserve an opt-in registry for others. Although we generally like this approach, there are some difficulties with it. One downside is that requiring a duty to rescue by all primary caregivers may risk overinclusiveness (and, thus, discourage persons from becoming primary caregivers) and some degree of vagueness—given that the tests for who is a primary caregiver will be hard to apply in some borderline cases.

A third option is another hybrid approach to reduce problems of underinclusiveness. First, retain the status-based duty for parents as a strong presumption that is rebutted only with the termination of parental rights; second, impose omissions liability on all other primary caregivers; and third, create an opt-in registry for all others. Our own view is that this option is probably the most feasible and attractive in part because it involves only an incremental adjustment from the current practice of most jurisdictions. There is not much difference between the second and third option, but the presumption of parent-based duties to rescue makes the third option arguably cheaper to administer from a social cost perspective and there is less need to worry about chilling effects because, under this regime, parents would generally have responsibility for children, whatever the status of other primary caregivers.

A fourth option is to require all persons to make easy rescues regardless of parental status. This option violates a thick commitment to voluntarism, perhaps, but it might be said that the compelling interest underlying the goal (saving vulnerable lives through actions that pose little to no risk to the rescuer) justifies the infringement here. Here, we note that such infringements on voluntarism occur in other contexts where the stakes are high, such as the lesser evils defense in criminal law,[10] compulsory vaccinations,[11] and conscription for armed services.[12] And as a practical matter, it reflects the prevailing norm by which most persons actually do undertake "easy rescues."[13]

Even though we can agree on the scope of duty attaching to parents and others regarding obligations to rescue minor children, we must also consider whether such obligations persist with children who are no longer minors. Should their primary caregivers still owe them a duty to rescue? If we take the fourth approach—by which we impose general duties to rescue—then the answer is yes. But two of us (Leib and Markel) believe that if we take any of the three approaches described that focus on the relationship between adult caregivers and children, then it makes sense to recognize that adult children typically stand in a different position than minor children—they can both utilize a registry system and have more options available to remove themselves from a dangerous situation.[14] In addition, the dynamics of the relationship may be very different with an adult child. It may seem justifiable for parents to wish to sever a relationship with a child who has committed a heinous crime or even victimized his parents, for example, whereas we would not allow parents of a minor child to walk away from their obligations to that child because of the child's misconduct unless they were prepared to terminate their parental rights. On the other hand, if an adult child is ill or incapacitated in some way, it does not seem unfair to require that the parental status-based or caregiver-based duty to rescue should apply. Professor Collins, by contrast, believes the parental duty to rescue one's child should persist into adulthood unless the parent has terminated his or her rights on grounds such as having been victimized by the child's criminal activity.

b. Minimalism and Means-Analysis

As to whether there are equally effective non-criminal alternatives available to the imposition of omissions liability, several options are worth considering. Most people would say that a parent's love and the social norm of being a Good Samaritan together mean that any legal remedy is unnecessary. But we often have criminal sanctions prohibiting or requiring conduct that would otherwise be obvious and attractive to most people. Thus, the criminal law and its concomitant sanction may be used to deny defendants the claim that the polity deprived them of fair notice of how they were expected to act to avoid reproach.[15]

Couldn't a tort remedy enunciate the same requirement of responsible behavior here? It might, but chances are that it will be less effective. For one thing, relying on the tort remedy here may be insufficient when there might not be a plaintiff to bring a claim against a parent who fails to rescue a child. Another issue is that the parent might be judgment-proof, which would give parents inadequate incentives to monitor their care of their children. Parents on the fence about the duty to rescue may be more likely to discharge the reasonable duties we impose in exchange for the benefits and latitude afforded to parenting.[16] So the criminal sanction here may serve to both educate the public about the obligation parents have toward children and to effectively punish parents for their failing to live up to the obligations that accompany the raising of children. When a parent fails to rescue a child under the restrictive conditions that make one eligible for criminal sanction, the parent is making a condemnable choice and is worthy of punishment for that breach of trust described above. The criminal sanction also is appropriate to ensure that parents do not skimp on their responsibilities because they know they might not be attractive tort defendants under existing law.

c. Gender, Inequality, and Discrimination

Even if omissions liability based on a parent's failure to rescue passes our voluntariness test and means test, we need to acknowledge that imposing liability on a parent for failing to protect a child from harm certainly has the potential to perpetuate inequality and discrimination. In those jurisdictions where gays and lesbians are prohibited from marriage and from adoption, these failure to rescue laws facially discriminate against families headed by homosexual couples or polyamorous unions.

For example, imagine a state that does not permit homosexual couples to adopt.[17] One adult, John, might nonetheless formally adopt a child, but John's long-standing partner, Larry, who may have informally taken on a parental role to the minor, will not be under the duty to rescue the child absent some contract or other basis for omissions liability as discussed in Chapter 4. Although this rule discriminates against Larry on the basis of Larry's lack of state-recognized family member status, the person who is harmed or left at risk by this discrimination is the minor child.[18] This is just one of the ways in which state default rules based on status of a certain kind can risk arbitrary and unintended harms against children.[19]

Because protecting minors from harm in the context of "easy rescues" is a compelling interest of the state, regardless of how one feels about discrimination against gays, even a state that does not grant homosexual couples adoption rights should make available a registry by which individuals may volunteer to take on the duty to rescue a minor (or anyone else). Getting "registered" might be a prerequisite that adoption agencies require of couples like John and Larry to ensure that the minor child is in a secure home. Moreover, if Larry were not willing to register then that might be a good information-forcing device relevant to John's choice to adopt the minor individually or to continue in a relationship with Larry.

In addition to concerns about inequality and discrimination, we are also worried about how prosecutorial practices regarding omissions statutes are used in a way that may perpetuate stereotypes about gender.[20] The first concern is that focusing on caregiving relationships that are voluntarily undertaken might have a chilling effect that exacerbates gender inequalities operating in the current practices of caregiving. In a recent article,[21] Professor Melissa Murray observed that allowing nonparental caregivers to have rights or authority over a child might deter parents from structuring care networks comprised of non-parental caregivers. In a note to us, Professor Murray suggests the same concerns might attend a policy that extends criminal liability to those who voluntarily provide care and thus risks further insulating families and caregiving within the private sphere, emphasizing caregiving as a "private" (and presumably, more female) responsibility.[22]

With respect, we think most parents, male and female, would be pleased to know that more caregivers for their children could face omissions liability because that would redound to the benefit and safety of their children. Indeed, to the extent that people are aware of broader omissions liability, it might make them more inclined to separate from their children under certain conditions and view caregiving as a task shared with the government or non-governmental organizations.[23] In other words, although we understand Professor Murray's concerns in the context of the extension of rights or benefits to non-parental caregivers, we think that in the context of *obligations* to children by non-parental caregivers this deterrent effect is unlikely to be realized except to the extent that some non-parental caregivers might be worried about their exposure to criminal omissions liability. But even in this context, this anxiety is misplaced since it is likely that omissions liability would already attach based on some of the other traditional bases for omissions liability discussed in Chapter 4.

The second gender-related worry is that prosecutions based on omissions liability disproportionately target women. Indeed, women are more likely to bear the brunt of such prosecutions than men simply by virtue of the fact that they are, more often, the custodial parent.[24] Further, women are commonly thought to be held by the public to a higher standard of care in childrearing relative to men.[25] As Naomi Cahn has argued, "Cultural middle-class norms expect all women to be primarily responsible for their children. The criminal justice system supports this norm by criminalizing the abusive and neglectful behavior of parents, penalizing mothers particularly harshly."[26]

We also cannot ignore the linkage between domestic violence and prosecutions for failing to protect a child from abuse by another. In our view, it is important to acknowledge that, in many cases in which children are being battered, a parent (usually the mother) may be the victim of battering as well.[27] To be sure, in particular situations, it might be a male father who is battered, and our approach to omissions liability does not hinge on the precise identity of the defendant *qua* mother. But the general point here is that the adult victims of violence may have few available options, from their perspective, to remove their children from an abusive situation.[28] They may (correctly) perceive that attempts to leave will escalate the violence.[29] Additionally, they may have no economic options in terms of being able to find housing or a job that will provide sufficient income to support a family.[30]

These issues are weighty and important, and thus, we need to consider practical options to help mitigate the potential disparate impact of omissions liability. As a policy matter, we should partner any attempts to hold parents accountable for their failure to protect with efforts to make it more viable for battered spouses to leave abusive partners—for example, by ensuring adequate funding for shelters, job training, and child care resources.[31] The question remains, however, whether the existence of domestic violence should preclude prosecuting a parent for failing to rescue the child. Supporters of prosecutions of passive parents argue that even a parent's status as a victim of domestic violence cannot categorically excuse a failure to act to prevent the abuse of a child. Professor Mary Becker has suggested that "mothers, even when abused themselves, should be held to a high standard of care for their children and should normally be held responsible for their own abuse or neglect of their children and for failing to protect their children from others' abuse and neglect, provided that they knew or had reason to know of the harm to their children."[32] That's because even though the mother may have been weakened physically or mentally by virtue of the abuse she has suffered, unless she is "literally a hostage," she still has options to employ in an attempt to protect her child that are not available to the child itself; young children, after all, are utterly defenseless and completely dependent upon adults for their protection.[33]

In domestic violence cases in which prosecution may be appropriate because the parent did have some protective options available, there should be some strict limitations on when the state seeks to impose liability.

The focus needs to be on the easy rescue; thus, in cases involving child abuse, we should limit omissions liability to those circumstances where a parent had prior knowledge of past abuse and had the practical opportunity to seek help, such as access to a telephone to contact law enforcement authorities.[34] Second, parents who fail to protect in a case involving a fatality should only face the same homicide charge as the actual killer if they had the same (or worse) *mens rea*; otherwise, a lesser (and perhaps non-homicide) charge is appropriate to reflect the reduced culpability.[35] And of course, in some cases, no conviction is appropriate if the defendant had no easy rescue to make based on her own circumstances or diminished capacity as a battered spouse.

Another option legislatures should consider is adopting a statutory scheme that recognizes the defendant's omission as a distinct and separate crime of failure to rescue like reckless endangerment. A separate charge by a prosecutor would better reflect the idea that there is a meaningful moral distinction between actually inflicting the fatal blows and, for example, making the mistake of leaving a child alone with an individual who has been abusive in the past.

2. Spousal Obligations to Rescue Each Other

Regarding spouses, the foregoing analysis calls for refinement though it also tracks the discussion above. The plausibly strong interests the state has in penalizing a failure to rescue between spouses are (1) saving human lives in danger and (2) affirming the significance of marital obligations.

The problem with the first interest is that the means used here—spousal obligations to rescue each other, policed through the criminal law—is woefully underinclusive, so much so that it's hard to take seriously the idea that this is what's motivating the use of this family ties burden. The second objective, by contrast, makes more sense. Although the obligation to undertake easy rescues is not specifically articulated in many wedding vows, it reasonably falls under the language that often is used in those vows.[36] Thus, it makes sense to impose the duty to rescue on those who become vulnerable after they have already made commitments to each other to serve as caregivers.

The notion undergirding the legal obligation here is that spouses who have voluntarily chosen to obtain the benefits conferred by the spousal relationship should endure some burdens in return, and facilitating the safety of a spouse is a reasonable burden. When a person opts to marry, the person is, as we suggested earlier, signaling to others that he or she will be a first responder. In this respect, imposing a duty to rescue here is analogous to the imposition of liability on those people who have "waved away" others. Just as with children, the goal here is not to tie an albatross around the neck of every spouse. Omissions liability does not create a responsibility to rescue against unreasonable risks. Rather, it simply punishes the breach of a trust relationship that marriage creates between the parties to the marriage and those creating the political community around them.

But let's consider further how our normative framework applies to this family ties burden. We note at the outset that even more so than with children who may not have been "wanted," spouses have already evidenced their commitment to take care of each other. Thus, we view obligations to spouses as grounded in voluntarily created commitments to care for each other and that easily includes the duty to undertake an easy rescue. Together, married couples share a freedom to pursue in concert those goals and goods they cannot or will not pursue alone or without the stamp of social recognition.[37]

With respect to minimalism, we need to examine the same arguments about whether an effective alternative to criminal sanction is available. As with children, the need to create a spousal obligation seems practically redundant because most people would say that romantic love would render any legal strategy unnecessary. Nonetheless, it is not unreasonable to legislate criminal sanctions prohibiting or requiring conduct that would otherwise be obvious and attractive to most people; as explained above, the criminal law and its concomitant sanction may be used to deny defendants the claim that they were denied fair notice of how they were expected to act with respect to certain conduct.

As with children, here, too, reliance on tort remedies as a substitute seems unhelpful. There might not be a plaintiff to bring a claim against a spouse who fails to rescue another spouse (though a plaintiff is more likely in this context than in that of the wrongful death of a child). Moreover, the spouse might be judgment-proof in a civil case involving money damages, and knowledge of one's inability to pay may marginally cause spouses (on the fence) to have inadequate incentives to rescue. So the criminal sanction here may serve to both educate the public about the obligation spouses have toward each other and to effectively punish spouses for their failing to live up to their caregiving obligations. In other words, when a spouse fails to rescue a partner under the conditions eligible for criminal sanction, the spouse-defendant is making a condemnable choice and is worthy of punishment for that breach of trust described above. The criminal sanction also is appropriate to ensure that spouses do not renege on their responsibilities because they know they might not be attractive tort defendants under existing law.

Any law calling for the prosecution of a person for failing to protect his or her spouse from harm also has the potential to have a discriminatory impact, in a different and critical sense: it treats differently those who cannot or choose not to enter a spousal relationship recognized by the state.[38] For example, these laws currently do not clearly give the family members of homosexual couples the comfort of knowing that omissions liability is parceled out in a non-discriminatory fashion. One way to see this discrimination is through analogy: if omissions liability were distributed on the basis of race, such that whites had a duty to rescue their spouses but blacks did not unless they separately contracted for that duty, what message would that send? It clearly exhibits a lack of respect to the value of the spouses of black people.[39] The same inference of disrespect is true when a state restricts omissions liability along lines that are tethered to the few family status relationships recognized by the state. Why should a heterosexual man have an obligation to protect his spouse from harm while a gay man in a similarly meaningful and voluntary partnership does not?[40] In both instances, imposing liability serves the same valuable functions: increasing safety and promoting an ethos of caregiving relations triggered by voluntary choices. Thus, limiting omissions liability to those in a state-sanctioned relationship seems plainly underinclusive—it leaves out those who *cannot* get married because of a plainly troubling moral choice made by the state.[41]

For the most part, we do not have much problem with marriage being an overinclusive obligation because divorce is an option by which the obligation can be terminated. But because marriage is an underinclusive basis for imposing omissions liability, we think several options should be explored.

One solution would be to decouple omissions liability from marriage altogether and instead ask parties to any relationship to register *sua sponte*.[42] This would treat all persons the same and without favor. But a no duty to rescue rule in marriage could act like a penalty default rule. On the one hand, it would probably encourage more people outside of marriage to think about whom they wish to rescue. On the other hand, it might also add needless costs associated with persons who by virtue of marriage would already be willing to undertake a duty to rescue. A better solution, based on reducing the social costs of the scheme, would be to require duties to rescue in marriages and to create a registry for all others who want to participate in a "covenant of care" such that they have a duty to perform easy rescues. Marriages would simply have the implicit term of duty to rescue built into them and others outside marriage (including those in polyamourous relationships) could opt into it. This would also allow persons to insist on seeing evidence of opt-in by another person before they decide to jointly acquire property, cohabit, or perform caregiving tasks for one another.

3. Duties to Rescue in Other Relationships

Some might raise concerns that we are too focused on spouses and parents as paradigmatic relationships here. The worry here would be that we are constructing the sexual family or marriage as the normative ideal for adult interactions with each other. We respectfully disagree. Indeed, the point of our registry system is to obviate this concern entirely. People who are not married do not have to register, but they may choose to do so. In any given relationship, just one person may decide to do so for the other since the registry is a place of declaring one's assumption of obligation—it is not predicated on norms of reciprocity, nor does it require contractual formalities. To be sure, our slight preference for assigning duties to rescue in the context of marriage and custodial parenting is responsive to what we think of as the specific features of caregiving written into the "scripts" of marriage and parenting, but no one should be forced into assuming those burdens otherwise.

That said, people should be free to and encouraged to assume these obligations outside the scripts of marriage and parenting. The registry we discussed in Chapter 5 permits siblings or cousins or roommates or friends to enter into covenants of care, but the idea is not to require it through the criminal law outside voluntary choices or the specific circumstances of the parent-child or spousal relationships. Indeed, we would resist any state's attempt to impose a duty to rescue on those persons outside the parent-child or spousal context because we simply cannot say these relationships have been entered into voluntarily. In the context of platonic roommates, imposing a duty of rescue through the criminal law would be drastic restructuring of the traditional boundaries of that relationship. On the other hand, we certainly believe that individuals should be able to create a legally enforceable relationship of caregiving through the use of a registry. This allows individuals to signal their commitment both to each other and to those around them.[43]

It is, of course, possible that very few individuals will choose to register—why would they voluntarily assume the risk of a legal liability that they currently do not face? But if that is the outcome, we are no worse off than we are now, as these individuals do not currently face liability. If, on the other hand, some individuals do choose to undertake an obligation to rescue, the benefits that decision conveys in terms of promoting safety and promoting an ethos of care and compassion certainly seem worth the effort. We can also imagine the state incentivizing such registrations through small tax breaks or norm entrepreneurs (private employers or faith groups) that mobilize "opt-in days" to foster solidarity among members of their communities. And because people's relationships ebb and flow, we could imagine that the registry would permit people to withdraw from these covenants of caregiving when adequate notice is given to the affected parties.

Allowing more private-ordering in the context of criminal law regulation (with sufficient attention to third-party harms) is also consistent with the suggestions we make later in the contexts of incest, bigamy, and adultery.

B. Parental Responsibility Laws

When adults have committed an affirmative act contributing to a minor's delinquency with a culpable state of mind, the traditional core requirements for a crime have been satisfied; moreover, in those situations in which the laws speak to a *general* obligation by *all adults* to forbear from contributing to a minor's truancy or curfew violation or criminal misconduct, there is no specific family ties burden. But as we saw in Chapter 4, some states and more municipalities have created criminal liability for parents when their children commit some misconduct based on nothing more than a failure to supervise theory. It is these laws we focus on here because parental status is an element of liability.

Discussions of these laws suggest several reasons for their passage: first, they are thought to reduce crime; second, they are viewed as vehicles to project norms of parental conduct by instructing parents to monitor their children carefully and to remain actively involved in parenting; third, these laws are regarded as an avenue of restitution to victims for the harms committed by the minors. Despite these plausible justifications, we view these laws as normatively troublesome and think they should be jettisoned for the reasons we articulate below.

We are willing, for the purposes of argument, to stipulate that the state has compelling interests in the reduction of crime, whether by minors or adults; the proper instruction of parental obligations in supervising minor children; and ensuring adequate compensation to victims of crime. However, we are not of the view that the state claiming to pursue these objectives has shown that the means used here are appropriately tailored to these ends, especially if other non-criminal alternatives are available and equally effective.

To begin with, if the goal is to reduce crime, why not require all adults who are aware of criminal mischief by a child to prevent the crime and/or report it if prevention fails? It does not make sense to restrict failure to supervise laws to parents for the sake of reducing crime. The second argument, restricting the reach of these laws to parents, makes sense if the state's goal is to instruct parents to be involved in raising their children and to act diligently in the supervision of their children. But if that is the case, then it is not clear why mandatory parenting classes, public advertising, civil recovery statutes, and a showing of an affirmative culpable act or omission by the parent would be insufficient, as we explain below. The use of strict liability and a criminal sanction are unnecessary and have problematic effects. As to the adequate compensation of victims, every state has a civil recovery statute or tort in place by which victims can seek compensation from parents for harms perpetrated by their minors.[44] The criminal sanction is redundant in that respect.

1. Voluntary Caregiving and Liberty Interests

Admittedly, these laws attach obligations only to the person who voluntarily creates a relationship (*i.e.*, the parent, not the child). In that respect, these laws are consistent with one aspect of liberalism.

However, because these laws create strict criminal liability by punishing parents without proof of a choice to commit an action, they fail to respect a reasonable liberty-maximizing rule by ensuring that the defendants have performed a voluntary action or omission with a culpable mind that warrants condemnation and punishment. To visit the full weight and condemnation of a criminal sanction upon an individual for an action by another person beyond his or her control is antithetical to the spirit of a liberalism that respects individuals and their liberties.

A plausibly fair interpretation of the failure to supervise theory requires proof that the parents could reasonably have done something to prevent the minor's misconduct and chose not to. But the statutes as drafted, which hold parents criminally and strictly liable for the misconduct of their children, leads to absurd results in some situations: for instance, parents could be liable for prosecution when they themselves were the victims of the minor's misconduct. To be sure, some jurisdictions allow this or other reasons (*e.g.*, the parent acted reasonably in the situation) as an affirmative defense,[45] but the absence of reasonableness by the defendant should be part of the government's case-in-chief—not a burden allocated to the defense in a criminal case.

2. Minimalism and Means Analysis

As suggested above, we think imposing criminal liability is misplaced in the absence of a blameworthy state of mind and a wrongful action or omission by the caregiver in question. If a parent acted with something approaching at least criminal negligence, we could better understand the impetus to punish the parent with a light sanction. But imposing criminal responsibility on a strict liability theory does not seem to promote more effective caregiving than a negligence standard. Rather, it would only chill the underlying activity of raising or adopting children or foster children and/or force parents to take unreasonable steps in monitoring their children. This would undermine the very point of trying to cultivate and support voluntary caregiving relationships through family ties burdens. Some examples can illustrate our point.

Imagine a parent goes out on a date and leaves a fourteen-year-old alone in the house with unsecured firearms and an unlocked liquor cabinet, even though the parent knows the child has attempted to play with the guns and drink liquor on prior occasions. If the fourteen-year-old proceeds to get drunk and use the parent's gun to shoot up the neighbor's car, the parent has been reckless, or at a minimum, criminally negligent by "failing to exercise reasonable control" over the child. Imposing liability in this scenario will signal both to this particular caregiver, and other caregivers in the community, that caregivers must supervise their children more vigilantly.

But imagine instead that the child buys the gun on his own with his money from an after-school job and shoots up the neighbor's car on the way home from school, despite repeated admonitions by his parents to stay away from guns and people with guns. Under an ordinance like the one passed in Silverton, Oregon, and other jurisdictions, parents could face prosecution on a strict liability theory because their child had been charged with a crime. But such a prosecution would have little impact in terms of promoting better caregiving in situations like the one that gave rise to the misconduct in our hypothetical—there is very little caregiving the parent could have done that would have prevented the crime in question. Perhaps the parent could prevent the child from earning extra money or going to school independently, but children who are determined to find trouble can do it, notwithstanding all reasonable efforts by parents.

The consequences of parental responsibility laws warrant consideration too. To the extent that criminal law successfully projects norms about correct values, the strict liability standard in some parental responsibility laws will deter people from becoming foster parents, adoptive parents of teenagers, or on the margins, parents of their own biological children. That's not the signal regarding the promotion of caregiving that society should emit.

As to restitution, there is no reason that a civil tort remedy against the parents (or the minor) would not suffice in providing an avenue of repair for the harms caused by a minor. After the children themselves, parents are likely the next cheapest cost avoider, and so pinning parents with obligations under civil recovery statutes gives parents a strong incentive to monitor their children closely and provide an avenue of compensation for victims.[46] To be sure, there is the possibility—as there was above—of parents being judgment-proof and of there being no available plaintiff to sue. But if parents were reasonably nowhere near the misconduct of the minor—if, for example, the child goes on a supervised school trip with teachers—then, quite generally, the assumption that parents are the next least cost avoider may be misplaced. In any event, under the parental liability laws we discuss, the defendant is not being forced merely to pay for harm; the defendant is being condemned through criminal punishment for wrongdoing that someone else committed even if the defendant was non-culpably unaware of and did not participate in the wrongdoing and even though the defendant instructed the wrongdoer that such misconduct was forbidden.

To be sure, we allow vicarious liability elsewhere in the criminal justice system: for example, in the crime of conspiracy. Co-conspirators have been permissibly held liable for substantive crimes committed by another member of the conspiracy, through the *Pinkerton* doctrine,[47] even if they are not present at the scene of that crime or aware of the crime's commission.[48] These efforts are controversial and have been subject to substantial criticism.[49]

But the parental responsibility law differs significantly from the *Pinkerton* scenario. To impose liability under *Pinkerton*, the defendant must have committed the act of joining a conspiracy, and the additional crime by the co-conspirator must be committed in furtherance of the conspiracy and be reasonably foreseeable. In a recent article, Professor Kreit excavates the constitutional foundations for *Pinkerton*, noting that many courts have acknowledged the *Pinkerton* criteria—that the co-conspirator's crimes be in furtherance of the conspiracy and reasonably foreseeable—to be due process requirements.[50] If *Pinkerton* can be read roughly to establish a floor of a negligence rule in the context of vicarious liability for conspiracy then why, we might ask, doesn't the negligence rule operate in other cases of criminal vicarious liability, such as felony murder, or for our purposes, parental responsibility laws?

Putting the constitutional issue aside, we do well to consider whether these laws are likely to be effective at reducing the incidence of crime by minors. Professor Dan Filler suggests that such statutes could be effective if the consequences for violation were sufficiently severe and certain, although, of course, we might not be willing to live with stakes of such high magnitude.[51] For example, if parents whose children threw an alcohol-filled party for their friends faced a felony conviction and a lengthy prison term, most reasonable parents, Filler argues, would quickly "lock up the booze and perhaps install a nanny-cam to monitor the house."[52] We think they might take even more drastic measures—put their children on lockdown. Moreover, to be effective, the government would have to enforce these laws more often. The fact remains that though these statutes are on the books in a number of jurisdictions, criminal prosecutions remain extremely rare.[53] The laws receive most of their attention in the media on account of those few prosecutions that have taken place, such as the St. Clair prosecution discussed in Chapter 4.

But even if these statutes could be made effective, would it be appropriate to use them? We have already articulated some reasons for thinking that other alternatives might better achieve the goals sought by these parental responsibility laws. But it is also important to question the assumptions associated with these laws. Support for these statutes is motivated in part by the belief that "poor parenting" is a root cause of much of the juvenile crime in this country. As one family outreach worker exclaimed, "We have an adult problem, not a children problem . . . If we can get our adults together, the children will naturally fall in line."[54] One commentator has suggested that that "the rationale behind the parental liability laws—punishing the parents to reduce acts of juvenile delinquency by their children—must be based on a series of interconnected assumptions:" first, that the nature of the child's behavior is directly—if not primarily—caused by the quality of the parenting in the household; second, that we can somehow create a "universal model of adequate parenting," which all parents can and should adopt regardless of their circumstances; and third, that the threat of punishment will induce parents to adopt this government-sanctioned model of parenting.[55]

Critics of these statutes contend that the link between poor parenting and juvenile crime is far less certain than their proponents suggest.[56] Juveniles are no doubt also profoundly influenced by their peers, their schools, their communities, the media, and perhaps their genetic makeup.[57] In addition, the threat of criminal liability might actually negatively impact parenting, rather than enhance it. One critic suggests that parental responsibility statutes will induce some parents to "over-parent[], that is by either severely restricting their child's freedom or by excessively punishing the child."[58] Other parents might respond by "under-parenting," that is, by distancing themselves from their children "by filing ungovernability or similar petitions to transfer responsibility to the state."[59] In either case, the relationship between parent and child would become more adversarial and negative, rather than more productive and positive.[60]

3. Gender, Inequality and Discrimination

From the preceding discussion, one can see why we are dubious about the value of these statutes as to their capacity to reduce crime through parental vigilance, to signal commitment to parenting values, or to provide restitution not available through other measures. Here we note that limiting vicarious liability to those parents within a state-sanctioned family unit seems underinclusive as well and, therefore, discriminatory. If vicarious liability is embraced by legislatures because of its crime-reduction promise, then it should be applied whenever there is a relationship of asymmetrical dependency and voluntary caregiving, and not just when there is a strictly construed version of the parent-child relationship.[61] For at least in this way, more of the deterrence will be achieved by extending vicarious liability's ambit to same-sex or non-married child-rearing partners, and the importance of the supervision as part of caregiving will be communicated to those who have opted to raise or supervise minors. A narrower structure would be to restrict the reach of parental responsibility laws to the same class of people who constitute voluntary "primary caregivers" that would face a duty to rescue children.

Having already considered heteronormativity concerns, here we want simply to recognize that women will likely bear the brunt of these duties to supervise in light of the fact that women currently most often serve as the heads of single-parent homes. Although women may be deemed to have voluntarily assumed their parenting duties, it is critical to understand that, based on a variety of factors, it might be difficult to conclude that parents can effectively control their minor children, especially in the context of a single-parent home. For one thing, the number and/or physical strength of some children may prove overwhelming in particular situations. The parent might also be a victim of a child's misconduct. Additionally, parents might fear that reporting their children to the police will lead to the involuntary termination of their parental rights. All these serve as additional independent reasons to be concerned with the structure of parental responsibility statutes or ordinances. In omissions liability, the parent being held responsible is the last lifeline to prevent real harm to vulnerable and innocent children; in the context of parental responsibility laws, by contrast, the children are generally neither wholly innocent nor in danger.

4. Summary

Although the burdens associated with parental responsibility statutes attach to voluntarily created caregiving relationships, and therefore deserve some leeway, our view is that they fail to be fully justified as drafted because of the ways in which they raise substantial concerns under our minimalism, gender, and inequality inquiries. It bears emphasis that our critique does not affect those criminal laws that apply to any adult who commits a culpable act or omission that proximately contributes to the delinquency of a minor or endangers the minor's welfare—assuming the statutes and courts define those terms with reasonable specificity.

C. Incest

At the outset, we acknowledge that the topic of incest, like that of bigamy, which follows, is a complicated one. Our modest goal is to contribute some preliminary thoughts to a difficult dialogue about whether the criminal law is an appropriate vehicle to regulate the intimate activities of mature persons. As we discussed in Chapter 4, there are various kinds of incest rules: some regulate conduct regardless of the age of participants, some regulate conduct regardless of the consent of the participants, and some regulate conduct among intimates regardless of an actual blood relationship. Unsurprisingly, there is overlap across these categories depending on the jurisdiction.

We emphasize that our focus here is on those criminal laws that punish a person's conduct that, but for the family ties of the defendant, would otherwise be lawful in a given jurisdiction. We are specifically *not* talking about the sexual abuse of children, which is sometimes referred to as incest but is clearly and rightly illegal conduct regardless of the identity or family status of the perpetrator. As we explain below, we will focus our discussion on consensual sexual conduct between adults, but our analysis also has potential implications for how states regulate sexual conduct between minors and adults and between minors and other minors, which we touch on toward the end of this section.

Consistent with our positions developed in Chapter 5, we think that in situations where genuine and mature consent between the parties is possible and where negative externalities can be eliminated, the criminal law should prescind from application. If genuine and mature consent cannot be presumed or achieved, then the sexual activity should be investigated and punished largely in the way other sexual misconduct is punished—though we have some concern that coercion is too narrowly defined in some jurisdictions. Nonetheless, we also believe that sentencing enhancements based on breach of trust can be justified in contexts where a primary caregiver has abused a minor child or other person who might be incapacitated (*e.g.*, an elderly parent or disabled adult child).[62]

Let's begin by determining the objectives articulated on behalf of incest statutes. The most commonly cited rationale for prohibiting consensual relations is that incestuous relationships have the potential to create children with genetic problems if the parties reproduce.[63] Moreover, incestuous relationships have special potential to be abusive and nonconsensual, and this coercion may be difficult to detect, thus calling for a separate and perhaps more severe set of penalties.[64] Additionally, some have viewed the incest taboo as a way to "prevent intrafamilial sexual jealousies and rivalries," when a parent figure has relations with both another parent and a child.[65]

Yet, these rationales cannot account for the scope of the incest prohibition in almost all American states. For example, *consensual* relationships between adult siblings who were adopted from different birth parents, and thus share no genetic link, raise none of the concerns associated with genetic difficulties, and raise fewer relevant concerns related to sexual jealousies or coercion.[66] It is therefore impossible to underestimate the influence of the "disgust factor."[67] In large part, these relationships are criminalized because Americans view them with distaste or because they are, in some situations, religiously proscribed.[68] As we develop below, we think that at least as to some of these relationships, the state should step in to proscribe the sexual conduct—and with regard to others, the state should step aside and refrain from using the *criminal justice system* to sanction the conduct.

1. Voluntary Caregiving and Liberty Interests

In most jurisdictions, incest laws apply to both voluntarily and involuntarily created relationships—parents are prohibited from sex with their children the same way that siblings are prohibited from having sex with each other.[69] To the extent that these family ties burdens are placed on relationships that are involuntarily created, we think these prohibitions fail one of our liberal concerns and should be regarded very carefully before being legally implemented. However, to the extent they apply to voluntarily created relationships of caregiving, we have little problem in extending some deference to legislative decisions to penalize these relationships.

Our reasons for doing so, however, are not predicated on the biological issues undergirding support for most incest laws. Rather, we think a general rule is appropriate, one that prohibits sexual relations between an adult and any person for whom the adult provides caregiving functions such that the other person is involved in a relationship of asymmetrical dependency—regardless of whether the dependency relationship is established through consanguinity. Examples of asymmetrical dependents include, on the one hand, foster parents, adoptive parents, stepparents, and biological parents and, on the other hand, all minors under their charge and responsibility until that dependent is no longer under their charge and responsibility.[70] Our concern is that the relationship of asymmetrical dependency lends itself to peculiar risks of abuse such that establishing a norm of protecting vulnerable persons from coercion or improper pressure requires a rule that may be overprotective in some cases. Such a law would emit a clearer signal of which relations are prohibited than the mishmash that characterizes current incest laws.[71]

This more general rule ties in with our liberal concern that seeks to assess whether the family ties burden in question unnecessarily infringes on one's liberty. With respect to sex crimes, it is the lack of (intelligent and mature) consent that should drive the liberal state's punishment of offenders. When a person stands in a position of asymmetrical dependency, it is very hard to determine whether truly voluntary consent was given. There are also complicated questions about whether persons who were once in relationships of asymmetrical dependency, but now are not, could voluntarily consent to have relations with persons with whom they were once vulnerable; thus, at a minimum, some regulatory speed bumps should be erected to ferret out the existence of genuine and meaningful consent in those contexts.[72]

As to relationships between independent adults, we believe that a respect for autonomy and limited government should permit consenting individuals to engage in the sexual relations they deem appropriate without fear of criminal sanction.[73] That is not to say we endorse any of these relations; rather, we simply think the state should not be using the *criminal* law to tread upon the intimate associational rights of mature individuals. As they stand, the current laws chill consensual activities by adults that should be unencumbered by threats of arrest, prosecution, and punishment.[74] Indeed, criminal prosecution is ordinarily unnecessary to prevent this conduct; most of these relationships will be deterred by social stigma. We recognize the concern that incestuous relationships have the potential to be abusive and nonconsensual,[75] and we think that these concerns are substantial and important. But in the context of adults, these problems can ordinarily be punished through the traditional crimes tracking lack of consent, *i.e.*, the crimes regulating sexual assault.[76]

We acknowledge that, in some circumstances, those available "background" laws may be unsatisfactory. For example, it is quite possible that the coercion involved in an incestuous relationship would be psychological rather than physical, and many states still do not consider psychological coercion sufficient to satisfy the required elements of their rape or sexual assault statutes.[77] Thus, although our background laws forbidding sexual assault and rape may be sufficient bases for prosecuting and punishing offenders in cases involving physical coercion, it is important to recognize that the current status of rape law may leave some non-consensual incestuous relationships outside the reach of criminal law sanctions. Thus, reform of current rape laws continues to be an important goal. It is also important to recognize that various gender inequities within households raise questions about whether consent to an incestuous relationship could ever truly be voluntary, but these are fact-bound inquiries. Assuming there are such consensual relations between mature adults, then prohibiting adult step-siblings or any other adult couple from having consensual relations is primarily a form of squeamishness—at least from a liberal criminal justice perspective that does not seek to impose a particularly traditional vision of sexual morality.[78]

In the absence of consent between adults, as we've qualified it here, we think sexual misconduct should be punished as if the crime were committed by an acquaintance or stranger. However, we support legislative decisions to impose breach of trust enhancements—whether treated as elements of a crime or sentencing factors—for crimes by primary caregivers against persons in relationships of asymmetrical dependency, where the caregiver voluntarily assumed the caregiving relationship.[79]

2. Minimalism and Means Analysis

In this sub-section, we explore whether the purported objectives of the incest prohibition match up to the laws we have, focusing on the degree of narrow tailoring extant in the current practices. Let's begin with the concern about coercion. This problem, which we think is the government's most compelling interest, can be punished through general laws prohibiting coercive sex. Thus, the need for articulating a specific family ties burden requires justification. One argument associated with coercion is that it is very difficult to achieve adequate deterrence in the family context because of the problems associated with getting minor victims to report parental misconduct because of the supervisory relationship. But if that's the case, we can have, as suggested above, heightened penalties in any context where a breach of trust with a supervisory adult arises—whether schools, churches, or the home. In other words, the breach of trust enhancement need not be limited to family status, even though family status in some contexts creates the inference of betrayal of trust. Admittedly, this strategy won't do the work of addressing the reluctance of a minor to report a sibling's or cousin's improper conduct, but that same reluctance can easily arise if it is a close family friend or neighbor who commits the sexual misconduct.

As to the sometimes articulated goal of preventing intrafamilial sexual jealousy, there are reasons to doubt that this is truly a governmental interest of the sort that can vindicate the use of the criminal sanction. For one thing, it is hard to understand why sexual jealousy is a form of jealousy that the state should be particularly worried about, as opposed to the jealousy and rivalry that may arise from economic disparities, parental favoritism, or other forms of rivalry. Second, incest laws do not currently attach to whole clusters of possible relationships that might also give rise to intrafamilial sexual jealousy—thereby creating serious underinclusiveness relative to this goal. A heterosexual woman may marry a man and also sexually desire his father or brother; a heterosexual man might marry a woman and desire her mother or sister. If persons act on these desires, they are not subject to incest laws in the vast majority of jurisdictions, but they will surely trigger intrafamilial jealousies.

As to the genetic concerns, there are several responses. First, for persons not engaged in activity capable of causing genetic repercussions—gay cousins, elderly siblings, etc.—the rules prohibiting their relationships are overbroad and cannot be justified on this ground. With respect to those not related by consanguinity, there is no basis for genetic fears at all. Admittedly, such fears increase when talking about closely related persons, such as brothers and sisters.[80] But as others have noted, "in no other legal realm does the government criminally prohibit two people from having children because their offspring are more likely to inherit genetic defects."[81] Put simply, we have long since retired the idea that eugenics preferences are a reasonable basis for criminal justice policy.[82]

Related to the genetics-based fears is concern for the economic costs of allowing incestuous relationships. In other words, some might be tempted to justify criminal law incest prohibitions to reduce the costs associated with increased medical care for children of consanguineous parents. But again, the solution of using incest prohibitions is both overbroad and underinclusive. First, some couples deemed incestuous may choose not to have children or may not be able to have children, and yet their conduct would still be subject to criminal sanction. Second, we do not use the criminal law as a tool to reduce potential medical costs in any other context, so it would be hard to justify its use here. When we criminalize murder or theft, it is not because we want to keep insurance payments down; it is because murder or theft is wrong. Third, if we were genuinely concerned about increased medical costs, we could test all couples with high risks of disease or complications who are contemplating having children. But this would be both an offensive policy to many people, and it would sweep in far more persons than those who are blood relatives.

The preceding discussion of narrow tailoring has largely addressed family ties burdens in the context of relations between adults. We acknowledge that concerns about family ties burdens on persons engaged in relationships with minors raise weightier concerns than those arising in the context of consenting adults.[83] Although all of us agree that the possibility of coercion is far more significant in this context and that it is less likely that the minor in question is capable of truly informed consent, we disagree among ourselves how much to credit the consent of minors who choose to have sex with adults to whom they are related, and what measures might be taken to prove such consent to the state.[84] Although many states have a variety of statutory rape laws available to punish and deter adult-minor and minor-minor sex, these laws may not be sufficient to address all the possible concerns arising from these relationships where incest is involved. Thus, we address below the use of family ties burdens in these contexts.

As to sexual relations strictly among minors, we are not all of one mind—proving the point, perhaps, that our framework for analyzing these laws does not require a single conclusion on all family ties burdens. One of us (Markel) thinks that sex with and between minors should also be regulated in family-neutral ways. This would mean that either the criminal law applies to prohibit sexual activity for all persons under a certain age or that the criminal law does not apply in the context of consensual relations among those credited with the capacity to consent. (This would be in addition to the general rule that would prohibit sexual activity between supervisory caregivers and dependent caretakers.) Thus, there would be no categorical rules prohibiting sexual conduct between, say, seventeen-year-olds on the basis of family status alone. Under this view, those worried about physical or psychological coercion or abuse or retaliation can simply rely on the laws available to punish that independent misconduct. If sexual relations are to be decriminalized for those over an age of consent, then it should be immaterial from the state's perspective whether they are brothers or first cousins or friends. The key would be to ensure an absence of coercion or abuse.[85]

But at least one of us (Collins) finds these conclusions troubling. Sex between minor siblings, for example, does not implicate a significant liberty interest that is worth protecting. In addition, some of the concerns used to justify incest bans take on heightened importance in the context of minors. For example, because the potential public health ramifications of incestuous sex are admittedly non-negligible—and because it would be extremely hard for minors to give meaningful consent to such complex sexual relations—there may be sound reasons to preserve criminal statutes against incestuous sex among minors. Minors, because of their emotional immaturity, are more vulnerable to psychological coercion. In addition, minors in incestuous sexual relationships may be less likely and able to seek outside help in ending the relationship. It would seem far easier, for example to report one's forty-year-old uncle to the authorities than it would to report one's brother.

One of us (Leib) cannot make up his mind, though his sympathies are largely with Collins. Indeed, not only are Collins' concerns serious, there are serious costs associated with creating new and complicated institutions and bureaucracies—would minors be expected to use registries too?—to channel and sanction conduct (minor sex with family members) that hardly seems like an especially grave liberty interest for the state to protect. There is also, finally, the reality that the juvenile justice system is a different beast from the adult system and probably raises different concerns, which have not been systematically examined or considered sufficiently here to reach a clear conclusion on the merits.

3. Gender, Inequality, and Discrimination

There are a couple of important points about inequality and discrimination that bear mention regarding the use of family ties burdens in the incest context. First, as we have noted above, incest laws appear motivated in part by concerns about genetic repercussions in the offspring. That implicates both heteronormativity and repronormativity—and signals to the polity that we expect couples engaged in sex to procreate. We note, additionally, that to the extent that the family ties burden operates *ex ante* in a protective manner (of a particular model of family relations), it denies that protection to those whose families do not fit the particular model of family relations informing the contours of most incest statutes. Thus, if a gay couple lives in a state where they cannot adopt as a couple together, then the incest statute will not "protect" a child who has been adopted by *X* against the sexual misconduct perpetrated by *X*'s partner, *Y*—assuming that *Y* has not been able to create a legally binding relationship to the child. Of course, *Y* is susceptible to the general statutes prohibiting sexual misconduct, but that just shows the general redundancy of most incest statutes. Last, we note that the incest statutes around the country are generally drafted and, to our knowledge, prosecuted in manners that do not especially and unfairly burden one sex over another.

4. Summary

Having applied our normative framework from Chapter 5, we see that in many jurisdictions, incest laws by their scope create family ties burdens not only in the context of consensual sexual conduct between adults, but also when states otherwise permit consensual sexual conduct between adults and minors, and between minors and minors. In the context of adults, and subject to the caveats discussed above, we find this burden on the intimate associational rights of consenting mature individuals unjustifiable because the interests underlying incest laws can be promoted through more appropriate measures short of invoking the particular power of the criminal law. In the context of incestuous sex between adults and minors, and minors and minors, we are divided about whether incest laws—which create specific family ties burdens that create liability where, in the absence of a family relationship as designated by the state, none would otherwise exist—should survive scrutiny. That said, we agree that when sexual misconduct occurs in a relationship of asymmetrical dependency, a sentencing enhancement is warranted for the breach of trust created by that dependency. Those enhancements would be sensibly extended even to those secondary caregivers who exert supervisory powers over minors—including teachers, scout leaders, and faith group leaders.

However one redrafts criminal law in the incest arena to address the various difficult issues surrounding adult-adult, adult-minor, and minor-minor incest, we doubt we will gain much traction with the political community that favors these laws in the near future. In large part, these relationships are criminalized because Americans view them with distaste or because they are, in some situations, religiously proscribed. That said, the topic of consensual adult incest has actually been the subject of some legal and political discourse of late because of its links to the same-sex marriage debate. Some have suggested—with an intention to alarm—that if we legalize (as we have in some jurisdictions) same-sex marriage, the legalization of incest is sure to follow.[86] But in contrast to the issues of gay rights and same-sex marriage,[87] there is no committed and vociferous mainstream advocacy movement of which we are aware that is currently arguing for the liberalization of incest laws.[88]

Similarly, there is very little legal scholarship seeking to make an affirmative case for greater recognition of intrafamilial romantic relationships; discussions about incest usually involve simply pointing out that many of the arguments made in favor of the criminal laws are problematic. For example, commentators remark that the evidence related to the possibility of genetic harm is far less certain than once believed, and, in any event, many of the relationships currently prohibited do not trigger this concern at all.[89]

There are a few recent exceptions in the academic literature to this general pattern. For example, Christine Metteer argues that the individual's constitutionally protected right to marry trumps the state's interest in prohibiting incestuous marriages when the parties are related only by affinity rather than consanguinity.[90] More provocative is a recent article by Ruthann Robson, who suggests that "the proffered explanations for incest prohibitions should be deeply problematic for any same-sex marriage advocate."[91] She argues that attempts to justify prohibitions against incest by appealing to religion or longstanding community mores should be soundly rejected, because "tribal customs should not govern our current cultural mores and constitutional notions any more than Leviticus should prevail."[92] She also argues that we should reject the genetics justification, because it "rests upon identity between marriage and procreation—the same logic that is used to resist same-sex marriage."[93]

Our own view of the matter is, as we have said, limited to the reach of the criminal law. We think these criminal prohibitions, regardless of their motivation or provenance, are problematic from our liberal minimalism perspective, as well as from the viewpoint that considers how family ties burdens trigger concerns of inequality and discrimination, especially in the context of mature individuals engaging in consensual sexual relations.

D. Bigamy

Our analysis of bigamy takes some cues from the preceding discussion of incest. The rationales for bigamy laws (by which we refer to the criminal bans on the practice of polygamy) are familiar and, in America, deeply rooted.[94] They are nonetheless underscrutinized,[95] something we hope to remedy below. In describing the objectives of bigamy laws, some have adverted to the many "[p]opular depictions of polygamists in the media and in society, [which] generally focus on the prevalence of underage brides, accounts of sexual abuse, and the subservient role of women in these relationships."[96] Indeed, historically, polygamy has been decried by some as a tool to subordinate women and so bigamy laws would presumably be responsive to those concerns. Some supporters of bigamy laws have also noted their importance in reducing the costs of social welfare programs. The underlying assumption here appears to be that if a person has eight spouses (and their offspring) for whom she or he must provide care and resources, there is greater concern that these people might become charges of the welfare state. Last, some critics of polygamy have stated that polygamy is especially dangerous to the governance of the liberal state itself. We flesh out these claims on behalf of bigamy below. Our perspective on how to approach this family ties burden will, we hope, illuminate the debate—and raise questions about whether the criminal law is the proper tool with which to respond to the practice of polygamy.

1. Voluntary Caregiving and Liberty Interests

To begin, we note that bigamy laws satisfy our first liberal concern in that the legal burden of a criminal penalty only applies to someone who has previously created a voluntary caregiving relationship. Thus, when a criminal penalty based on family status is imposed on *X*, who is married to *Y*, for also marrying *Z* during an extant and valid marriage to *Y*, that is a burden that can be regarded as one for which *X* was on notice. That notice and implicit consent to the burden partially diminishes the problem of bigamy laws, but it does not provide an affirmative and independent justification for these family ties burdens. They must still undergo further scrutiny.

Our second inquiry asks whether there is some liberty at stake that a society committed to advancing one's liberty should respect. Our view is that the act of plural marriage itself can be expressive of one's basic rights to establish intimate associational relationships without undue intrusion by the state. We also believe that the right to terminate those marriages is a right properly belonging to individuals within a liberal state. So, using the terms above, if *X* marries *Z* even though *Y* opposes *X*'s second marriage to *Z*, *Y* should be able to terminate his marriage to *X* via divorce for this reason. And if *X* and *Y* had signed an agreement that *X* would not undertake a second marriage, then that should be enough to keep *X* from marrying *Z* while *X* is also married to *Y*. But statutes simply and completely criminalizing polygamy infringe on the fundamental rights of consenting mature individuals to enter into covenants of mutual care with other persons. Thus, if we are to criminalize this behavior, the reasons should be very substantial.

2. Minimalism and Means Analysis

a. Coercion and Minors

Recall that the first objection to repealing bigamy laws is that polygamous practices are thought to entail the frequent coercion of underage persons, usually females.[97] In light of the recent events involving the Fundamentalist Church of Jesus Christ of the Latter-Day Saints (FLDS) community in Texas,[98] we view this as a very substantial (though obviously contingent) consideration, especially because such girls often have had little recourse to reach beyond the relatively insular communities in which they were raised. To be sure, the problems that arise in prosecuting persons guilty of misconduct—the unwillingness or inability of family members to testify against the perpetrator, and the participation or enabling of the family members in the abuse—arise in monogamous situations too. But the problems are especially stark where an entire community may be supportive of the polygamist adult male and not his underage wives. Indeed, these problems also exist for potential wives who are technically of legal age because they are eighteen but may also face intense pressures from their communities and have no avenues of economic or social support outside them.

There is another important consideration related to the coercion of underage women. Some practitioners of polygamy seek to evade criminal sanctions by simply not declaring to the state that the parties have entered into what would otherwise be a formal marriage relationship.[99] Yet, bigamy laws are not always drafted or interpreted to target this wrong.[100] Indeed, they sometimes render the coerced parties themselves as criminals.[101] That we must vigilantly guard against harm to minors does not mean that we must necessarily prohibit the decision of three or more consenting adults to enter into a polygamous relationship. Using broadly written polygamy bans to fight coercion or exploitation of minors is overinclusive and facially discriminatory because it punishes those adults with polyamorous desires or dispositions who are willing to abide by norms requiring both consent and maturity.

There are other laws currently available, or that could be enacted, to punish the commandeering of immature or unconsenting minors without infringing upon legitimate associational rights and interests. First, as we suggested in connection with the discussion about incest, we should make sure the law is especially scrutinizing of and skeptical toward sexual and marital relationships involving minors generally and especially minors or other persons in relationships of asymmetrical dependency. Thus, under our approach, relationships established upon pressure or coercion would be prohibited (though the "poly" aspect of this prohibition is essentially irrelevant since it would apply to monogamous marriages too). We should also be vigilant about allowing parental authorization of marriages below an age of maturity and consent because that could facilitate abuse within communities committed to flouting those normative benchmarks. We emphasize, however, that the concern for coercion of minors (and adults) is relevant in the context of both monogamous marriages and polygamous ones. This concern would entail, perhaps, criminal prohibitions on persons knowingly facilitating or solemnizing marriage ceremonies regardless of whether they involve a license.[102]

In sum, although we need laws that prohibit the coercion of persons into marriage or sex, we do not believe these laws need to be drafted in such a way that unnecessarily infringe upon the rights of mature persons to structure their family lives in the way they feel appropriate. Rather, the government can develop specific strategies for dealing with acute dangers of coercion of minors or adult victims trafficked into marriages. In light of our commitment to being minimalist about the criminal law's reach, if policy-makers are determined to encourage particular structures within the household, they should not do so though the criminal law, especially when there are alternative civil options that can incentivize monogamous marriages.

b. Economics

Another reason some might think criminalizing polygamy is appropriate is based on the economics of social welfare. If a person has eight spouses (and their offspring) for whom she or he must provide care and resources, there is greater concern that these people might become charges of the welfare state. The problem with this argument is its contingent and highly speculative nature: as scholars have shown, the economics of polygamy are quite complicated and thus might not justify any criminal encroachments on the rights people have to intimate association.[103]

First, in any given polygamous cluster, there might be economies of scale that attach to family units that allow for optimization of human capital. One woman who is a polygamy activist in Utah paints her participation in a polygamous relationship in exactly such a manner.[104] Her husband has eight other wives and children with a number of them. One of the wives is employed by the others to tend to the collective children for several years at a time while the other wives are free to pursue careers of their choosing for longer periods. Indeed, some research shows that women are materially better off in societies in which polygamy is allowed or encouraged.[105] To be sure, it is not our goal to improve the lot of women at the needless expense of any other group, but we advert to such studies simply to show that who benefits from polygamous arrangements is a more complicated matter than often assumed.

Second, if an economic burden on the state were a sufficient reason to infringe upon an otherwise important liberty in associational freedom and privacy, the state could take a more narrowly tailored measure to ensure the financial viability of such unions, *i.e.*, the disqualification of additional spouses from social benefits.[106] Indeed, one could insist that adding more spouses is subject to higher taxes or proof of assets—both of which are non-criminal rules that can achieve the same end of reducing numbers on the dole.[107] Obviously, these rules should be crafted in gender-neutral terms.

Polygamous arrangements are not to everyone's taste, but in a world in which women, empirically, continue to shoulder the brunt of childrearing at the cost of their careers, flexibility in marital arrangements might be a way to minimize the social and personal costs of abiding by these extant social norms.

c. Bigamy Laws as a Safeguard Against Defiance of the Liberal State

As alluded to earlier, some propose banning polygamy because of the general injuries that the practice inflicts on liberal democratic states. For example, Professor Strassberg argues, with respect to some polygynous communities,[108] that children from polygamous unions impose an unusual burden on the state because they are often concealed; that polygamous practices conduce to create theocratic communities that fail to abide by or support the government's rules; that these practices create a secrecy that leads to the denial of individual civil rights; and, last, that these polygynous communities fail to pay sufficient taxes.[109]

These arguments, while well-motivated, are largely misplaced. Concealment-based harms are only a challenge in the context of a state that criminalizes polygamy. It is the threat of criminal liability that often drives the parties underground. Putting aside social norms that will bend over time, and recognizing that these norms have already changed somewhat, there is no *legal* need to conceal polygamous relations if bigamy laws are repealed. If we were worried that people were denied their civil rights, then that would be a separate reason to intervene in any specific situation, but there is nothing inherently denigrating of civil rights by expanding options for plural marriage. If we are worried about concrete legitimate wrongs (such as the failure to pay taxes) resulting from the theocratic tendencies of certain polygynous communities, we have separate laws available to punish violations of any given law. It is not as if polygamous communities are the only communities in which fundamentalist views pose a threat to the vitality and security of a liberal state. Using polygamy bans to remedy these harms on these grounds is unjustifiable as a government policy.[110]

3. Gender, Inequality, and Discrimination

Some arguments Professor Strassberg mentions bear special scrutiny because they run parallel to arguments opposing polygamy based on cultural or racial bias. As various scholars have shown, with ample record in the Supreme Court's nineteenth-century cases to support the argument,[111] opposition to polygamous practices is often rooted in prejudice against other cultural practices.[112] Although opposition to polygamy today is not usually expressed in racial or ethnic undertones,[113] it does sometimes take on a cast of hostility to religious views.[114]

A more powerful reason to be worried about decriminalizing bigamy is that polygamy, in some views, serves to facilitate the subordination of women, even if they are adults.[115] Although bigamy statutes are facially neutral to women, and thus prohibit both polygyny and polyandry,[116] we acknowledge the sociological and anthropological evidence showing that polyandry is much rarer.[117] Nonetheless, the research on this topic indicates that the claims that polygamous relationships subordinate all its female participants go too far in light of the diverse reasons that polygamy erupts and the diverse forms polygamy takes under different conditions.[118] Moreover, it is a mistake to resist polygamy (or more specifically, polygyny) as oppressive to women without noting that the same norms that exist within some polygamous communities also exist within some monogamous communities.[119]

There is also some empirical evidence indicating that abuse is no more likely in polygynous communities than monogamous ones.[120] Indeed, perhaps because of the marginalization of polygamous practices, polygamy supporters argue that it is harder for female victims or allies of victims to report abuse because it might lead to bad consequences for the victim.[121] Of course, this same reluctance to report abuse or coercion is a concern in monogamous relationships; but unlike in monogamous relationships, the victims of abuse in polygamous relationships might face serious collateral consequences from the state, such as the termination of parental rights.[122]

Consequently, we have to sift carefully among the potential causes of harms to women. As Professor Shayna Sigman trenchantly writes:

> The belief that polygyny causes gender discrimination or a low status of women in a given society is a classic example of the fallacy of post hoc ergo propter hoc. That polygyny can be found in societies that treat women poorly does not mean that the practice itself causes the gender inequality. Often, the true culprit of oppression merely lies in limitations on property rights for women, a practice that can be facilitated through polygamous life, but need not be. Indeed, where polygyny can help women economically by linking them with men who can provide more resources, it is the societies with less gender discrimination that are found to have this arrangement.[123]

Moreover, there is the quite powerful point that taking away a woman's right to participate in a polygamous arrangement (whether with men or women or both) is itself a way of subordinating women. Again, as Professor Sigman observes: "prohibiting polygamy infantilizes women, declaring them incapable of providing consent and foreclosing true choice by criminalizing one of their options for family living."[124]

In response to the claim that bigamy laws work to protect women from subordination, we note that many of the claims about how women are subservient in plural marriages have been said many times about monogamous marriage itself and the legal institutions accompanying it. So if antisubordination is the goal, then two questions arise: first, whether, as an empirical matter, plural marriage prohibitions in fact achieve marginal harm reduction—or, alternatively, whether marriage as a legal institution should be abolished.[125] In light of the fact that many prominent feminists have over the years argued for decriminalizing bigamy, including active support by Susan B. Anthony and Elizabeth Cady Stanton,[126] we should evaluate more carefully blanket claims about the subservience of women in plural marriage made in the absence of hard empirical evidence—and note that empirical evidence of polygamy's harms in liberal democracies would be difficult to come by in light of the prevalence of the ban on the practice.

Last, we think bigamy laws' effects on gay unions of two or more persons warrant attention. Obviously, to the extent gays are denied the right to marry one partner, they are also denied the right to marry two partners simultaneously. To gays, bigamy laws just add further insult to injury since whatever protective benefit or function the bigamy laws were designed to achieve for heterosexuals is denied to homosexual families. Despite this problematic discrimination, however, we note that the particular problem can be solved either by leveling down (decriminalization for all) or leveling up (expanding criminalization).[127] Thus, discrimination on the basis of sexual orientation could also be overcome by an *expansion* of bigamy laws, one that would encompass and sanction the misconduct of gays who have chosen to register their union with the state for this purpose alone or for other protections and benefits the state might offer to homosexual couples.

4. A Solution

Assuming the liberty to enter multiple covenants of mutual care is at least morally defensible on grounds of respecting the autonomous and honest choices of mature persons, then it seems that the state should abandon the business of criminalizing polygamy and let private ordering, and perhaps civil taxes and subsidies, determine who marries whom. This would entail, of course, that persons with same-sex poly-orientations should be able to group together as well without fear of prosecution.

In practical terms, here is what we propose. We would start with the decriminalization of bigamy as between mature and consenting individuals. Partners who wanted to secure exclusivity of marital relations could contract around such a rule through a private contract calling for, if desired, liquidated damages. This would place the burden of talking about the preference for imposing the family ties burden on the person who wanted the family ties burden imposed. Given our general concerns about family ties burdens, this burden-shifting makes sense as a penalty default rule.[128]

Several advantages from this regime obtain. First, it encourages couples to discuss in advance of their marriage whether both parties have a desire to keep the union monogamous. Second, it allows couples the flexibility to work out these issues without fear of the criminal law sanction.

In other words, couples could create agreements in which polygamy is prohibited, but without the involvement of criminal law penalties. Third, it allows those who want the benefits that accrue from having a penalty to opt in to a regime of regulation by contract. To be sure, a regime like the one we endorse still forces individuals to have conversations that might be deemed uncomfortable, but it seems that such a statute would prove to be a powerful information-forcing device prior to marriage. Fourth, because liquidated damages provisions are only enforceable to the degree that they are a reasonable estimation of the damages to an individual, they can be set at a level sufficient to communicate condemnation of the breach of trust, while still ensuring that the breacher can remain a productive member of society and caregiver to any dependents. How exactly one should estimate the worth of the breach is surely a difficult question. But we suspect a common sense judgment can be made about what might count as an impermissible penalty clause.

That we think bigamy should be decriminalized does not mean the state must affirmatively endorse "poly" relationships. Emphatically, the views developed here (as in our discussion of all these family ties burdens) are limited to the proper scope of the *criminal* law. Our argument does not require that the state forbear from promoting certain kinds of relationships through the civil system—and if the state wanted to endorse the view that children are better raised through monogamous marriages,[129] then it could do so through the use of civil subsidies and taxes, rather than criminal penalties. We do not necessarily agree that the state should use the civil justice system in this way, but at the very least, the civil justice system's carrots and sticks do not trigger the most fundamental liberty interests of citizens.

Despite the appeal of some of these recent arguments in favor of decriminalizing bigamy, opposition to the practice continues to be widespread in American society. As of 2004, more than ninety percent of Americans still viewed polygamy as immoral.[130] If polygamy activists will have their say, they will have to demonstrate to Americans that the parties to these unions are genuinely consenting and that the externalities of such practices, both on the state and on any resulting children, will be close to trivial.

E. Adultery

As we saw in Chapter 4, almost half the states in the United States still retain adultery laws. Even though they are sparingly used to prosecute individuals outside the military context, their existence on the books could have important collateral effects in various civil proceedings affecting child custody, adoption, and employment. To be sure, some might view this state of prosecutorial desuetude as a sign of progress that we are no longer interested in pursuing "mere" morals legislation. However, there is still support in various regions to retain these prohibitions, even if they are largely symbolic.[131] And the reasons for this support are worth consideration: some may view adultery's potential wrongful harm to children or to spouses who do not consent to their partner's non-exclusivity as profound and worthy of criminal sanction. Indeed, a decision to commit adultery has the potential to undermine an individual's ability to perform necessary care-giving functions, in that one's energies and attention will be focused outside the family unit rather than within it. Moreover, some may view these laws as helping to further the state's interest in keeping the institution of marriage strong and stable.

1. Voluntary Caregiving and Liberty Interests

As with bigamy laws, the current prohibitions on adultery attach only to voluntarily created relationships—indeed, the paradigmatic one of marriage. So in that sense, adultery laws meet the first liberal concern we highlighted in Chapter 5. However, there are still other considerations. When adultery is defined simply as a married person's sexual relations with a person not his or her spouse, then the question is whether there is some normatively attractive liberty to commit adultery such that a liberal society should respect it or at least tolerate it by not harnessing the condemnatory power of the criminal law upon it. On the one hand, if adultery is performed with duplicity, it hardly warrants praise; but it still leaves the question of whether it warrants the condemnation associated with criminal sanction, especially if non-criminal alternatives are available, as we discuss below. On the other hand, imagine a devoted couple wherein one person faces prolonged illness or some emotional development precluding the desire or capacity for sex or intimate companionship. One can easily imagine couples who might jointly authorize, either through a prenuptial agreement, or through open or tacit consent, to a partner's sexual relations with someone outside the marriage. It is hard to understand why a liberal state should be opposed to that private ordering arrangement if harms to third parties are trivial to non-existent.

2. Minimalism and Means Analysis

The objective of preventing betrayals of the marriage bond can be achieved through various non-criminal law norms, though admittedly it is hard to tell whether these non-criminal means are equally effective (though the degree of non-enforcement suggests that deterrence is not really the rationale). In those states without adultery laws, however, there are still strong social norms against cheating in one's marriage. The strength of these social norms should not surprise. In various states in the United States or in liberal democratic countries around the globe, strong social norms persist against stigmatized activities: gambling and private tobacco use come to mind. It is hard to believe that the modern state could not adopt effective norm-shaping and regulatory strategies that encourage faithful monogamous unions without the use of the criminal law.[132]

3. Gender, Inequality, and Discrimination

Because only a very few jurisdictions permit same-sex marriage, it bears emphasis that adultery laws work primarily for the benefit of partners (and, *arguendo*, children) of heterosexual marriages and not for the benefit of partners (or children) of gay unions.

Although we think adultery laws should generally be abolished based upon the very limited state interest in proscribing this conduct, we think this added discrimination is very problematic. We note, however, that, like the bigamy laws, the discrimination can be overcome by an *expansion* of adultery laws, one that would sanction the misconduct of gays who have chosen to register their union with the state for this purpose alone or for other protections and benefits the state might offer to homosexual couples. Yet this expansion to alleviate discrimination sits in tension with our commitment to minimalism.

4. A Solution

We understand the viewpoint that, at least in certain contexts involving duplicity, adultery statutes help punish and deter injury to persons who did not consent to extramarital sex—for example, the spurned spouse. But what adultery laws don't permit, and what they should, is a life in which both parties consent to one or both parties living in marriage but outside the bonds of monogamy, whether permanently or temporarily. This would have the effect of destabilizing the conflation of marriage with persistent *sexual* companionship.

As with bigamy, we view adultery laws that criminalize the extramarital sex of married persons as facial family ties burdens warranting careful scrutiny despite the fact that they are triggered by virtue of a voluntarily created relationship of caregiving. That's because, in the absence of such adultery laws, the proscribed activity would otherwise be lawful. Given that adultery laws are drafted in gender-neutral terms across the country, we do not believe they inherently raise issues of patriarchy or gender bias against women.[133] Nonetheless, because same-sex marriage is not permitted in almost all American jurisdictions, adultery laws protect the interests of (potentially) betrayed heterosexual partners while not being similarly available to those in same-sex partnerships. For us, that is a basis for rethinking adultery laws.

Assuming that adultery statutes could be made indifferent to sexual orientation, would there be any reason to retain them in some fashion? We think the strategy we endorsed in the bigamy context is instructive. We would begin with a default rule that decriminalizes adultery because of the way adultery intrudes on the choices of autonomous and consenting individuals. But we would encourage prospective partners to contract around that default rule if they wished by agreements that called for liquidated damages.[134] As with polygamy, several advantages from this regime obtain.

First, it will give couples an undoubtedly useful incentive to have an important conversation before marriage about whether both parties want their relationship to be monogamous, and it will give couples the flexibility to address these issues without fear of the criminal law sanction. Couples could create agreements in which adultery is prohibited, not by the criminal law, but by allowing a regime of regulation by contract. In addition, because liquidated damages provisions are only enforceable to the degree that they are a reasonable estimation of the damages to an individual, they can be set at a level sufficient to communicate condemnation of the breach of trust, while still ensuring that the breacher can remain a productive member of society and caregiver to any dependents. The same disclaimer we referenced above applies here too: these reasonable liquidated damages are hard to set in the abstract but we are confident courts could find a way to determine when the damages clauses become impermissibly high penalties.

It needs to be emphasized that the burden for contracting around the default rule of permitting adultery falls upon the individual who has information regarding his or her preference for monogamous relations.[135] Thus, the person wanting the extra burden imposed has to raise the issue and force a conversation about monogamy. We think that, in light of the difficulties raised by many family burdens, the burden should lie with this party. This is also consistent with our sense that if we are to have other family ties burdens like duties to rescue or supervise, the benefits flowing from these duties should be available for a wide range of persons who either have signaled their caregiving commitments through parenthood or partnership or those who are not in such relationships but nonetheless want to create a covenant of caregiving.

Admittedly, we toyed with an idea—inspired by an article by Professor Elizabeth Emens—that parties should be able to opt into a regime of voluntary criminal law regulation, such that breach of a contract for monogamy could lead to criminal prosecutions for bigamy or adultery.[136] But upon further consideration, we recognized the unfairness of using public resources to investigate, prosecute, and punish conduct that amounted to a breach of private promises between individuals. The notion that average people would have to pay more taxes or suffer the effects of diverting scarce prosecutorial resources to prosecute the failure of a private party to live up to its contractual sexual expectations seemed ultimately unsupportable. By contrast, even in the absence of the "contractual criminal law regulation" of adultery or polygamy, parties of any sexual preference can contract for monogamous commitments on pain of liquidated damages, and private ordering could thus be made to supplant the clunky machinery of the state's prosecutorial apparatus.[137]

In sum, because we believe the protections of the criminal law should not be arbitrarily denied to couples of different stripes, and because we think there are serious minimalism concerns and some liberalism concerns with categorical rules against adultery, we support the decriminalization of adultery laws. This would put everyone on the same footing. At the same time, it would permit parties of all sorts to contract around a world without criminal penalties.[138] As we explained above, we would prefer to set the default rule in a way that incentivized the person wanting the family ties burden imposed to secure the agreement of the other spouse.

Thus far, we have not said much about what criminal law consequences, if any, should be visited upon a person who has sexual relations with a married person.[139] (Recall that in some jurisdictions, adultery statutes encompass the "outside" person who intrudes upon the marital relationship.) We think the reach of these statutes goes too far, violating our second liberalism principle, and that such adultery statutes should also be modified to end criminal liability for those persons. But note that if the adultery statutes extend criminal liability to those third persons, there is no family ties burden imposed on the basis of *that person's* familial status or familial connection to the crime. Properly understood, those provisions of adultery laws are not family ties burdens as we define them.

F. Nonpayment of Child Support

As we described in Chapter 4, criminal sanctions have been adopted across the country to ensure that parents do not flout their obligations to provide material support for the well-being of their children. This development has occurred, no doubt, for a few reasons. First, it is politically attractive for elected officials to stand against parents who neglect their children.[140] Second, and more importantly, the nonpayment of child support is a serious problem in our society.[141] It obviously harms children, who rely on support payments for subsistence. Moreover, it harms the single parents left to struggle alone for the care of their children. And because more single parent households are headed by mothers, it leaves women to bear most of the brunt of parenthood and its unique challenges.[142] It also harms society at large, in that taxpayers may be forced to shoulder the burden of financially supporting those children who end up on the welfare rolls as a consequence of the nonpayment of child support. It is, accordingly, unsurprising that our criminal justice system takes special interest in child support debts. Additionally, when we know the "creditors" are especially vulnerable children with very little recourse to self-help options, we can see why it would be appealing at first blush for policymakers to look to the criminal justice system to help make sure these debts are paid. Nonetheless, we must see if these laws stand up to scrutiny.

1. Voluntary Caregiving and Liberty Interests

Criminally punishing parents for debts to their children clearly triggers the concern that most family ties burdens do: it punishes the same conduct—failure to pay a debt—differently based on the familial status of the debtor. This is a straightforward family ties burden. For the reasons we adverted to earlier in Chapter 5, we think we can explain why these family ties burdens continue to have some appeal or at least seem somewhat fair: because parents can be plausibly deemed to have consented to assume certain obligations and responsibilities by having their children. The family ties burden here is one that should be imposed on persons voluntarily creating these caregiving relationships.

But the case of a criminally punished obligation to support one's children may reveal a limitation of our approach because one could plausibly retort that it is too facile to say that the nonpayment of a contractual debt to a phone company, for example, is the *same conduct* as the nonpayment of child support. In other words, one could argue that our society has differential views about the inherent *blameworthiness* of these two forms of nonpayment precisely because we see them as different sorts of conduct, not as the same conduct treated differently on the basis of status. We cannot deny that this re-description of the burden has some rhetorical force; however, we still think our organizing method of scrutiny helps expose something deep and pervasive about how the criminal justice system in the United States interacts with a normative conception of the family.

Although our first liberal concern focusing on autonomy seems met by these laws, our second liberal concern asks whether there is some underlying liberty worthy of respect to the act of not satisfying one's obligations to support one's child. Our short answer is that it depends. As we discussed in Chapter 5, there are some situations in which we agree the obligation should not attach. A sperm donor may be the genetic parent, but if he disclaims, prior to the donation of the sperm, all future rights to the resulting offspring, he should not be held to pay child support. Similarly, a parent who gives a child up for adoption and thus terminates his or her parental rights should not be on the hook. But someone who has voluntarily entered into a parenting relationship should not be able to enjoy the benefits associated with parenting without also facing the obligations to be a minimally competent and supportive parent. The question is whether those obligations should be fixed by criminal law, and if so by what kinds of sanctions.

2. Minimalism and Means Analysis

We think that the criminal sanction should be used sparingly if there are non-criminal alternatives that might be equally effective at satisfying the goals here. Our sense is that using the criminal justice system with respect to this particular duty to support is not likely to be good—or effective—use of criminal sanctions. First, depending on the sanction imposed, criminal sanctions might risk putting "deadbeat" parents in prison, where they certainly will not be able to earn money to help support their children. Prison and other forms of forced separation also prevent the debtor parent from having meaningful relationships with their children—even if their only failure as parents was being too poor to pay support. If the sanction is a fine that goes to the state, then that is money that might otherwise be needed for the child.

But these criticisms of imprisoning or fining deadbeat parents do not close the debate, especially since a pretty basic empirical question is in play. We have earlier acknowledged that the ability of the criminal law to have an educative or expressive effect is worth careful attention. Having a criminal statute apply in a way that does not itself make matters worse for the child may be possible through alternative or intermediate sanctions.[143] For one thing, in these contexts, the adjudication alone may be valuable for both general deterrent and specific communicative purposes—when a public body declares, "you have flouted one of your most pressing obligations, the support of the children, and you warrant condemnation for that," that can be a powerful tool in shaping attitudes. But it might be that alternative non-criminal measures can also bring home that message to the offender in question, and to the public at large. Moreover, our anxiety about using the criminal sanction promiscuously here is that it focuses attention too narrowly on the economic aspects of parenthood, devaluing other important contributions to parenthood. When applied mostly to fathers, as is typical, it further reinforces outdated views about fathers discharging their parental obligations through money rather than direct caregiving.[144] To be sure, some fathers who are failing to pay financial support are likely failing to provide emotional support as well. But the fact that the criminal law takes an interest only in financial support in these statutes can have the effect of reinforcing gender stereotypes.

Our minimalist approach would try to ensure that we have considered how else to reduce the incidence of nonpayment of child support. First, we think it is worth noting that a number of other non-criminal enforcement mechanisms already exist to induce individuals to comply with their mandated child support payments. For example, wages can be garnished, tax refunds can be intercepted, and licenses and passports can be suspended.[145] Further, these remedies can often be pursued outside the criminal courts, for example, through state administrative agencies or through mediation. These civil proceedings can potentially promote the important ends that animate the current laws with more sophisticated, more sensitive, and less troublesome means—and without the stigma of criminal conviction, debtor parents can more easily get the jobs, education, and housing needed to get on their feet and meet their obligations. Primarily, these other enforcement mechanisms might be sufficient to keep deadbeat parents in their children's lives while at the same time ensuring that the children receive the funding to which they are entitled.

We cannot avoid the core question, however: if these mechanisms fail, say with repeat offenders, should enforcement through the criminal justice system, and in particular the use of incarceration, be an option of last resort? There is at least one study, albeit somewhat dated, that suggests that criminal sanctions can be effective in reducing the incidence of the problem. Professor David Chambers "found a close parallel between payments and jailing: the counties that jailed more did in fact collect more."[146] But other mechanisms have been shown to be even more effective than incarceration, with suspension of driver's licenses being the most effective stick.[147] That is not to say the criminal justice system cannot play any role in regulating parental behavior; conviction and probation may well be valuable in inducing a repeat offender to pay. But we generally do not think incarceration should be an available sentencing option for this offense, because, among other reasons, incarceration affirmatively *impedes* caregiving instead of fostering it. More empirical evidence would be helpful in finally resolving this issue since, if jailing were the most effective means of making deadbeat parents pay support, we would concede that the case for criminalization and incarceration would be stronger.

3. Gender, Inequality, and Discrimination

Although the statutes that criminally punish deadbeat dads are drafted in gender-neutral ways, fathers are most often the ones imprisoned under these laws.[148] We think it is undeniable that punishing mostly men for failing to pay child support contributes to a gender stereotype that assumes that men are supposed to be breadwinners and women are supposed to be caregivers. This system contributes to and reinforces gender stereotypes in our society—and it therefore raises our general concerns about family ties burdens.[149]

Although we applaud the drafting of these laws in gender-neutral language, we think more work can be done to take the focus off the family in particular, and instead focus more on voluntary caregiving relationships. Because our general approach is to deflect attention away from state-sanctioned families and promote the reorientation of family ties burdens to target relationships of voluntary caregiving, we suggest broadening the ambit of whatever approach the law takes to include all nonpayment of debts of support to those in asymmetrical relationships of voluntary caregiving. So, if we are to have a criminal sanction imposed, its reach should encompass all individuals who have assumed that responsibility by becoming a primary caregiver for the child in question. That would avoid the discrimination typically occurring *ex ante* against persons in same-sex or polyamorous relationships and at the same time would extend to the children of such unions the "protective" benefit these burdens are supposed to achieve.[150]

4. A Solution

We cannot deny that there are countervailing values that justify these laws in many people's minds. As we suggested, these debts, when unpaid, can largely harm vulnerable children and even primary caregivers themselves. So what does our particular framework offer to the public policy community on the issue of nonpayment of child support? Must the legal system get out of the business of these prosecutions?

Based on what we noted above, we would favor a solution that minimizes the use of the criminal sanction to ensure these obligations are met. One possibility, the use of restorative justice processes, would simultaneously help communicate the nature of the wrong to the debtor parent while also furnishing a forum in which the debtor can explain why the debt is not yet paid. And, in those cases where the criminal sanction is used to condemn unjustified selfish behavior by the debtor parent, it should be applied using a sanction to only and all those persons who have undertaken a voluntary caregiving role towards the child, thus using a sanction that actually promotes or is consistent with the caregiving obligations of the offender.

G. Nonpayment of Parental Support

In Chapter 4, we described the family ties burden created by criminal statutes that punish adult children who fail to provide financial support to their indigent parents. Because of the rarity with which prosecutions are brought under these laws, we will be relatively brief in our assessment, which is, on the whole, negative.

The plain objective of these laws is, first, to ensure aid to those who are vulnerable in old age, and second, to educate the public and to reinforce a sense of obligation through the criminal law to parents based on gratitude or a notion of unbargained-for reciprocity. Do these laws pass muster under our normative framework?

1. Voluntary Caregiving and Liberty Interests

These laws fail our initial concern regarding voluntary caregiving because it creates a family ties burden on a person who did not voluntarily establish a relationship with the indigent parent. The adult child is penalized simply by virtue of being the indigent parent's child.

From the perspective of our second concern with liberty, we ask whether an adult child should retain the liberty to support only those he volunteered to support. We think the answer to this, at least from a liberal legal perspective, is yes. Obviously, it is appropriate and praiseworthy for an adult with means to support his parents, whether based on love, reciprocity, or gratitude. But we think it is not the business of the criminal law to require that support, and, when it does, it violates a basic precept by condemning a person for failing to act gratefully. This seems too slender a reed to justify criminal sanctions.

2. Minimalism and Means Analysis

We begin by looking at the first objective of these laws. Here it is to ensure necessary aid to indigent and vulnerable persons, usually when they are elderly and without physical means to help themselves. To our mind, the obligation to help such persons is one that is agent-neutral, and thus, if it is to be undertaken, it should be undertaken and funded by the public at large; otherwise, it discriminates against those indigent elderly persons without children or those whose children predeceased the parents. In any event, there is no special need for using the criminal sanction to ensure support, when social services funded out of taxes could more readily ensure that the public interest in protecting the indigent elderly is satisfied.

As to the second objective, we note that, given our liberal orientation, we are doubtful that the state has an important public interest in vindicating norms of care based on gratitude. Assuming *arguendo* that we stipulate to the compelling or important nature of the second goal—of educating the public and reinforcing an obligation to parents based on gratitude—we do not understand why the civil remedies available to enunciate this obligation would be insufficient.

As with duties to support children, if the goal is ensuring norm projection and compensation, the goal can be expressed and the money can be obtained through civil actions or garnished through wages and tax refunds. If a criminal penalty were to attach, such that the person went to prison or had to pay a fine to the state, then that sanction would usually impede the first goal of ensuring adequate resources to the vulnerable elderly parent *ex post* even though it might achieve some marginal deterrence *ex ante* against the prospect of adult children walking away from their parents. We would invite empirical scholars to weigh this cost based on existing data, but we would not really seek out new legislative experiments based on our view that imposing this family ties burden on children is improper because of its incompatibility with the voluntarist underpinnings of an attractive criminal justice system in a liberal society.

Regarding the concerns about gender, inequality, and discrimination, we note first that imposing criminal liability on those violating filial responsibility norms discriminates *ex ante* against children raised by parents in those gay or polyamorous unions that are not recognized by the state; these children are told, effectively, that they are not viewed as "children" of this or that person to whom they properly regard as a parent. The discriminatory injury to the child is admittedly quite slight. But these laws also have the effect of denying to gay and polyamorous parents the "protective" benefit these burdens are supposed to achieve.

Although the urge to promote an ongoing ethos of reciprocal care between parents and children is powerful in some cultures, we must bear in mind that a child's relationship with his parents is not voluntary in the same sense as a parent's relationship to his children; after all, no child asks to be born, let alone to *these* parents. Thus, it is no surprise to us that many jurisdictions are reluctant to impose such liability now, even if that position leads to seemingly harsh results.[151] Because of the voluntariness problem, an opt-in registry makes sense in the context of adult children who wish to signal their covenants of care with their parents. And if they want, parents can opt to signal their ongoing commitment to their children by agreeing to face liability for failing to protect or support them as adults.

But, in the end, we think the current state of affairs, in which about a dozen states use the criminal sanction to establish filial responsibility norms,[152] violates our normative framework on every dimension. Therefore, we think these laws should be abandoned. However, if these criminal laws are to be retained for their expressive and/or compensatory purposes, we think that they should at least not involve fines or incarceration, and that the reach of the law should be expanded to include, under its umbrella, persons who would otherwise be excluded based on discrimination against children from same-sex or polyamorous unions.

Last, we think it bears mention that although there was once wide legislative support for filial responsibility laws in both civil and criminal form, these norms no longer act with much force. The reason for that desuetude, we think, is an increased appreciation for the voluntarist basis for holding people criminally liable. We also think the significance of that norm helps explain why, for example, we almost never see family ties burdens prominently used against persons—siblings, grandparents, aunts—who did not themselves voluntarily undertake to create that relationship of caregiving. That norm—of promoting voluntarily caregiving—illuminates much of the terrain we have surveyed here, and it lends promise to the project of how better to reform our existing laws.

*****

We hope to have accomplished three things here. Most concretely, we have demonstrated that there are a series of burdens that defendants face in the criminal justice system on account of their family status, when that status is recognized as part of a state-sanctioned family unit. Although our work in Part I on the range of family ties benefits might suggest that family status could only help a defendant, our exploration here reveals that such a picture is incomplete. Indeed, there are also some ways that the criminal justice system goes out of its way to punish persons on account of their family status. The extent of this phenomenon has not, to our knowledge, been previously examined systematically and we hope to get scholars and policymakers to take interest in these findings.

Second, we made an effort to organize a normative framework for thinking through whether special penalties should attach to family status. What we discovered is that these sorts of penalties are more palatable when they are efforts to reinforce relationships of voluntary caregiving. Accordingly, we developed a set of tests or questions that we used to assess these family ties burdens. First, did the burden fall on persons who had voluntarily created a relationship of care? Second, did the burden impinge on some liberty that should be recognized as deserving of protection in a liberal society? Third, were the laws drafted in such a way as to be narrowly tailored to the governmental objectives? Fourth, were there non-criminal measures that could be equally effective in achieving these government objectives, assuming these government objectives were sufficiently compelling or important to vindicate through law? Last, in what ways do the existing family ties burdens contribute to concerns about gender inequality and discrimination?

Finally, we tried to spell out how our normative framework might contribute to thinking through each of the family ties burdens we were able to identify here. We recognize, however, that ultimately we cannot hope to have analyzed each family ties burden exhaustively—for they are each embedded within a policy space of their own and each burden functions differently to control different kinds of conduct. Nevertheless, our hope has been to respond to older debates and start new ones through the framework we have adopted and the policy choices we have suggested. Indeed, we hope that looking at these burdens synthetically will illuminate how the criminal justice system is tempted to use each particular family ties burden to punish family status in several ways—and how we might reorient these burdens in a more normatively attractive light.

Coda

WE BELIEVE THAT THERE very well may be appropriate places for the modern liberal state to recognize and accommodate the significance of family life and caregiving networks. Indeed, the general subsidization that the family receives throughout our legal system is probably a fact of life that would be too utopian to oppose (though we remain discomfited by the way in which the family is too often defined in terms that are not true or respectful to the ways many people choose to organize their circles of affection). More than that, there is potentially some increase in compliance the legal system achieves by having family ties benefits and burdens. But even these relatively straightforward statements trigger some fundamental questions: how should we be defining the term *family* to achieve these possible, though ultimately speculative, gains in compliance? Is there any reason to assume that compliance would go down if we moved from a focus on family status to voluntary caregiving? And, in any event, even if such gains existed, might there not be a moral constraint on using the criminal justice apparatus to further a particular conception of which relationships constitute a family?

As we hope we have shown in this book, the criminal justice system, with a few exceptions, is not generally an appropriate place to foster a particular vision of family life. While our criminal justice system haphazardly reflects many values, surely its critical and appropriately dominant ones are the promotion of accurate and fair determinations of guilt or innocence and the protection of citizens from serious wrongful harm. As we saw in Part I, privileging individuals because of their membership in a state-denominated family unit can threaten these core functions. Conversely, as we saw in Part II, burdening defendants because of family status also threatens to extend the criminal justice system into an arena beyond its proper scope. We are mindful that a criminal justice system can do many other things, incident to its central functions. But we have endeavored to analyze and explain why propping up a narrow conception of the family through facial benefits and burdens is unacceptable from the standpoints of liberalism, minimalism, and criminal justice.

The conclusions we have drawn in our comprehensive investigation of the intersection of family ties and the criminal justice system are as follows. We think marital and other intrafamilial evidentiary privileges are troublesome; familial exemptions for harboring fugitives cannot be tolerated; and that violence within the family cannot be punished less severely than stranger violence. Yet we think certain benefits that family members get in pretrial release contexts, sentencing practices, and prison visitation and furlough policies can remain viable in a liberal criminal justice system so long as these benefits are extended more broadly on the basis of relationships of caregiving, rather than arbitrary familial status, which is itself highly contested, gendered, and otherwise unjustifiable.

On the burdens side of the ledger, we support decriminalization in the cases of parental responsibility laws (based on strict and vicarious liability), bigamy, adultery, and nonpayment of parental support; we endorse decriminalizing incest between most adults, though we are divided on certain subissues in the incest context; and we are highly skeptical of criminalization in the nonpayment of child support context, though we concede that more research needs to be done on just how effective criminalization is in achieving compliance. The only area in which we are largely unconflicted about criminalization on the burden side is the omissions (duty to rescue) context.

We are open to being proven wrong through credible empirical evidence that would show that the benefits or burdens are necessary to achieve some compelling state goal that cannot be achieved through less discriminatory means. At the very least, we hope our evaluation of the benefits and burdens defendants receive throughout the criminal law encourages other thinkers and policymakers to develop more refined and systematic thinking about these pervasive practices. It will not do, for example, to simply suggest that the benefits and burdens somehow balance one another out, rendering the system equitable. For that balance to happen, there would likely have to have been some evidence of intentional action by either legislators or courts, even though such evidence appears scant; moreover, it would be hard to understand, for example, what the logical nexus is that translates, say, the burden of being susceptible to prosecution for incest into an entitlement for testimonial privileges or harboring fugitives.[1]

It also bears mentioning here that the somewhat different foci of the two Parts' normative frameworks (essentially Chapters 2 and 5) might mislead readers in the following way: although Part II focuses on voluntary relationships of caregiving as central to the justificatory apparatus that could render "burdens" legitimate, one might—in our view, mistakenly—conclude that this justificatory apparatus could underwrite all the benefits we describe in Part I. That is, just because we think some legitimate criminal justice burdens may be placed upon people in relationships of voluntary caregiving does not mean that we think the criminal justice system is necessarily the best place to incentivize these relationships by affording caregivers all the perquisites surveyed in Part I. Rather, we carved out just a few of these benefits that make sense to apply to such caregivers: sentencing discounts for the non-violent irreplaceable caregiver and certain prison policies and practices. Ultimately, the primary criminal justice values—prosecuting the guilty fairly and protecting the innocent from crime and prosecution—warrant more respect in a liberal criminal justice system than the possibility that these family ties benefits can contribute to promoting and sustaining caregiving relationships. So we do not think giving caregivers of any sort (within the extended family or outside it) the right to harbor fugitives, say, is a benefit worth extending broadly to promote caregiving relationships. When, however, the caregiving rationale does not endanger those fundamental pursuits of fair and accurate retribution and reasonable crime control (as it might not in some pretrial and post-sentencing contexts, for example), we think it is important not to run afoul of the heteronormativity and repronormativity concerns that characterize so many of these policies as they are currently constructed.[2]

*****

We cannot leave the topic of the challenges the family poses to the criminal justice system without offering a few thoughts on the special and pronounced problem of domestic violence. We have not addressed it in depth in Parts I or II because state statutes regarding domestic violence cannot neatly be characterized as representing either a benefit or a burden on the basis of family status; indeed, different states take wildly inconsistent positions. For example, one jurisdiction makes domestic violence offenders eligible for a diversion program whereas another jurisdiction bars domestic violence offenders from diversion even though defendants charged with other misdemeanor offenses might be eligible.[3] Indeed, some jurisdictions may decide to codify approaches to domestic violence that simply do not vary in any important way from stranger violence. In light of this diverse set of possible structures, we can only try to offer some general observations that bring to bear the insights of the book on this important and challenging issue.

First, any jurisdiction that might persist in treating domestic violence offenders *better* than offenders who victimize acquaintances or strangers, either through the law on the books or the law "on the streets," clearly would run afoul of the principles for analyzing family ties benefits that we set forth in the first half of the book. Such practices would probably have patriarchal origins and would certainly have gendered effects. They would thus offend our core concerns about equality and justice. To be sure, our analysis has focused on facial benefits, and the law "on the streets" falls a bit outside the purview of our book. Still, at least in this application, it is easy to see how we would react to such a family ties benefit as a matter of principle.

Second, any jurisdictions that utilize traditional, circumscribed notions of the family in their domestic violence statutes would also run afoul of the concerns about discrimination and heteronormativity that we have discussed in this book. For example, Professor Ruth Colker undertook a comprehensive survey of state domestic violence statutes in 2006.[4] She concluded that four states—Delaware, Louisiana, North Carolina, and South Carolina—only extend certain protections of their domestic violence statutes to opposite sex or married partners, thereby excluding individuals in same sex relationships who are not married.[5] Some other states, such as Massachusetts and New Mexico, limit coverage to individuals in a long-term romantic relationship.[6] Like Professor Colker, we would endorse using a functional approach to determining which individuals should receive the protections of domestic violence statutes. If individuals voluntarily perform primary caregiving roles to another, then they should be included within the coverage of a state's domestic violence statutes, regardless of whether they are part of a formal heterosexual marriage relationship. Thus, for those individuals who choose to utilize the registry that we described in Chapter 5, in which people opt into certain obligations of caregiving to affected parties, we would fully support including as part of the obligations covered by that registry a willingness to be bound by any reasonable state statutes proscribing domestic violence or state statutes that especially burden those voluntary caregivers in their domestic violence regulation.

Yet, there are more subtle and difficult issues raised by domestic violence statutes, to which our normative frameworks can also make a modest contribution. In some jurisdictions, domestic violence statutes can be construed as a family ties burden upon a defendant rather than as a family ties benefit. That is emphatically not to suggest that domestic violence laws are currently doing a good job of protecting women; as Professor Deborah Tuerkheimer has forcefully argued, "the disconnect between battering as it is practiced and battering as it is criminalized is vast and it is significant."[7] But on its face, as Professor Ruth Colker has argued, "the law is not 'neutral' with respect to domestic violence; it now articulates the presumption that domestic violence is worse than other kinds of violence." She adds that "this evolution in the law has not been accompanied by the development of a theory to explain why we have an enhanced, rather than neutral, law of domestic violence."[8]

Although the full articulation of such a theory would be far beyond the scope of this project, we hope that we have contributed some ideas to a dialogue about when and why such an enhanced law might be appropriate. The criminal justice system possesses its greatest moral force for intervention in relationships between individuals when it is necessary to protect persons from wrongful harms. Omissions liability, as we discussed in Part II, is a classic example. By entering into a relationship of voluntary caregiving, presumed in the case of a parent-child relationship and available for voluntary entry in the case of mature adults, we argued that one has signaled a willingness to be a first responder when a party to the relationship is in peril. If an individual has signaled a willingness to be a first responder, to rescue a vulnerable member of the relationship from harm, that individual has also signaled a willingness to forego being the actual cause of any harm and that individual's exploitation of—and failure to protect—the consequent vulnerability is itself an independent wrong that exacerbates the wrong of harming in the first place. Breaking a covenant of care by inflicting injury is thus a greater moral wrong than inflicting injury on an individual to whom such a specific covenant of care is not owed because exploitation of a particular vulnerability is a separate wrong. Accordingly, enhanced penalties (or separate charges) for that breach would seem to be appropriate to reflect the greater moral wrong that has been committed.

Ultimately, the issues surrounding the criminalization of domestic violence are tremendously complex and difficult, and we do not mean to suggest here that we have addressed them in any sort of comprehensive way. We have obviously not adequately addressed issues related to race or class—or the ways in which criminalization may itself be threatening to women's autonomy, to name just a few of the important questions that are beyond the scope of our limited efforts here. We simply wish to suggest that domestic violence policy may implicate some of the concerns about the criminal justice system's reflexive reliance on family status in setting legislative policy that we have discussed throughout this book, and we hope that legislators, courts, and policymakers will take a hard look at some of the questions that we have suggested might be useful in analyzing any particular policy a state is considering implementing regarding criminal justice and the family.

*****

In sum, whether benefits or burdens, privileging or punishing, is at issue, the core inquiry is in a fundamental sense the same: how should family status be used by the criminal justice system? We conclude that, in general, it should only rarely and cautiously serve as a vehicle for directly promoting the institution and goods of family life. The American family is a far more complex entity today than our current system of benefits and burdens acknowledges. Thus, in the final analysis, family ties benefits and burdens should be viewed with skepticism for two reasons. First, they undermine the core functions of a fair and attractive criminal justice system within a liberal democracy. Second, using the criminal justice system to reflect and constitute traditional ideals of the family is ineffective at best and, more often, plainly and perniciously discriminatory.

Notes

Introduction

1. *See* David Johnston & Janny Scott, *Prisoner of Rage: The Tortured Genius of Theodore Kaczynski*, N.Y. TIMES, May 26, 1996, at 1; Serge F. Kavaleski, *His Brother's Keeper*, WASH. POST, July 21, 2001, at W10.
2. *See* David W. Chen, *The Unabomber Case: The Survivors; Sadness Now Mixes with Relief and Regret*, N.Y. TIMES, Jan. 23, 1996, at A18.
3. *See* David Kaczynski, Editorial, *Death Penalty Turnaround*, L.A. TIMES, Apr. 12, 2005, at B13.
4. Indeed, recently, the Suffolk County District Attorney asked parents in the community to turn in their children involved in crime. *See* John R. Ellement, *Man Tells Police His Son Shot Teen—In Self-Defense*, BOSTON GLOBE, Jan. 19, 2006, at B7 (quoting Suffolk District Attorney Daniel F. Conley as saying, "I would urge parents, though it is difficult, to turn in their children if they have in fact committed a violent crime"); *cf.* Kevin Rothstein & Jessica Fargen, *Kin Turn in Suspect for School Shooting*, BOSTON HERALD, Dec. 6, 2005, at 6 ("'They definitely did the right thing. The police can't handle the situation alone,' Police Commissioner Kathleen O'Toole said of the arrest. 'It takes community and it takes responsibility.'").
5. *See* Manuel Perez-Rivas & Maria Good, *Md. Teen Sought in Dismemberment Slaying; Warrant Charges Student with Murder After Burned Body Is Found in Vacant House*, WASH. POST, Sept. 23, 1997, at D1.
6. *See* Barton Gellman & Steve Vogel, *Israel Bars Return of Md. Teen, May Hold Murder Trial There; Father, Brother Accused of Helping Aspen Hill Youth Flee*, WASH. POST, Sept. 30, 1997, at A1. Because Samuel's father had been born in Israel, the Israeli authorities considered Samuel to be an Israeli citizen. *See id.* Samuel's lawyer admitted that her client had deliberately fled to Israel because he preferred to be tried and incarcerated there rather than in the United States. *See Montgomery Co. Seeks U.S. Help in Slaying Suspect's Extradition; Teen Fled to Israel, Wants to be Tried There*, BALT. SUN, Oct. 1, 1997, at 2B.
7. *See* Katharine Shaver & Lee Hockstader, *Charge Filed Against Sol Sheinbein for Helping His Son Flee to Israel*, WASH. POST, Aug. 28, 1998, at C1. Sheinbein also apparently agreed to tell the police if he learned of his son's location but drove to New York to help his son flee to Israel rather than disclosing that information. *See* Andrea F. Siegal, *Silver Spring Man Fights to Keep Law License; Accused of Helping Son Flee Md. Murder Charges*, BALT. SUN, Sept. 11, 2002, at 2B.

8. *See* Barton Gellman & Karl Vick, *Parents Allege Sheinbein Was Being Robbed*, WASH. POST, Oct. 1, 1997, at B1; *see also* Katharine Shaver, *Patent Office Bars Wanted Lawyer; Ex-Md. Resident Helped Son Flee After '97 Killing*, WASH. POST, June 24, 2005, at B4 (indicating that Sol Sheinbein continued to work on behalf of Israeli clients despite issuance of Maryland arrest warrant in 1998 and disbarment in 2002, filing sixty-four patent applications in the United States since 2001).
9. *See* Shaver, *supra* intro., n 8, at B4.
10. *See* Lee Hockstader & Craig Whitlock, *Sheinbein Sentenced to 24 Years: Israeli Court Accepts Recommendation of Plea Agreement; Teenager Can Apply for Parole at 33*, WASH. POST, Oct. 25, 1999, at B1.
11. Ramit Plushnick-Masti, *A Family's Shame: Sheinbein's Parents Describe Their Pain, Bafflement*, WASH. POST, Nov. 5, 1999, at B1.
12. Lee Hockstader, *Judge Says Israel Can Extradite Sheinbein: Appeal of Ruling May Take Months*, WASH. POST, Sept. 7, 1998, at A1. Remarkably, two judges on Maryland's highest court agreed with Sheinbein's mother. Judge Eldridge, who dissented from the majority's opinion disbarring Sol Sheinbein from the practice of law in Maryland, suggested that Sheinbein had done no more than "forum shop" for the most advantageous jurisdiction in which to have his son tried. *See* Att'y Grievance Comm'n v. Sheinbein, 812 A.2d 981, 1007–09 (Md. 2002) (Eldridge, J., dissenting, joined by Judge Raker).
13. *See, e.g., Long Thought Dead, Suspect Turns up Alive*, ST. PETERSBURG TIMES, Sept. 25, 2005 (describing role that the son of a man, suspected of murder, played in helping the world think his father was dead); *Reported As Dead, a Suspect in 1964 Killings Is Found Alive*, N.Y. TIMES, Sept. 25, 2005, at A26.
14. *See* Carrie Johnson, *Prosecutors Making Fraud Cases Relative: Government Targets Family of Accused*, WASH. POST, Nov. 27, 2003, at A1 (discussing the Adelphia case in which prosecutors indicted the founder of the company and his two sons); Press Release, Securities and Exchange Commission, SEC Charges Adelphia and Rigas Family with Massive Financial Fraud (July 24, 2002), *available at* http://www.sec.gov/news/press/2002-110.htm.
15. *See* Kurt Eichenwald, *Ex-Chief Financial Officer of Enron and Wife Plead Guilty*, N.Y. TIMES, Jan. 15, 2004, at C9 (noting that Lea Fastow, Mr. Fastow's wife, who was a former assistant treasurer at Enron, entered a separate guilty plea to a single tax felony stemming from efforts she made to hide income that came from one of her husband's secret dealings with an Enron colleague).
16. A few legal scholars have addressed Antigone's plight, *e.g.*, Martha Grace Duncan, *"A Strange Liking": Our Admiration of Criminals*, 1991 U. ILL. L. REV. 1, 17–18; Mark S. Howenstein, *The Tragedy of Law, and the Law of Tragedy in Sophocles'* Antigone, 24 LEGAL STUD. F. 493 (2000), but none, so far as we know, has systematically looked at the intersection of the criminal justice system and the role of family ties the way this book does.
17. The analogy to Antigone is admittedly imperfect. First, Creon was also Antigone's uncle and arguably a paternal surrogate because her father, Oedipus, had been expelled from Thebes. Consequently, one could view the conflict Antigone faces as intrafamilial, as well as a duel between the family and state. Second, we are more

sympathetic to Antigone's plight because the edict she was flouting was unreasonable and oppressive, and an especial affront to the social norms of Greek times, which required proper burial for the dead lest their souls wander forever after. *See* Duncan, *supra* intro., n. 16, at 18. Thus, Antigone's defiance of Creon may be viewed as rebellion against an unjust law, whereas Sheinbein's father, for example, cannot fairly protest the justice of the relevant law prohibiting murder.

18. Although we use the phrase "the American criminal justice system," there are actually many criminal justice systems in the United States operating at the local, state, and federal level under a host of laws, ordinances, principles and policies. Consequently, not all the practices we describe exist around the country in every single system. In most instances, we try to explain how pervasive the reach is of each family ties benefit or burden we examine.
19. The family status in question is the status classification defined by the government of the jurisdiction involved. Our normative posture is to refrain from defining the family in the criminal justice system because the criminal law should generally be drafted in terms that are neutral to the status of a family member. As we explain, our concern is that that the state's definitions of who counts as family within the criminal justice system tend to exclude persons who, from a functional perspective, should not be excluded.
20. *See* DONALD BRAMAN, DOING TIME ON THE OUTSIDE (2004).
21. *See* SANDRA ENOS, MOTHERING FROM THE INSIDE: PARENTING IN A WOMAN'S PRISON (2001) (descriptive treatment of challenges of parenting in prison).
22. *See* JOAN PETERSILIA, WHEN PRISONERS COME HOME: PAROLE AND PRISONER REENTRY (2003).
23. Here, we develop an account drawing on several sources, including Linda McClain's work. *See, e.g.*, LINDA C. MCCLAIN, THE PLACE OF FAMILIES: FOSTERING CAPACITY, EQUALITY AND RESPONSIBILITY (2006); Linda C. McClain, *The Domain of Civic Virtue in a Good Society: Families, Schools and Sex Equality*, 69 FORDHAM L. REV. 1617, 1624–27 (2001).
24. For examples of scholarship advocating such benefits, *see* Leslie Acoca & Myrna S. Raeder, *Severing Family Ties: The Plight of Nonviolent Female Offenders and Their Children*, 11 STAN. L. & POL'Y REV. 133 (1999); Myrna S. Raeder, *Gender and Sentencing: Single Moms, Battered Women, and Other Sex-Based Anomalies in the Gender-Free World of the Federal Sentencing Guidelines*, 20 PEPP. L. REV. 905 (1993) [hereinafter Raeder, *Gender and Sentencing*]; Milton C. Regan, Jr., *Spousal Privilege and the Meanings of Marriage*, 81 VA. L. REV. 2045 (1995).
25. When we use the term inaccuracy, we are using that term to refer to the idea that justice is not being accurately realized (in terms of the effective prosecution of the guilty and exoneration of the innocent). In this sense, inaccuracy might also indicate an unjustified leniency (or harshness), which is a matter that can also be seen when considered in the context of equality issues.
26. For the most part, our discussion centers on legal policy issues, which are, in many cases, more appropriately developed by legislatures. However, our argument does address the issue of new intrafamilial privileges, as well as the use of some common law defenses, which are typically addressed in the courts in the first instance.

Part 1. Privileging Family Status

1. In the course of our exposition, we tend not to use the word "privilege" to help avoid confusion between the species and the genus; evidentiary privileges are just one example of these family ties benefits. Some might think these benefits merely "respect" family ties rather than benefit them, but we think that because these benefits have real consequences (as opposed to simply conveying attitudes of respect), it is better to characterize them as actual benefits (or in the case of our titles, *privileges*).

Chapter 1. A Survey of Family Ties Benefits

1. *See* Louisiana v. Taylor, 642 So. 2d 160 (La. 1994) (describing facts of case). The Louisiana Supreme Court ultimately carved out an exception to the spousal privilege in cases in which the spouse was the victim of the charged crime and the evidence supported a conclusion that the spouse was refusing to testify because of fear or coercion.
2. 8 JOHN H. WIGMORE, EVIDENCE § 2192 (John T. McNaughton ed., rev. ed. 1961). *See generally* United States v. Bryan, 339 U.S. 323, 331 (1950).
3. United States v. Nixon, 418 U.S. 683, 710 (1974).
4. The law has several sources for testimonial privileges. Most commonly, the common law is the root of them. The attorney-client privilege, for example, is one of the oldest recognized privileges in the common law—and every court recognizes it to some extent. *See, e.g.*, Swidler & Berlin v. United States, 524 U.S. 399, 403 (1998). The Fifth Amendment is another source of a testimonial privilege in that it gives persons a privilege against self-incrimination. US CONST. amend. V ("No person shall be . . . compelled in any criminal case to be a witness against himself.").
5. As a general rule, federal courts are cautious before creating new mechanisms to allow people to refuse to help the justice system. State systems, by contrast, tend to be a bit more generous, recognizing clergyman-parishioner and doctor-patient privileges, as well as journalist-source and accountant-client privileges rejected under Federal Rule of Evidence 501. *See generally* 2 SCOTT N. STONE & ROBERT K. TAYLOR, TESTIMONIAL PRIVILEGES § 3 (2d ed. 1995) (explaining the accountant-client privilege and where and when it applies); *id.* § 6 (addressing the clergy-penitent privilege); *id.* § 7 (doctor-patient privilege); *id.* § 8 (journalist-source privilege).
6. *See, e.g.*, Regan, *supra* intro., n. 24, at 2119.
7. To see which states have adopted this privilege and which version, *see* 2 STONE & TAYLOR, *supra* chap. 1, n. 5, § 5.02, nn.4, 8, 12, 13.
8. "[I]t hath been resolved by the Justices that a wife cannot be produced either against or for her husband." 1 E. COKE, A COMMENTARIE UPON LITTLETON 6b (1628); *see also* 8 WIGMORE, *supra* chap. 1, n. 2, § 2227. Some have contested this story and have argued that the immunity has its roots in *petit treason*, the crime of violence against a head of household. *See* WIGMORE, *supra*, at § 2227.

9. *See Developments in the Law—Privileged Communications*, 98 HARV. L. REV. 1450, 1564 (1985) [hereinafter *Developments in the Law*].
10. 290 U.S. 371, 380–82 (1933).
11. 358 U.S. 74 (1958).
12. *Id.* at 78.
13. *Id.* at 79.
14. 445 U.S. 40, 52 (1980). The Court's claim is not always true; prosecutors can threaten spouses and offer them fairly substantial incentives to testify against their loved ones, even if the relationship is otherwise strong.
15. To see which states have adopted this privilege and in what way, *see* 2 STONE & TAYLOR, *supra* chap. 1, n. 5, § 5.09.
16. 291 U.S. 7, 14–15 (1934).
17. 340 U.S. 332, 333–34 (1951).
18. *Cf.* FRIEDRICH NIETZSCHE, HUMAN, ALL TOO HUMAN, (Ernst Behler ed., Gary Handaerk trans., Stanford Univ. Press 1995) (1878) ("Marriage as a long conversation. In entering into a marriage we should put the question to ourselves: Do you believe that you will enjoy conversing with this woman all the way into old age? Everything else in marriage is transitory, but most of the time together is spent in conversation.").
19. *See, e.g.*, Maureen P. O'Sullivan, *An Examination of the State and Federal Courts' Treatment of the Parent-Child Privilege*, 39 CATH. LAW. 201 (1999); Catherine J. Ross, *Implementing Constitutional Rights for Juveniles: The Parent-Child Privilege in Context*, 14 STAN. L. & POL'Y REV. 85 (2003); Amee A. Shah, *The Parent-Child Testimonial Privilege—Has the Time for It Finally Arrived?*, 47 CLEV. ST. L. REV. 41 (1999); Erica Smith-Klocek, *A Halachic Perspective on the Parent-Child Privilege*, 39 CATH. LAW. 105 (1999); Shonah P. Jefferson, Note, *The Statutory Development of the Parent-Child Privilege: Congress Responds to Kenneth Starr's Tactics*, 16 GA. ST. U. L. REV. 429 (1999); Kimberly L. Schilling, Note, *Intrafamilial Communications: An Analysis of the Parent-Child Privilege*, 37 FAM. & CONCILIATION CTS. REV. 99 (1999).
20. *See, e.g.*, United States v. Dunford, 148 F.3d 385 (4th Cir. 1998) (no recognition of privilege when the defendant father was charged with gun crimes and abusing children with those guns; protection of this family unit not warranted); *In re* Grand Jury, 103 F.3d 1140 (3d Cir. 1997) (no confidential communication privilege in child-parent relationship because the overwhelming majority of states and federal courts reject the privilege); *In re* Erato, 2 F.3d 11 (2d Cir. 1993) (no recognition of the mother's asserted right not to testify against her adult son, particularly when she benefited from her son's illegal activity); *In re* Doe, 842 F.2d 244 (10th Cir. 1988) (no parent-child privilege recognized); United States v. Ismail, 756 F.2d 1253 (6th Cir. 1985) (children have no right not to testify against parents and can be forced to do so); *In re* Santarelli, 740 F.2d 816 (11th Cir. 1984) (no federal support for a family privilege); United States v. Penn, 647 F.2d 876 (9th Cir. 1980) (no "family" privilege so a five-year-old had to testify against his mother).
21. *See In re* Agosto, 553 F. Supp. 1298 (D. Nev. 1983) (recognizing a parent-child privilege); *see also* cases cited *infra* chap. 1, n. 29.
22. 518 U.S. 1 (1996).

23. *See, e.g., In re Grand Jury*, 103 F.3d 1140 (3d Cir. 1997).
24. *See generally* Kelly Korell, *Testimonial Privilege for Confidential Communications Between Relatives Other Than Husband and Wife—State Cases*, 62 A.L.R. 5th 629 (1998).
25. IDAHO CODE ANN. § 9-203(7) (2008) ("Any parent, guardian or legal custodian shall not be forced to disclose any communication made by their minor child or ward to them concerning matters in any civil or criminal action to which such child or ward is a party."). The privilege does not apply in all cases, including cases involving allegations of child abuse.
26. CONN. GEN. STAT. ANN. § 46b-138a (2008) ("In any juvenile proceeding in superior court, the accused child shall be a competent witness, and at his or her option may testify or refuse to testify in such proceedings. The parent or guardian of such child shall be a competent witness but may elect or refuse to testify for or against the accused child except that a parent or guardian who has received personal violence from the child may, upon the child's trial for offenses arising from such personal violence, be compelled to testify in the same manner as any other witness.").
27. MASS. GEN. LAWS. ANN. ch. 233, § 20 (2008) ("An unemancipated, minor child, living with a parent, shall not testify before a grand jury, trial of an indictment, complaint or other criminal proceeding, against said parent, where the victim in such proceeding is not a member of said parent's family and who does not reside in the said parent's household.").
28. MINN. STAT. § 595.02.1(j) (2008) ("A parent or the parent's minor child may not be examined as to any communication made in confidence by the minor to the minor's parent. . . . This exception may be waived by express consent to disclosure by a parent entitled to claim the privilege or by the child who made the communication or by failure of the child or parent to object when the contents of a communication are demanded."). The statutory privilege in Minnesota does not apply in all circumstances, including cases involving allegations of child abuse or the termination of parental rights.
29. *See In re* A & M (People v. Doe), 403 N.Y.S.2d 375 (N.Y. App. Div. 1978) (common law recognition of a parent-child privilege through the constitutional right to family privacy); People v. Fitzgerald, 422 N.Y.S.2d 309, 312 (N.Y. App. Div. 1979) (extending the parent-child privilege to an older child; holding that the privilege is not limited to minors); *In re* Ryan, 474 N.Y.S.2d 931, 931 (N.Y. Fam. Ct. 1984) (recognizing a grandmother as a parent for parent-child privilege purposes). *But see* People v. Hilligas, 670 N.Y.S.2d 744, 747 (N.Y. Sup. Ct. 1998) (rejecting *Fitzgerald* for independently living adults).
30. *See* Diehl v. Texas, 698 S.W.2d 712, 717 (Tex. App. 1985) (Levy, J., dissenting); Belmer v. Virginia, 553 S.E.2d 123, 129 (Va. Ct. App. 2001) (Elder, J., dissenting).
31. *See* IDAHO CODE ANN. § 9-203(7).
32. *See* CONN. GEN. STAT. § 46b-138a (2004).
33. *See* MASS. GEN. LAWS ch. 233, § 20 (2005).
34. *Compare* IDAHO CODE ANN. § 9-203(7) *with* MASS. GEN. LAWS ch. 233, § 20.
35. *See* MINN. STAT. § 595.02.1(j) (2004).

36. Joe Lawlor, *What's a Parent To Do? Escaped Convict Case Raises Questions*, FLINT J., June 11, 2008, http://www.mlive.com/flintjournal/index.ssf/2008/06/whats_a_parent_to_do_escaped_c.html.
37. For similar examples of a brother making the same decision as David Kaczynski, *see* Cantu v. State, 939 S.W.2d 627, 631 (Tex. Crim. App. 1997); Elise Ackerman & Marianne Lavelle, *Thicker Than Blood*, U.S. NEWS & WORLD REP., Dec. 1, 1997, at 30, 32 (describing the case of Joe Cantu, who turned his younger brother in to the police after hearing his brother laughing about the fact that he had just participated in the gang rape and murder of two young girls); Linda Grace-Kobas, *Death Penalty Offers Families No Closure, Law School Speakers Say*, CORNELL CHRON., Mar. 20, 2003, *available at* http://www.news.cornell.edu/Chronicle/03/3.20.03/death_penalty_forum.html (describing case of Bill Babbitt, who told the police that he believed his brother Manny had killed an elderly woman and then was horrified when Manny, a paranoid schizophrenic, was eventually executed for the crime); Serge F. Kovaleski, *His Brother's Keeper*, WASH. POST, July 21, 2001, at W10.
38. *See* Beth Shuster, *Veteran LAPD Officer Aided Fugitive Son, Panel Finds*, L.A. TIMES, Mar. 27, 1996, at B3. The sergeant ultimately received a thirty-three-day suspension. *See also* Andrew Blankstein, *Member of Robbery Ring Convicted*, L.A. TIMES, Apr. 25, 1997, at B4.
39. *See* Mandy M. Goodnight, *Vernon Deputy Sentenced to Jail*, ALEXANDRIA DAILY TOWN TALK (Alexandria, La.), May 24, 2003, at 4A. The deputy was convicted of assorted criminal charges related to his assistance and sentenced to spend one year in prison.
40. *See* David Chanen, *Woman Charged As Accomplice to Her Sons in Shooting Death*, STAR TRIB. (Minneapolis-St. Paul, Minn.), Dec. 15, 1998, at 5B. For other examples, *see* Ackerman & Lavelle, *supra* chap. 1, n. 37, at 30 (describing how the brother of Thomas Capano, a well-known political figure in Delaware, helped him dump the body of his former mistress into the ocean); M. Hernandez, *Woman Sentenced for Role in Killing*, VENTURA COUNTY STAR, Apr. 26, 2005, at 2 (describing how a mother, who had witnessed her son stab a man to death, helped her son flee to Mexico to avoid arrest); Ed Pope, *Police Charge Father in Fugitive Insurance Fraud Case*, SAN JOSE MERCURY NEWS, Mar. 2, 2000 (describing how a father destroyed evidence to prevent police from locating his daughter, who was charged with participating in a $10 million insurance fraud scheme).
41. *See* William Booth, *Kaczynski's Brother Expresses Sadness, Relief in Aftermath of Plea; Accuser Still Feels Powerful Sibling Connection*, WASH. POST, Jan. 24, 1998, at A3; Don Oldenburg, *What If He Were Your Brother? When David Kazcynski Fingered the Unabomber Suspect, He Became the Star in a Morality Play*, WASH. POST, Apr. 11, 1996, at C1.
42. *See* Oldenburg, *supra* chap. 1, n. 41 (describing comments by G. Gordon Liddy). We were unable to locate any rigorous empirical work attempting to answer the question of what most Americans would do if they learned a family member had committed a serious crime. *USA Today* conducted a telephone poll of 305 adults in 1990 that was prompted by the Charles Stuart case in Boston, in which Stuart murdered his pregnant wife and famously accused a black man of committing

the crime. Stuart became a suspect only after his brother went to the police. Eight percent said they would not turn in a family member accused of murder; 79 percent said that they would. Tom Squitieri & John Larrabee, *Poll: 79% Say They'd Turn in Kin Who Killed*, USA TODAY, Jan. 15, 1990, at 3A. The newspaper acknowledged two problems with the survey: first, the outcome might well have been affected by the outrageous facts of the Stuart case itself. *See id.* (quoting criminologist James Fox, who stated that "[t]hese poll results would have been very different if the survey had been done last year.... It's not what they would do, but what they would have liked the Stuarts to do."). Second, "experts" acknowledged that the results might "reflect the 'socially desirable response' rather than the real-life action" that people would take if actually confronted with the situation. *Id.* We suspect that relatives' decision-making would vary on two vectors: the severity of the crime and the degree of closeness of the relative (whether closeness is measured in emotional closeness or bloodline closeness). It probably would be hard, for example, to turn in a child for all but the most heinous crimes, and it would be comparatively less heart-wrenching to turn in a distant cousin when a more serious crime is involved.

43. In the Enron case, for example, Enron Chief Financial Officer Andy Fastow and his wife Lea were both indicted in connection with the fraud. *See* Carrie Johnson, *Prosecutors Making Fraud Cases Relative: Government Targets Family of Accused*, WASH. POST, Nov. 27, 2003, at A1. In the Adelphia case, prosecutors indicted the founder of the company and his two adult sons. *Id.* Similarly in ImClone, executive Sam Waksal pled guilty to fraud charges "in an attempt to spare his daughter and his [eighty-year-old] father from being charged with insider trading." *Id.* Johnson also cites the case of Aldrich Ames, whose deal to plead guilty to espionage charges included a promise of leniency for his wife. *Id.*

44. A principal in the first degree is a person who physically commits the offense. Joshua Dressler defines a "principal in the second degree" as "one who is guilty of an offense 'by reason of having [intentionally assisted]... in the commission thereof in the presence, either actual or constructive, of the principal in the first degree.'" JOSHUA DRESSLER, UNDERSTANDING CRIMINAL LAW 464 (3d ed. 2001).

45. Dressler describes an accessory after the fact as "one who, with knowledge of another's guilt, intentionally assists the felon to avoid arrest, trial, or conviction." *Id.* at 465. Although most states have eliminated the various common law categories of principal and accomplice liability, many states still treat accessories after the fact as a separate category of offender. *Id.* at 432–33.

46. The states that provide exemptions for family members are Florida, Illinois, Indiana, Iowa, Kentucky, Massachusetts, Nevada, New Mexico, North Carolina, Rhode Island, Vermont, Virginia, West Virginia, and Wisconsin. *See* FLA. STAT. ANN. § 777.03 (2008); 720 ILL. COMP. STAT. ANN. 5/31-5 (2009); IND. CODE ANN. § 35-44-3-2 (2009); IOWA CODE ANN. § 703.3 (2009); KY. REV. STAT. ANN. § 520.110 (2008); MASS. GEN. LAWS ANN. ch. 274, § 4 (2009); NEV. REV. STAT. ANN. § 195.030 (2008); N.M. STAT. ANN. § 30-22-4 (2008); N.C. GEN. STAT. ANN.

§ 14-259 (2008); R.I. GEN. LAWS ANN. § 11-1-4 (2008); VT. STAT. ANN. tit. 13, § 5 (2008); VA. CODE ANN. § 18.2-19 (2008); W. VA. CODE ANN. § 61-11-6 (2009); WIS. STAT. ANN. § 946.47 (2008).

47. *See* FLA. STAT. ANN. § 777.03. Iowa is more restrictive in that it only exempts spouses from criminal liability. *See* IOWA CODE ANN. § 703.3. Illinois and North Carolina do not include grandparents or grandchildren within their exemptions. *See* 720 ILL. COMP. STAT. ANN. 5/31-5; N.C. GEN. STAT. ANN. § 14-259. Indiana does not include grandparents, grandchildren, or siblings. *See* IND. CODE ANN. § 35-44-3-2.
48. These states are Arkansas, New Jersey, Washington, and Wyoming. *See* ARK. CODE ANN. § 5-54-105 (West 2007); N.J. STAT. ANN. § 2C:29-3 (West 2007); WASH. REV. CODE ANN. § 9A.76.070 (West 2007); WYO. STAT. ANN. § 6-5-202 (West 2007). Washington, for example, typically treats rendering criminal assistance to a murder suspect as a Class C felony, but only as a gross misdemeanor if committed by an immediate family member. *See* WASH. REV. CODE ANN. § 9A.76.070.
49. *See* FLA. STAT. ANN. § 777.03 (1)(a).
50. *See id.* § 777.03 (1)(b).
51. *See* WILLIAM BLACKSTONE, 4 COMMENTARIES *38–39 ("So strict is the law where a felony is actually complete, in order to do effectual justice, that the nearest relations are not suffered to aid or receive one another. If the parent assists his child, or the child his parent; if the brother receives the brother, the master his servant, or the servant his master, or even if the husband relieves the wife, who have any of them committed a felony, the receivers become accessories *ex post facto*. But a feme-covert can not become an accessory by the receipt or concealment of her husband; for she is presumed to act under his coercion, and therefore she is not bound, neither ought she, to discover her lord."); Leo Gerard Smith, Note, *Family Member Exemption for Accessory After the Fact*, 20 J. FAM. L. 105, 107–09 (1981) (discussing common law exemption for wives).
52. MODEL PENAL CODE § 242.3 cmt. at 237 (1980).
53. *Id.*
54. *See* Smith, *supra* chap. 1, n. 51, at 123–24 (discussing the treatment of family member exemptions in the federal system).
55. 21 F. Supp. 281, 282 (E.D.N.Y. 1937).
56. *Id.*; *see also* Haupt v. United States, 330 U.S. 631 (1947). In *Haupt*, the defendant was charged with treason for aiding his saboteur son during World War II, but the Supreme Court noted that the possibility the defendant's acts were motivated by "parental solicitude" rather than "adherence to the German cause" was certainly a relevant factor for the jury's consideration. *Id.* at 641.
57. State v. C.H., 421 So. 2d 62, 65 (Fla. Dist. Ct. App. 1982).
58. *See* State v. Lucero, 541 P.2d 430, 434 (N.M. 1975).
59. United States v. Hill, 279 F.3d 731, 733–34 (9th Cir. 2002).
60. *See id.*
61. *Id.* at 736.
62. *Id.* at 737.

63. *See, e.g.*, Jane C. Murphy, *Rules, Responsibility, and Commitment to Children: The New Language of Morality in Family Law*, 60 U. PITT. L. REV. 1111, 1165 (1999) ("One of the most deeply embedded principles in American family law is the principle of family autonomy, which limits the state's intervention in the affairs of the intact family."); Carl F. Schneider, *Moral Discourse and the Transformation of American Family Law*, 83 MICH. L. REV. 1803, 1835–39 (1985) (discussing the "legal tradition of noninterference in the family"); Elizabeth S. Scott & Robert F. Scott, *Parents As Fiduciaries*, 81 VA. L. REV. 2401, 2406 (1995) (noting that academic commentators have begun to argue that "the latitude given to parents in rearing their children is. . . excessive, allowing some parents to inflict unmonitored and unsanctioned harm on their children" and that "the tradition of legal protection of parental rights has deep historical roots"). *But see* Carolyn B. Ramsey, *Intimate Homicide: Gender and Crime Control, 1880–1920*, 77 U. COLO. L. REV. 101, 101 (2006) (revising the "feminist understanding of the legal history of public responses to intimate homicide by showing that, in both the eastern and the western United States, men accused of killing their intimates often received stern punishment, including the death penalty, whereas women charged with similar crimes were treated leniently" for the period under review).
64. *See generally* Donna Coker, *Crime Control and Feminist Law Reform in Domestic Violence Law: A Critical Review*, 4 BUFF. CRIM. L. REV. 801 (2001) [hereinafter Coker, *Crime Control*].
65. *See* Michelle J. Anderson, *Marital Immunity, Intimate Relationships, and Improper Inferences: A New Law on Sexual Offenses by Intimates*, 54 HASTINGS L.J. 1465, 1485 (2002–2003) (stating that since the mid-1970s, marital immunity for sexual offenses was eliminated in twenty-four states and the District of Columbia).
66. *See generally* EVE S. BUZAWA & CARL G. BUZAWA, DOMESTIC VIOLENCE: THE CRIMINAL JUSTICE RESPONSE (2d ed. 1996) (describing reform efforts in police and prosecutors' offices); Jeannie Suk, *Criminal Law Comes Home*, 116 YALE L.J. 2, 7 (2006) (appraising critically the "use of protection orders to prohibit the cohabitation and contact of intimate partners" where domestic violence has occurred).
67. *See* ELIZABETH PLECK, DOMESTIC TYRANNY: THE MAKING OF SOCIAL POLICY AGAINST FAMILY VIOLENCE FROM COLONIAL TIMES TO THE PRESENT 173 (1987) (noting that "no other piece of modern social legislation has been so quickly adopted by all the states").
68. *See* State v. DeLeon, 813 P.2d 1382 (Haw. 1991); *see also* Deanna Pollard, *Banning Child Corporal Punishment*, 77 TUL. L. REV. 575, 641 n.415 (2003) (discussing the DeLeon case).
69. Pollard, *supra* chap. 1, n. 68, at 641.
70. *Id.* at 621.
71. *Id.* at 634–35. Professor Pollard's article contains an excellent discussion of different approaches states take in evaluating parental claims that the injuries they inflicted upon their children should not be considered child abuse because they were simply disciplining their children. *Id.* at 635–46. She also notes that, despite mounting evidence about the dangers posed by spanking, ninety percent of American parents still hit their children. *Id.* at 577.

72. *See id.* at 586.
73. *See* Legal Reforms, Center for Effective Discipline, at http://www.stophitting.com/laws/legalReform.php (visited November 21, 2008).
74. *See* MODEL PENAL CODE § 3.08 (1985); *see also* Pollard, *supra* chap. 1, n. 68, at 641 (discussing the Model Penal Code's adoption of a parental discipline defense).
75. Tamar Lewin, *What Penalty for a Killing in Passion?*, N.Y. TIMES, Oct. 21, 1994.
76. *See* Donna K. Coker, *Heat of Passion and Wife Killing: Men Who Batter/Men Who Kill*, 2 S. CAL. REV. L. & WOMEN'S STUD. 71, 72 (1992) [hereinafter Coker, *Heat of Passion*].
77. People v. Thompkins, 240 Cal. Rptr. 516, 518–19 (Ct. App. 1987) ("At least as early as Manning's Case (1793) 83 Eng. Rep. 112, an archetypical illustration of adequate provocation to invoke the common law heat-of-passion theory for voluntary manslaughter has been the defendant's discovery of his wife in bed with another man."); *see also* Coker, *Heat of Passion*, *supra* chap. 1, n. 76, at 72; Laurie Taylor, *Provoked Reason in Men and Women: Heat of Passion Manslaughter and Imperfect Self-Defense*, 33 UCLA L. REV. 1679, 1692–96 (1986).
78. Girouard v. State, 321 Md. 532, 538 (1991).
79. People v. Chevalier, 544 N.E.2d 942 (Ill. 1989) ("In Illinois, adultery with a spouse as provocation generally has been limited to those instances where the parties are discovered in the act of adultery or immediately before or after such an act, and the killing immediately follows such discovery."); People v. McDonald, 212 N.E.2d 299 (Ill. 1965) (mitigation available only to persons who kill lawful spouses, not girlfriends or mistresses).
80. MD. CODE ANN., CRIM. LAW § 2-207 (b).
81. Tripp v. Maryland, 374 A.2d 384 (Md. 1977) ("The modern tendency is to extend the rule of mitigation beyond the narrow situation where one spouse actually catches the other in the act of committing adultery.").
82. Victoria Nourse, *Passion's Progress: Modern Law Reform and the Provocation Defense*, 106 YALE L.J. 1331, 1332 (1997)
83. *Id.* (footnotes omitted).
84. *See generally* WAYNE A. LOGAN, KNOWLEDGE AS POWER: CRIMINAL REGISTRATION AND COMMUNITY NOTIFICATION LAWS IN AMERICA (forthcoming 2009).
85. *See* Rose Corrigan, *Making Meaning of Megan's Law*, 31 LAW & SOC. INQUIRY 267, 291 (2006). Corrigan notes this exclusion was supported by rape care advocates in order to promote victim confidentiality. Even if the exclusion does protect victims, however, it clearly gives offenders the obvious benefit of avoiding identification as a sex offender to friends, employers, and other members of the community. It bears emphasis, however, that charging decisions (like prosecuting a sex offender for incest rather than rape or sexual abuse) really do not come within the ambit of our discussion, since they are not a formal family ties benefit. Indeed, as Chapter 4 reveals, incest is a *family ties burden*, as we define that term.
86. *See* Anderson, *supra* chap. 1, n. 65, at 1486.
87. *See id.* at 1472–73.
88. *Id.*

89. *See* Associated Press, *Child Molester Charged in Assault on Boy, 5*, MIAMI HERALD, Jan. 21, 1987, at 10A. We recognize this story does not necessarily involve a family ties benefit, but it illustrates the kind of risks associated with such benefits in the context of pretrial release.
90. For an overview of pretrial release patterns, *see* MARC L. MILLER & RONALD F. WRIGHT, CRIMINAL PROCEDURES 847–80 (3d ed. 2007).
91. Bail Reform Act of 1966, Pub. L. No. 89-465, 80 Stat. 214 (codified as amended at 18 U.S.C. 3142 (g)(3)(A) (2000)).
92. *See, e.g.*, ALA. R. CRIM. P. 7.2(a)(1) (2006) (requiring court to consider a range of factors in determining pretrial release, including "the age, background and family ties, relationships and circumstances of the defendant"); FLA. STAT. ANN. § 903.046(2) (West 2001) (mandating court to consider "[t]he defendant's family ties[and] length of residence in the community"); Watson v. State, 158 S.W.3d 647, 648 (Tex. Crim. App. 2005) (noting that the Court of Criminal Appeals has determined that a court in setting bail should consider, among other things, the "defendant's: work record, family ties, . . . length of residency").
93. 725 ILL. COMP. STAT. 5/110-10(b)(10) (2002).
94. *See* Suk, *supra* chap. 1, n. 66, at 2 (describing use of protection orders as a form of "state-imposed de facto divorce that subjects the practical and substantive continuation of intimate relationships to criminal sanction").
95. 725 ILL. COMP. STAT. 5/110-10 (c).
96. United States v. Johnson, 964 F.2d 124 (2d Cir. 1992).
97. *Id.* at 126; *see also* Karin Bornstein, Note, *5K2.0 Departures for 5H Individual Characteristics: A Backdoor out of the Federal Sentencing Guidelines*, 24 COLUM. HUM. RTS. L. REV. 135, 135 (1993); Gregory N. Racz, Note, *Exploring Collateral Consequences:* Koon v. United States, *Third Party Harm, and Departures from Federal Sentencing Guidelines*, 72 N.Y.U. L. REV. 1462, 1480 (1997).
98. CHRISTOPHER J. MUMOLA, BUREAU OF JUSTICE STATISTICS, SPECIAL REPORT: INCARCERATED PARENTS AND THEIR CHILDREN NCJ 182335, at 1 tbl.1 (reporting figures for 1999, "an estimated 721,500 State and Federal prisoners were parents to 1,498,800 children under age 18"), *available at* http://www.ojp.usdoj.gov/bjs/pub/pdf/iptc.pdf.
99. United States v. Booker, 543 U.S. 220, 246 (2005). In his remedial opinion, Justice Breyer highlighted the provision in 18 U.S.C. § 3661, which says that "[n]o limitation shall be placed on the information concerning the background, character, and conduct of a person convicted of an offense which a court of the United States may receive and consider for the purpose of imposing an appropriate sentence." *Id.* at 252.
100. *See, e.g.*, United States v. Menyweather, 431 F.3d 692, 699 (9th Cir. 2005) ("[F]amily circumstance is a discouraged factor under the Guidelines."); U.S. SENTENCING GUIDELINES MANUAL § 5H1.6 (2000) (stating that "family ties and responsibilities and community ties are not ordinarily relevant" in deciding if a departure is warranted); *see also* United States v. Aguirre, 214 F.3d 1122, 1127

(9th Cir. 2000) (referring to family circumstance as a "discouraged" factor). *See generally* Melissa E. Murray, *The Networked Family: Reframing the Legal Understanding of Caregiving and Caregivers*, 94 VA. L. REV. 385 (2008) (canvassing family circumstances departures in federal courts).

101. Koon v. United States, 518 U.S. 81, 96 (1996).
102. United States v. Haversat, 22 F.3d 790, 797 (8th Cir. 1994) (price fixing); United States v. Sclamo, 997 F.2d 970, 974 (1st Cir. 1993) (drug distribution); United States v. Johnson, 964 F.2d 124, 125 (2d Cir. 1992) (bribery and theft); United States v. Alba, 933 F.2d 1117, 1122 (2d Cir. 1991) (drug offenses); United States v. Pena, 930 F.2d 1486, 1494–95 (10th Cir. 1991) (drug distribution); *see also* United States v. Gaskill, 991 F.2d 82, 86 (3d Cir. 1993) (fraud case).
103. United States v. Aguirre, 214 F.3d 1122, 1127 (9th Cir. 2000) (upholding four-level departure "based on the fact that there is an 8 year-old son who's lost a father and would be losing a mother for a substantial period of time"). However, in cases where another parent (aside from the defendant) was available, courts routinely rejected the downward departure by the trial court. *See, e.g.*, United States v. Miller, 991 F.2d 552, 553 (9th Cir. 1993). *But see* United States v. Chestna, 962 F.2d 103, 107 (1st Cir. 1992) (stating that, although defendant was single with four small children, this was not "an unusual family circumstance"); United States v. Mogel, 956 F.2d 1555, 1565 (11th Cir. 1992) (declining to view a single mother of two minor children as warranting extraordinary family circumstances); United States v. Headley, 923 F.2d 1079, 1083 (3d Cir. 1991) (stating that "the imprisonment of a single parent was not extraordinary," even where the woman had five minor children).
104. *See* ROGER W. HAINES, JR., FRANK O. BOWMAN III, & JENNIFER C. WOLL, FEDERAL SENTENCING GUIDELINES HANDBOOK 1445 (2006) (addressing whether "the departure effectively will address the loss of caretaking or financial support"); United States v. Leon, 341 F.3d 928, 931 (9th Cir. 2003); *see also* United States v. Roselli, 366 F.3d 58, 68–69 (1st Cir. 2004) (looking at whether "there are *feasible* alternatives of care that are relatively comparable" to the defendant's).
105. *See* U.S. SENTENCING GUIDELINES MANUAL § 5H1.6 cmt. n.1(B) (2006).
106. The implication is that if the departure simply reduces rather than eliminates the difficulty, the departure should not be awarded. Thus, courts have been reluctant, given the state of the law, to confer departures to minimize all the disruptions typically caused by incarceration of a family member. *See, e.g.*, United States v. Wright, 218 F.3d 812, 815–16 (7th Cir. 2000) ("Today we conclude that a downward departure for extraordinary family circumstances cannot be justified when, even after reduction, the sentence is so long that release will come too late to promote the child's welfare."). This state of affairs leads some judges to believe that the law they must apply here is quite "cruel." United States v. Jurado-Lopez, 338 F. Supp. 2d 246, 254 n.17 (D. Mass. 2004) (Gertner, J.) (excoriating case law prohibiting departures for ordinary family responsibilities as "cruel"). Commentators often agree. *See* Raeder, *Gender and Sentencing*, *supra* intro., n. 24, at 960; Myrna Raeder, *Remember the Family: Seven Myths About Single Parenting*

Departures, 13 FED. SENT'G REP. 251 (2001) [hereinafter Raeder, *Remember the Family*]; Jack B. Weinstein, *The Effect of Sentencing on Women, Men, the Family, and the Community*, 5 COLUM. J. GENDER & L. 169, 169 (1996) (stating that section 5H1.6 "is so cruelly delusive as to make those who have to apply the guidelines to human beings, families, and the community want to weep").

107. United States v. Spero, 382 F.3d 803, 805 (8th Cir. 2004) (affirming downward departure for defendant who provided critical care for autistic son and other three children, notwithstanding that defendant had a spouse); United States v. Jebara, 313 F. Supp. 2d 912, 919–20 (E.D. Wis. 2004) (splitting defendant's sentence between incarceration and home confinement due to judge's view that a short-term disruption to the defendant's children would be tolerable but not a long-term one).
108. *See, e.g.*, United States v. Sweeting, 213 F.3d 95, 104 (3d Cir. 2000) (invalidating a Section 5H1.6 downward departure for a single mother of five children (one afflicted with some neurological disorders)). *Sweeting* might be distinguished on account of the defendant's substantial criminal history and the severity of the penalty under the guidelines, which in this case exceeded five years.
109. United States v. Menyweather, 431 F.3d 692, 703–08 (9th Cir. 2005) (Kleinfeld, J., dissenting).
110. *Id.* (criticizing lower court's departure on grounds of family responsibilities because the sentence failed to adequately reflect seriousness of the offense).
111. *See, e.g.*, United States v. Duarte, 901 F.2d 1498 (9th Cir. 1990) (holding that trial court may properly consider defendant's stable family ties and responsibilities in setting sentence within the prescribed range).
112. *See* Dan Markel, *Luck or Law? The Constitutional Case Against Indeterminate Sentencing Schemes* 28–38 (unpublished manuscript on file with authors).
113. *See* U.S. SENTENCING COMM'N, FINAL REPORT ON THE IMPACT OF UNITED STATES V. BOOKER ON FEDERAL SENTENCING (2006), *available at* http://www.ussc.gov/booker_report/Booker_Report.pdf (summarizing results).
114. 18 U.S.C. § 3553(a)(1) (2000).
115. *Menyweather*, 431 F.3d at 700 (noting that, after *Booker*, district court judges "have the discretion to weigh a multitude of mitigating and aggravating factors that existed at the time of mandatory Guidelines sentencing, but were deemed 'not ordinarily relevant,' such as age, education and vocational skills, mental and emotional conditions, employment record, and *family ties and responsibilities*") (citation omitted). Thus, for example, "[t]he difficulty of providing appropriate care for a child of a single parent may, when balanced against factors such as the nature of the offense, § 3553(a)(1), deterrence to criminal conduct, § 3553(a)(2)(B), and protection of the public, § 3553(a)(2)(C), warrant a sentence outside the Guidelines." *Id.* at 700.
116. LINDA DRAZGA MAXFIELD, U.S. SENTENCING COMM'N, FINAL REPORT: SURVEY OF ARTICLE III JUDGES ON THE FEDERAL SENTENCING GUIDELINES 8 (2003), *available at* http://www.ussc.gov/judsurv/jsfull.pdf ("More than half of all judges would like to see more emphasis at sentencing placed on an offender's mental condition or the offender's family ties and responsibilities."); *cf.* STANTON

WHEELER ET AL., SITTING IN JUDGMENT: THE SENTENCING OF WHITE-COLLAR CRIMINALS 154 (1988) (quoting a judge who explains that "[w]hether there are people who are dependent on him or her [i.e., the defendant], . . . whether there is going to be an injury to others if I incarcerate him: that has a profound effect on me and when I sense that, I am more inclined to be lenient").

117. *See, e.g.*, United States v. Ranum, 353 F. Supp. 2d 984, 990–91 (E.D. Wis. 2005) ([D]efendant is fifty years old, had no prior record, a solid employment history, and is a devoted family man. He has two children, one of whom is still in school. Prior to his recent marriage, he was a single father who did an excellent job of raising two daughters. He also provides care and support for his elderly parents. His father suffers from Alzheimer's disease and is particularly dependent on defendant—defendant is one of the few people he still recognizes. Defendant's mother is also elderly and suffers from depression. I concluded that defendant's absence would have a profoundly adverse impact on both his children and his parents."); United States v. Jaber, 362 F. Supp. 2d 365, 383 (D. Mass. 2005) ("Measuring a departure for 'extraordinary family obligations' now in the light of *Booker* and the purposes of sentencing (particularly the likelihood of recidivism), I would find that Momoh qualified for a downward departure on these grounds."). *But see* Myrna Raeder, *Gender-Related Issues in a Post-Booker World*, 37 McGeorge L. Rev. 691, 716 (2006) (contending that "many judges are not exercising their *Booker* discretion" and that "a relative handful of judges" are responsible for most of the family ties departures").

118. Gall v. United States, 128 S. Ct. 586 (2007).

119. United States v. Kimbrough, 128 S. Ct 558 (2007).

120. Richard S. Frase, *State Sentencing Guidelines: Diversity, Consensus, and Unresolved Policy Issues*, 105 COLUM. L. REV. 1190, 1191 (2005).

121. *See, e.g.*, CAL. PENAL CODE § 3003(b)(4) (West 2007) (including family ties within a list of "suitability factors" that the Parole Board is to consider in awarding parole).

122. State v. Killpack, 276 N.W.2d 368, 373 (Iowa 1979); State v. Warner, 229 N.W.2d 776, 782–83 (Iowa 1975); *see also* State v. McKeever, 276 N.W.2d 385, 387 (Iowa 1979) ("Punishment must fit the particular person and circumstances under consideration; each decision must be made on an individual basis, and no single factor, including the nature of the offense, will be solely determinative").

123. For example, in Washington, the state guidelines contain "no provision comparable to U.S.S.G. § 5H1.6," which, as discussed above, expressly discourages the consideration of family ties and responsibilities. State v. Law, 110 P.3d 717 (Wash. 2005). Rather, the Washington sentencing scheme "explicitly prohibit[s] such considerations" when considering departures. *Id.* at 725. The state simply requires a "substantial and compelling reason[]" to depart from the state guidelines. *Id.* at 733 (Sanders, J., dissenting); *see also* People v. Coleman, No. 231299, 2002 WL 1340891, at *3 (Mich. Ct. App. June 18, 2002) (holding that under the sentencing statute in Michigan, a court may depart from minimum sentence if it finds "substantial and compelling reasons" to do so; defendant's family ties did not constitute a reason to depart downward).

124. Malone v. State, 58 P.3d 208, 210 (Okla. Crim. App. 2002) (stating that when jury decides punishment for noncapital offenses "there simply is no provision allowing for mitigating evidence to be presented in the sentencing stage of the trial. This is a limitation enacted by our Legislature, and the limitation is undoubtedly constitutional. . . . [A] criminal trial is not to be based upon so-called 'character' evidence, and the same principle applies to sentencing proceedings").
125. The courts in Florida must also bear in mind that the "primary purpose of sentencing is to punish the offender. Rehabilitation and other traditional considerations continue to be desired goals of the criminal justice system but must assume a subordinate role." FLA. R. CRIM. P. 3.701.
126. *See* Commonwealth v. Langill, No. ESCR2002-729, 2003 WL 22459077, at *3 (Mass. Super. Ct. Sept. 29, 2003) (enumerating a list of mitigating factors, including family ties and responsibilities, in MASS. GEN. LAWS ch. 211E § 3(d)); Commonwealth v. Morris, No. ESCR2002-1227, 2003 WL 22004943, at *6 (Mass. Super. Ct. Aug. 19, 2003) (legislature's intent was for the court to refer to the nonexclusive list of mitigating factors found in Massachusetts Sentencing Act, which included family ties and responsibilities of offender).
127. State v. Luke, 917 So. 3d 1226, 1228 (La. Ct. App. 2005) (stating that, when sentencing an offender, courts should consider, *inter alia*, "age, family ties, marital status" but noting that "[t]here is no requirement that specific matters be given any particular weight at sentencing"); State v. Douglas, 914 So. 2d 608, 610 (La. Ct. App. 2005) ("The important elements which should be considered are the defendant's personal history (age, family ties, marital status, health, employment record), prior criminal record, seriousness of offense and the likelihood of rehabilitation."); State v. Fultz, 591 So. 2d 1308, 1310 (La. Ct. App. 1991) (upholding sentence after trial court considered "defendant's age, employment, family ties and responsibilities, and criminal history").
128. Pennsylvania's sentencing guidelines themselves do not suggest specific mitigating factors, *see* 204 PA. CODE § 303.1 (2006), but the law in Pennsylvania does require consideration of alternatives to incarceration, and the rules for probation state that courts should, when deciding whether to impose probation instead of incarceration, consider whether "[t]he confinement of the defendant would entail excessive hardship to him or his dependents." 42 PA. CONS. STAT. ANN. § 9722 (2006).
129. Utah has sentencing guidelines that courts are encouraged to use as a starting point. UTAH CODE ANN. § 76-3-201(7)(e) (2002) ("In determining a just sentence, the court shall consider sentencing guidelines regarding aggravating and mitigating circumstances promulgated by the Sentencing Commission."). Those guidelines state that courts may consider mitigating a sentence when an adult offender has "exceptionally good . . . family relationships . . . [or i]mprisonment would entail excessive hardship on offender or dependents." UTAH SENT'G COMM'N, 2006 ADULT SENTENCING AND RELEASE GUIDELINES 17 (2006), *available at* http://www.sentencing.utah.gov/Guidelines/Adult/AdultGuidelineManual2006.pdf.

130. Wisconsin has a purely advisory guidelines system in place, and the guidelines provide that courts may mitigate the sentence of a defendant when he has "strong and stable ties to family and community." *See* WIS. SENT'G COMM'N, WISCONSIN SENTENCING GUIDELINES NOTES 7 (2003), *available at* http://wsc.wi.gov/docview.asp?docid=3297.

131. State v. Turner, No. M2003-02064-CCA-R3-CD, 2004 WL 2775485, at *6 n.2 (Tenn. Crim. App. Dec. 1, 2004) ("[T]his court has stated that . . . work ethic and family contribution are entitled to favorable consideration under Tennessee Code Annotated section 40-35-113(13)."); *see also* State v. McKnight, 900 S.W.2d 36, 55 (Tenn. Crim. App. 1994) ("The defendant would normally be due some favorable consideration based upon his family contributions and work ethic. Because, however, the 'help' he provided to young people was improperly motivated, the factor is inapplicable here."). The sentencing statutes in Tennessee also permit sentence mitigation if the defendant committed the offense in order to "provide necessities for the defendant's family or the defendant's self." TENN. CODE ANN. § 40-35-113(7) (2006).

132. State v. Johnson, 640 P.2d 861, 867 (Ariz. 1982) ("[S]entencing judge listened to the mitigating evidence before him and apparently concluded that appellant's family ties, military record, and good reputation did not offset the seriousness of appellant's murderous design.").

133. N.C. GEN. STAT. § 15A-1340.16 (2006). North Carolina's Sentencing Guidelines permit mitigation of sentences when "[t]he defendant supports the defendant's family" and when the "defendant has a support system in the community." *Id.*

134. LA. CODE CRIM. PROC. ANN. art. 894.1.B(31) (2006).

135. *See, e.g.*, State v. Baker, No. 02-1332, 2003 WL 22339644, at *2 (Iowa Ct. App. Oct. 15, 2003) (finding no abuse of discretion where trial court, which was required to state on the record its reasons for sentencing in a particular way, said to defendant, in explaining its imposition of sentence, that "you lack a stable residence; you have no family ties to the area, or [sic] no substantial family ties to the area").

136. FED. BUREAU OF PRISONS, PROGRAM STATEMENT 7300.4A(1) (2003); *see also* DANIEL GLASER, THE EFFECTIVENESS OF A PRISON AND PAROLE SYSTEM 366 (1964) (interaction with family members promotes rehabilitation); AM. CORRECTIONAL ASS'N, MANUAL OF CORRECTIONAL STANDARDS 542 (1966) (stating that family members "should be permitted and encouraged to maintain close contact with the inmate"); AM. PRISON ASS'N, A MANUAL OF CORRECTIONAL STANDARDS 342 (1954) (parole success depends on family ties during incarceration); COMM'N ON ACCREDITATION FOR CORRECTIONS, MANUAL OF STANDARDS FOR ADULT CORRECTIONAL INSTITUTIONS 88 (1981) (same). The Bureau provides in its bill of rights for inmates that inmates "have the right to visit and correspond with family members and friends." FED. BUREAU OF PRISONS, PROGRAM STATEMENT 5270.07 § 541.12(5) (1987).

137. *See generally* Virginia L. Hardwick, Note, *Punishing the Innocent: Unconstitutional Restrictions on Prison Marriage and Visitation*, 60 N.Y.U. L. REV. 275, 295–98 (1985) (arguing that families have a constitutional right to see their imprisoned family members).

138. *See, e.g.*, Bellamy v. Bradley, 729 F.2d 416, 420 (6th Cir. 1984) ("Prison inmates have no absolute constitutional right to visitation."); Craig v. Hocker, 405 F. Supp. 656, 674 (D. Nev. 1975) ("So long as there are reasonable alternative means of communication, a prisoner has no First Amendment right to associate with whomever he sees fit."); *see also* Bazzetta v. McGinnis, 124 F.3d 774, 779 (6th Cir. 1997) (citing and following *Bellamy*); Newman v. Alabama, 559 F.2d 283, 291 (5th Cir. 1977) (leaving visitation regulations to prison administrators); Harris v. Thigpen, 727 F. Supp. 1564, 1581 (M.D. Ala. 1990) (citing and following *Newman*); Thompson v. Bland, 664 F. Supp. 261, 262 (W.D. Ky. 1986) (same); White v. Keller, 438 F. Supp. 110, 115 (D. Md. 1977) (finding that the incarcerated have no right to visitation).

139. *See* Griffen v. Coughlin, 673 N.E.2d 98, 122–23 (N.Y. 1996) (finding a prison policy that required attendance in a religiously oriented substance abuse program to qualify for the prison's Family Reunion program to violate the Establishment Clause); McMurry v. Phelps, 533 F. Supp. 742, 764 (W.D. La. 1982) (rejecting policy preventing children under fourteen from seeing their jailed parents); Laaman v. Helgemoe, 437 F. Supp. 269, 322 (D.N.H. 1977) (holding that "visitation privileges may be curtailed as a punishment for disciplinary infractions" but "may not be so great as to infringe upon inmates' First Amendment rights to familial association").

140. *See, e.g.*, Block v. Rutherford, 468 U.S. 576, 586 (1984); Bell v. Wolfish, 441 U.S. 520, 547–48 (1979); Doe v. Coughlin, 518 N.E.2d 536, 538 (N.Y. 1987) (ruling that a prison can exclude inmates with HIV/AIDS from family visitation programs); *In re* Dyer, 20 P.3d 907, 912 (Wash. 2001) (finding that prison authorities have wide discretion to administer an extended visitation policy because "[i]t is not in the best interest of the courts to involve themselves in the 'day-to-day management of prisons, often squandering judicial resources with little offsetting benefit to anyone. Courts ought to afford appropriate deference and flexibility to state officials trying to manage a volatile environment.'" (quoting Sandin v. Conner, 515 U.S. 472, 482 (1995))).

141. *But see* Jeremy Travis, *Families and Children*, FED. PROBATION, June 2005, at 31, 37 ("[M]any prisons narrowly define the family members who are granted visiting privileges.").

142. *See* Overton v. Bazzetta, 539 U.S. 126, 133 (2003) (upholding prison regulations that impose two-year visitation bans and regulations that excluded visits by minor nieces and nephews and children as to whom parental rights had been terminated). As the regulations upheld in *Bazzetta* did allow visits between an inmate and her own children, grandchildren, and siblings, the Court did "not imply . . . that any right to intimate association is altogether terminated by incarceration or is always irrelevant" in evaluating the legitimacy of prison policies. *Id.* at 131. In *Bazzetta*, however, the Court found a legitimate penological interest in excluding certain extended family members from visitation. *Id.* at 126–27.

143. *See* FED. BUREAU OF PRISONS, PROGRAM STATEMENT 7300.4A(1) (2003).

144. *See* Lanette P. Dalley, *Imprisoned Mothers and Their Children: Their Often Conflicting Legal Rights*, 22 HAMLINE J. PUB. L. & POL'Y 1, 40–43 (2001); Philip M. Genty, *Permanency Planning in the Context of Parental Incarceration: Legal Issues and Recommendations*, 77 CHILD WELFARE 543, 545–46 (1998); Heidi Rosenberg,

California's Incarcerated Mothers: Legal Roadblocks to Reunification, 30 GOLDEN GATE U. L. REV. 285, 325–26, 329–30 (2000).

145. *See* CAL. WELF. & INST. CODE § 361.5(e)(1) (West 2007); N.Y. SOC. SERV. LAW § 384-b(2)(b), 7(f) (McKinney 2007).
146. FED. BUREAU OF PRISONS, PROGRAM STATEMENT 5270.07 (1987).
147. *Id.* § 570.32(a)(2).
148. *Id.* § 570.31(a)(1). Such furloughs are also granted "to enrich specific institution program experiences."
149. *Id.* § 570.32(a)(1) (defining immediate family as "mother, father, step-parents, foster parents, brothers and sisters, spouse, and children").
150. *Id.* § 570.32(a)(3).
151. 28 U.S.C. § 994(d) (2000).
152. Notably, it is easier to accomplish this accommodation for men than it is for women; there are many fewer prisons with female populations. *See* Myrna S. Raeder, *A Primer on Gender-Related Issues That Affect Female Offenders*, 20 CRIM. JUST. 4, 18 (2005) [hereinafter Raeder, *A Primer*].
153. 196 F.3d 800, 802 (7th Cir. 1999).
154. *Id.*
155. Raeder, *A Primer*, *supra* chap. 1, n. 152, at 11, 18.
156. *Id.* at 17.
157. *Id.*; *see also* Myrna S. Raeder, *Creating Correctional Alternatives for Nonviolent Women Offenders and Their Children*, 44 ST. LOUIS U. L.J. 377 (2000).
158. FED. BUREAU OF PRISONS, PROGRAM STATEMENT 5553.06, ESCAPES/DEATHS NOTIFICATION (updated 1999).
159. FED. BUREAU OF PRISONS, PROGRAM STATEMENT 5355.03, PARENTING PROGRAM STANDARDS (updated 1995).
160. *Id.*
161. It bears mention that our study of family ties benefits in this book is more focused than the one we wrote about in our article in 2007. *See* Dan Markel, Jennifer M. Collins & Ethan J. Leib, *Criminal Justice and the Challenge of Family Ties*, 2007 U. ILL. L. REV. 1147 [hereinafter Markel, Collins & Leib, *Family Ties*]. There we wrote about the criminal justice system's promotions of family interests without focusing our inquiry, as we do here, on the issue of whether a defendant's family status is examined by the law in question. Here we are focused on facial family ties benefits to defendants, though we acknowledge that this analysis may imperfectly survey that landscape.

Chapter 2. A Normative Framework for Family Ties Benefits

1. *See, e.g.*, Travis, *supra* chap. 1, n. 141, at 37 ("[M]any prisons narrowly define the family members who are granted visiting privileges. Michigan's corrections department, for example, promulgated regulations in 1995 restricting the categories of individuals

who are allowed to visit a prisoner. The approved visiting list may include minor children under the age of eighteen, but only if they are the prisoner's children, stepchildren, grandchildren, or siblings. Prisoners who are neither the biological parents nor legal stepparents of the children they were raising do not have this privilege. . . . Many prisoners' extended family networks, including girlfriends and boyfriends who are raising prisoners' children, are not recognized in these narrow definitions of 'family.'"). *See generally* Murray, *supra* chap. 1, n. 100.

2. As we explain in Chapter 3, we find the bright-line marriage rule impossible to justify. Others agree that same-sex partners ought to be granted the same privilege rights that married couples get. *See, e.g.*, Jennifer R. Brannen, *Unmarried with Privileges? Extending the Evidentiary Privilege to Same-Sex Couples*, 17 REV. LIT. 311 (1998) (arguing that same-sex couples should be entitled to claim spousal privileges); Elizabeth Kimberly (Kyhm) Penfil, *In the Light of Reason and Experience: Should Federal Evidence Law Protect Confidential Communications Between Same-Sex Partners?*, 88 MARQ. L. REV. 815, 845 (2005) ("[T]he debate between those who would protect communications between same-sex partners and those who would not more readily resembles the paradigmatic dispute between Antigone and Creon. Those who, like Creon, believe the current, state-imposed laws are inviolate will refuse the privilege. Those who, like Antigone, believe the eternal laws of family loyalty and ethical choice supercede the state's current pronouncement of the law will seek to apply the privilege."); Nancy D. Polikoff, *Ending Marriage As We Know It*, 32 HOFSTRA L. REV. 201, 202 (2003) (advocating "sweeping reform" in rewarding diverse adult relationships, rather than just marriage).
3. Of course, the exclusion of people here is not a problem unique to the criminal law context. And the fact of a benefit's underinclusiveness is not a sufficient reason to jettison the benefit, but rather is a potential reason to expand who receives it.
4. It bears mention, though, that many jurisdictions confer a right to a willing spouse to testify.
5. *See* Chapter 5.
6. *See* U.S. SENTENCING GUIDELINES MANUAL § 5H1.6 cmt. n.1(B) (2006).
7. Consequently, in the federal context, it might appear that family ties actually work against some defendants because of the broad network of persons on which they might rely. On this view, this could seem more like a burden on defendants with family ties than a benefit to them. We disagree. By narrowing the class of offenders who might benefit from family ties departures to simply those who occupy a role of irreplaceable caregiver, the cases implementing the 5H1.6 provision help ensure that defendants with family ties are not benefited *vis-à-vis* those similarly situated defendants without any special family ties or responsibilities.
8. The federal courts, in other words, expand the notion of family capaciously for purposes of sentencing but restrict it for purposes of extending evidentiary privileges.
9. *See* GEORGE P. FLETCHER, LOYALTY: AN ESSAY ON THE MORALITY OF RELATIONSHIPS 3 (1993).

10. *See* MEIR DAN-COHEN, *Responsibility and the Boundaries of the Self, in* HARMFUL THOUGHTS: ESSAYS ON LAW, SELF, AND MORALITY 199–200 (2002) (originally published at 105 HARV. L. REV. 959 (1992)).
11. *See* MILTON C. REGAN, JR., ALONE TOGETHER: LAW AND THE MEANINGS OF MARRIAGE 15–29 (1999); Regan, *supra* intro., n. 24, at 2067–89.
12. These accounts of the self have their roots in the early communitarian theories of Charles Taylor and Michael J. Sandel. CHARLES TAYLOR, SOURCES OF THE SELF: THE MAKING OF THE MODERN IDENTITY 3–24 (1989) (developing the idea that selves have "inescapable frameworks" that any theory of justice and the state must accommodate); CHARLES TAYLOR, THE ETHICS OF AUTHENTICITY 37–39 (1991) (developing the idea of the self with "horizons of significance"); MICHAEL J. SANDEL, LIBERALISM AND THE LIMITS OF JUSTICE (1982) (developing the idea of the "encumbered" self).
13. For more on the distinction between associative and general duties, *see* SAMUEL SCHEFFLER, *Families, Nations, and Strangers, in* BOUNDARIES AND ALLEGIANCES: PROBLEMS OF JUSTICE AND RESPONSIBILITY IN LIBERAL THOUGHT 48, 49–50 (2001).
14. A variant of this argument is offered by Roderick M. Hills, Jr., *The Constitutional Rights of Private Governments*, 78 N.Y.U. L. REV. 144, 147 (2003) [hereinafter Hills, *Constitutional Rights*]. Drawing on JOSEPH RAZ, THE MORALITY OF FREEDOM 38–69 (1986), Hills suggests that state officials should defer to decisions made by competent "private governments"—of which the family is an example. Hills, *supra*, at 193–96. Such private governments promote individual freedom and should be accorded special associational rights and liberties. Hills's presumption that families' internal decision-making processes should command deference holds so long as the decision at issue would be more likely to be handled appropriately by the private government than by the state. In what follows, we ultimately contest the notion that the family and its internal decision-making process should receive any deference by the state in the criminal law context. This is ultimately no real challenge to Hills, who concedes that deferring to private governments may be inappropriate if such deference does not improve decisions. *See id.* at 195–96. Nevertheless, with Hills, we are mindful that the state can draw on the family's comparative expertise and efficiency—and appreciate that these reasons may sometimes help as a basis for distributing certain benefits or burdens in the realm of distributive justice institutions.
15. *See* Paul H. Robinson, *Competing Conceptions of Modern Desert: Vengeful, Deontological, and Empirical*, 67 CAMBRIDGE L.J. 145 (2008) ("If the criminal law tracks the community's intuitions of justice in assigning liability and punishment, it is argued, the law gains access to the power and efficiency of stigmatization, it avoids the resistance and subversion inspired by an unjust system, it gains compliance by prompting people to defer to it as a moral authority in new or grey areas (such as insider trading), and it earns the ability to help shape powerful societal norms."); *see also* Paul H. Robinson & John M. Darley, *The Utility of Desert*, 91 NW. U. L. REV. 453 (1997).

16. PLATO, THE REPUBLIC 155–68 (Francis MacDonald Cornford ed. 1945).
17. Linda C. McClain, *Care As a Public Value: Linking Responsibility, Resources, and Republicanism*, 76 CHI.-KENT L. REV. 1673, 1674 (2001).
18. Linda C. McClain, *Negotiating Gender and (Free and Equal) Citizenship: The Place of Associations*, 72 FORDHAM L. REV. 1569, 1569 (2004); *see also* MARTHA FINEMAN, THE AUTONOMY MYTH, at xviii (2004) ("It is very important to understand the roles assigned to the family in society—roles that otherwise might have to be played by other institutions, such as the market or the state."). Although space constraints have prevented us from giving the subtle and important work of McClain and Fineman its due, we think it important to give a flavor of this form of argument in the text.
19. *See* JOAN C. TRONTO, MORAL BOUNDARIES: A POLITICAL ARGUMENT FOR AN ETHIC OF CARE 3 (1993); Deborah Stone, *Why We Need a Care Movement*, NATION, Mar. 13, 2000, at 13, 15.
20. Stone, *supra* chap. 2, n. 19, at 15.
21. Some feminists remain suspicious of the "ethic of care" because it seems intrinsically gendered—and using the state to promote care might only further ensnare women in particular into the hard work of caring. *See* JOAN WILLIAMS, UNBENDING GENDER: WHY FAMILY AND WORK CONFLICT AND WHAT TO DO ABOUT IT 179 (2000).
22. McClain, *supra* chap. 2, n. 18, at 1569.
23. *See* BRAMAN, *supra* intro., n. 20, at 6–7.
24. *See* NANCY COTT, PUBLIC VOWS: A HISTORY OF MARRIAGE AND THE NATION (2000); HENDRIK HARTOG, MAN AND WIFE IN AMERICA: A HISTORY (2000).
25. *See* Jill Elaine Hasday, *Intimacy and Economic Exchange*, 119 HARV. L. REV. 491, 530 (2005) (arguing that we can furnish respect for intimate relationships through various means—and need not pursue all strategies at once in every issue area).
26. SAMUEL SCHEFFLER, *Conceptions of Cosmopolitanism*, *in* BOUNDARIES AND ALLEGIANCES: PROBLEMS OF JUSTICE AND RESPONSIBILITY IN LIBERAL THOUGHT, *supra* chap. 2, n. 13, at 121.
27. *Cf.* Markus Dirk Dubber, *The Power to Govern Men and Things: Patriarchal Origins of the Police Power in American Law*, 52 BUFF. L. REV. 1277, 1345 (2004) (describing the patriarchal genealogy of the modern police power and noting that a clear view of the origins of state power can help achieve the legitimate use of power).
28. *See* Trammel v. United States, 440 U.S. 40 (1980) (describing the origin of the privilege).
29. Parham v. J.R., 442 U.S. 584, 602 (1979); *see also* Lehr v. Robertston, 463 U.S. 248, 256 (1983) ("The intangible fibers that connect parent and child have infinite variety. They are woven throughout the fabric of our society, providing it with strength, beauty, and flexibility.").
30. *See generally* Jennifer M. Collins, *Lady Madonna, Children at Your Feet: The Criminal Justice System's Romanticization of the Parent-Child Relationship*, 93 IOWA L. REV. 131 (2007).
31. *See* Wayne Logan, *Criminal Law Sanctuaries*, 38 HARV. C.R.-C.L. L. REV. 321 (2003).

32. Terry Davidson, *Conjugal Crime: Understanding and Changing the Wifebeating Pattern* 99 (1978); Logan, *supra* chap. 2, n. 31, at 339; *see also* Mason Thomas, *Child Abuse and Neglect Part I: Historical Overview, Legal Matrix, and Social Perspectives,* 50 N.C. L. REV. 293, 295 (1972) (explaining that doctrine of *patria potestas* also gave a father the right to "kill, mutilate, sell, or offer his child in sacrifice").
33. PLECK, *supra* chap. 1, n. 67, at 17–33.
34. *Id.* at 27–29; *see also* Logan, *supra* chap. 2, n. 31, at 340.
35. *See generally* Elizabeth Pleck, *Criminal Approaches to Family Violence, 1640–1980, in* FAMILY VIOLENCE 19, 19–57 (Lloyd Ohlin & Michael Tonry, eds., 1989) (describing the history of reform efforts in matters of family violence). Pleck notes that "[t]he greater the defense of the rights and privileges of the traditional family, the lower the interest in the criminalization of the family." *Id.* at 20.
36. *See, e.g.,* Fulgham v. State, 46 Ala. 143, 146–48 (1871); Commonwealth v. McAfee, 108 Mass. 458, 461 (1871).
37. *See* Reva B. Siegel, *"The Rule of Love": Wife Beating As Prerogative and Privacy,* 105 YALE L.J. 2117 (1996).
38. Logan, *supra* chap. 2, n. 31, at 341 ("Child abuse, by mothers and fathers alike, similarly continued without significant intervention." (citing 1 JOEL PRENTISS BISHOP, COMMENTARIES ON THE CRIMINAL LAW §§ 878–891 (Little Brown 5th ed. 1872) (elaborating upon the chastisement right in families))); Robert W. Ten Bensel et al., *Children in a World of Violence: The Roots of Child Maltreatment, in* THE BATTERED CHILD 3 (Mary Edna Helfer *et al.* eds., 5th ed. 1997) (providing historical survey of child abuse). As Logan explains, it was not until the widespread use of x-ray technology, which could discern evidence of abuse that children were too afraid to discuss, that the tide changed, and jurisdictions began adopting criminal laws against child neglect or abuse. Logan, *supra* chap. 2, n. 31, at 342–43.
39. According to Logan, "[m]arital rape, as of the mid-1980s, largely remained a legal impossibility, with the drafters of the influential Model Penal Code expressing concern over 'unwarranted intrusion of the penal law into the life of the family.'" Logan, *supra* chap. 2, n. 31, at 347; *see also* MODEL PENAL CODE § 213.1 cmt. 8(c) (1985).
40. *See* 42 U.S.C. § 3796hh(c)(1)(A) (2000) (requiring units of government to "encourage or mandate arrests of domestic violence offenders based on probable cause that an offense has been committed" to be eligible for certain grants); Miller & Wright, *supra* chap. 1, n. 90, at 331–40 (discussing changes in police responses to domestic violence); LAWRENCE W. SHERMAN ET AL., POLICING DOMESTIC VIOLENCE: EXPERIMENTS AND DILEMMAS (1992); Deborah Epstein, *Procedural Justice: Tempering the State's Response to Domestic Violence,* 43 WM. & MARY L. REV. 1843, 1851–56 (2002); Cheryl Hanna, *The Paradox of Hope: The Crime and Punishment of Domestic Violence,* 39 WM. & MARY L. REV. 1505, 1518–19 (1998).
41. *See* R. Michael Cassidy, *Reconsidering Spousal Privileges After* Crawford, 33 AM. J. CRIM. L. 339, 348 (2006) (distinguishing soft from hard no-drop policies).

42. *See* Coker, *Crime Control, supra* chap. 1, n. 64, at 803–05; Linda G. Mills, *Killing Her Softly: Intimate Abuse and the Violence of State Intervention,* 113 HARV. L. REV. 550, 569–70 (1999); Suk, *supra* chap. 1, n. 66, at 45. *But see* Annalise Acorn, *Surviving the Battered Reader's Syndrome, or: A Critique of Linda G. Mills'* Insult to Injury: Rethinking Our Responses to Intimate Abuse, 13 UCLA WOMEN'S L.J. 335, 340 (2005); Cassidy, *supra* chap. 2, n. 41, at 350 (surveying counter-arguments and studies supporting claim that welfare and autonomy of women are improved through tough policies on domestic violence).
43. Seymour Moskowitz, *Saving Granny from the Wolf: Elder Abuse and Neglect—the Legal Framework,* 31 CONN. L. REV. 77 (1998); Audrey S. Garfield, Note, *Elder Abuse and the States' Adult Protective Services Response: Time for a Change in California,* 42 HASTINGS L.J. 859 (1991).
44. Nancy J. Knauer, *Same-Sex Domestic Violence: Claiming a Domestic Sphere While Risking Negative Stereotypes,* 8 TEMP. POL. & CIV. RTS. L. REV. 325 (1999); Ruthann Robson, *Lavender Bruises: Intra-Lesbian Violence, Law and Lesbian Legal Theory,* 20 GOLDEN GATE U. L. REV. 567 (1990); Symposium, *Lesbian, Gay, Bisexual, and Transgender Communities and Intimate Partner Violence,* 29 FORDHAM URB. L.J. 121 (2001).
45. Logan, *supra* chap. 2, n. 31, at 347; *see also* Jill Elaine Hasday, *Contest and Consent: A Legal History of Marital Rape,* 88 CAL. L. REV. 1373, 1482 (2000) (noting the "partial norm and uneven" reform of marital rape law).
46. Logan, *supra* chap. 2, n. 31, at 347 (citing MURRAY A. STRAUS, BEATING THE DEVIL OUT OF THEM: CORPORAL PUNISHMENT IN AMERICAN FAMILIES (1994); Susan H. Bitensky, *Spare the Rod, Embrace Our Humanity: Toward a New Legal Regime Prohibiting Corporal Punishment of Children,* 31 U. MICH. J.L. REFORM 353 (1998); David Orentlicher, *Spanking and Other Corporal Punishment of Children by Parents: Overvaluing Pain, Undervaluing Children,* 35 HOUS. L. REV. 147 (1998)).
47. Logan, *supra* chap. 2, n. 31, at 372 (citing PATRICIA TJADEN & NANCY THOENNES, EXTENT, NATURE, AND CONSEQUENCES OF INTIMATE PARTNER VIOLENCE: FINDINGS FROM THE NATIONAL VIOLENCE AGAINST WOMEN SURVEY III (2000)) (estimating that 4.8 million women experience every year some form of sexual or physical abuse, and that annually about 2.9 million men endure physical assaults by their partners).
48. *Id.* at 348.
49. If our skepticism toward family ties benefits were implemented in law and practice, we might see the state's criminal justice system serve as a vehicle to interrupt and upend patterns of private patriarchy and domination. But this would only be a first step; as Laura Rosenbury pointed out to us in a comment on an earlier draft, reducing private patriarchy would not address the various ways the state's institutions historically perpetuated its own kind of public patriarchy.
50. *See supra* chap. 1.
51. FLETCHER, *supra* chap. 2, n. 9, at 81 (arguing that the perjury rationale for the intrafamilial privileges might justify it where other rationales fail).
52. *See* 5 JEREMY BENTHAM, RATIONALE OF JUDICIAL EVIDENCE 338 (1827).

53. *Cf.* MICHAEL WALZER, SPHERES OF JUSTICE 283 (1983).
54. *See* Mapp v. Ohio, 367 U.S. 643, 657 (1961) (holding that the exclusionary rule is an essential part of the Fourth and Fourteenth Amendments).
55. Moreover, with the right alternative measures available, some scholars have suggested that there is good reason to revisit the wisdom of the exclusionary rule. *See, e.g.*, AKHIL REED AMAR, THE CONSTITUTION AND CRIMINAL PROCEDURE: FIRST PRINCIPLES 20–31 (1997).
56. *See, e.g.*, Tracy E. Higgins & Laura A. Rosenbury, *Agency, Equality, and Antidiscrimination Law*, 85 CORNELL L. REV. 1194, 1198 (2000) (noting that liberal discourse normally entails commitments which respect that "individuals, and not groups, are the primary political units and bearers of rights; [and] that equality means, first and foremost, the right of every individual to 'equal respect and concern' in pursuit of her conception of the good").
57. *See* Dan Markel, *Against Mercy*, 88 MINN. L. REV. 1421, 1452–74 (2004) [hereinafter Markel, *Against Mercy*].
58. This account draws from Jean Hampton's discussion in JEFFRIE MURPHY & JEAN HAMPTON, FORGIVENESS AND MERCY 157–61 (1988), and Markel, *Against Mercy*, *supra* chap. 2, n. 57, at 1453–56.
59. Of course, the degree of disruption to the equality norm is diminished if the liability of the offender is established and the leniency affects only the sentence incrementally rather than the fact of being adjudged guilty.
60. Indeed, various feminist scholars have emphasized the importance of holding women accountable when they are offenders. *See* Kay Levine, *No Penis, No Problem*, 33 FORDHAM URB. L.J. 357, 385 n.125 (2006); *cf.* Martha Mahoney, *Women's Lives, Violence and Agency*, *in* THE PUBLIC NATURE OF PRIVATE VIOLENCE 59, 64 (Martha Fineman & Roxanne Mykituik eds., 1994) (discussing how it is "so difficult" for us "to see both agency and oppression in the lives of women").
61. Thus, when family members receive punishment discounts on account of who the victim was, we are saying that their victim is not worth the same amount as she would have been if the victim were not a family member. *Cf.* ANDREW VON HIRSCH, DOING JUSTICE: THE CHOICE OF PUNISHMENTS 73 (1976) ("[D]isproportionately lenient punishment for murder implies that human life—the victim's life—is not worthy of much concern.").
62. *But see* Peter Westen, *The Empty Idea of Equality*, 95 HARV. L. REV. 537 (1982) (arguing that the rhetoric of equality should be abandoned). It is true that Peter Westen cleverly shows why the concept of equality itself is, in some very real sense, tautological, circular, and uninteresting. That likes should be treated alike is also not actually true as an independent moral principle: if someone said to treat all murderers to green lollipops equally, we would think they were crazy, not egalitarians. His very reasonable point is that the substantive moral rules that tell us who are relevant equals and how to treat any one individual from that class contain all the relevant data to perform any moral calculus. The equality principle only contains what we already know—that the rule that prescribes conduct or treatment of one person in a group would likewise apply to anyone else with

the same relevant conduct or orientation. *Id.* at 572–73. He delightfully argues that "justice" fares little better, rendering "equal justice under law" one big empty redundancy. *See id.* at 558.

Still, we think Westen's thesis goes too far when he calls equality (and by extension, justice) an "empty vessel with no substantive moral content of its own." *Id.* at 547. For our purposes, the ideal of equality is a proxy for the uncontroversial claim that the criminal justice system's intrinsic legitimacy rests on its ability to treat all fairly, without favoring certain classes of citizens because of morally irrelevant characteristics. Having a family—like being of a certain race or religion—may be psychologically relevant to a person's identity; but it is often morally irrelevant from the standpoint of determining criminal liability. The principle of equality functions as a stand-in for the more general point that a person's status as a family member ought not, in principle, be a mitigating or aggravating factor in the administration of punishment. Making assumptions that family members are entitled to a special brand of criminal justice is inconsistent with the criminal justice system's focus on distributing punishment for culpability without favoring the status of an offender.

More generally, we are sympathetic to the response to Westen's article made by Kent Greenawalt. *See* Kent Greenawalt, *How Empty Is the Idea of Equality?*, 83 COLUM. L. REV. 1167, 1169–70 (1983) ("The applicability of the principle [of equality] provides an additional moral reason for complying with an established standard of how people are to be treated. In many situations the principle also affects the substantive conclusions that can properly be reached, bearing on whether differences in ultimate treatment are warranted and, if so, on the methods for determining how choices among individuals are to be made. [And s]omewhat less directly, the principle also affects how justifications of unequal treatment should proceed and what should be done in instances of uncertainty over whether people are relevantly alike or unalike."). *But see* Peter Westen, *To Lure the Tarantula from Its Hole: A Response*, 83 COLUM. L. REV. 1186 (1983).

63. *See generally* Darryl Brown, *Third Party Harms in Criminal Law*, 80 TEX. L. REV. 1383 (2004). Importantly, we recognize that many aspects of the criminal justice system have a disparate—and profoundly troubling—impact on family life in minority communities. *See, e.g.*, BRAMAN, *supra* intro., n. 20, at 1–11 (providing an ethnography of effects of incarceration on family and community life in the District of Columbia); Dorothy E. Roberts, *Criminal Justice and Black Families: The Collateral Damage of Over-Enforcement*, 34 U.C. DAVIS L. REV. 1005 (2001); Dorothy E. Roberts, *The Social and Moral Cost of Mass Incarceration in African American Communities*, 56 STAN. L. REV. 1271 (2004). We also recognize that our current sentencing regime has particularly harsh consequences for incarcerated mothers and their children. *See, e.g.*, Raeder, *supra* chap. 1, n. 117, at 678–99. Rather than use the criminal justice system to confer benefits just on members of favored groups such as traditional nuclear families, however, we believe a better response would be more sanity with respect to drug law enforcement, less harsh

sentencing policies, expanded use of the coercion or duress doctrines, and greater use of alternatives to incarceration. *See, e.g.*, Dan Markel, *Are Shaming Punishments Beautifully Retributive? Retributivism and the Implications for the Alternative Sanctions Debate*, 54 VAND. L. REV. 2157 (2001) [hereinafter Markel, *Shaming Punishments*]; Dan Markel, *Wrong Turns on the Road to Alternative Sanctions: Reflections on the Future of Shaming Punishments and Restorative Justice*, 85 TEX. L. REV. 1385 (2007). Additionally, if we want to direct benefits to improve family life, we believe it more appropriate to do so through the distributive-justice institutions of social policy and not through criminal justice "benefits" that are indirect and potentially more costly along other dimensions.

64. BENTHAM, *supra* chap. 2, n. 52, at 338.
65. *Id.* at 340.
66. "Criminal families" exist well beyond the *Godfather* trilogy. For a good introduction to scholarship about criminal families, *see* DIEGO GAMBETTA, THE SICILIAN MAFIA: THE BUSINESS OF PRIVATE PROTECTION (1993).
67. United States v. Menyweather, 431 F.3d 692, 708 (9th Cir. 2005) (Kleinfeld, J., dissenting).
68. United States v. Guy, 174 F.3d 859, 861 (7th Cir. 1999) (noting that the trial court acknowledged that incarcerating the defendant would impose hardship on her family but was averse to creating a situation "where a person could steal with relative impunity and not expect incarceration simply because they come from a large family, or have responsibilities for a large family").
69. *Cf.* JOSEPH GOLDSTEIN & JAY KATZ, THE FAMILY AND THE LAW 368 (1965) (quoting Dwight Eisenhower, who, when considering clemency for Ethel Rosenberg's espionage conviction, noted that "if there would be any commuting of the woman's sentence without the man's then from here on the Soviets would simply recruit their spies from among women.").
70. For example, do states with particularly vigorous parental discipline defenses have a higher rate of child abuse? In states that exempt family members from prosecutions for harboring fugitives, are prosecutors encountering significant obstructive activity from family members?
71. Importantly, we do not rank the relative importance of these concerns. Nor do we argue that a benefit must trigger a certain number of the relevant considerations to offend our normative framework.

Chapter 3. Applying the Framework to Family Ties Benefits

1. This refers to sentences to be served by an "irreplaceable caregiver" that are delayed until a point when the need for care is diminished or alternative means of care are secured.
2. *Developments in the Law*, *supra* chap. 1, n. 9, at 1577.

3. *Id.*
4. Hawkins v. United States, 358 U.S. 74, 77 (1958).
5. *See, e.g.*, HOMER H. CLARK, JR., THE LAW OF DOMESTIC RELATIONS IN THE UNITED STATES 544 (2d ed. 1988) (stating that spousal immunity "was never supported by any but specious reasons"); 8 WIGMORE, *supra* chap. 1, n. 2, § 2228 (arguing that spousal immunity is "the merest anachronism in legal theory and an indefensible obstruction to truth in practice"); David Medine, *The Adverse Testimony Privilege: Time to Dispose of a "Sentimental Relic,"* 67 OR. L. REV. 519 (1988).
6. *See* 2 STONE & TAYLOR, *supra* chap. 1, n. 5, § 5.08.
7. REGAN, *supra* chap. 2, n. 11, at 90. Most importantly, the spousal privilege disadvantages victims of domestic abuse, especially in a post-*Crawford* landscape. *See generally* Cassidy, *supra* chap. 2, n. 41 (describing how *Crawford v. Washington*, 541 U.S. 36 (2004), makes it much more difficult to prosecute domestic abusers).
8. It is worth noting that there are often exceptions to the spousal privileges: they tend not to apply in cases involving spousal violence, child abuse, or neglect. REGAN, *supra* chap. 2, n. 11, at 91. *But see* Cassidy, *supra* chap. 2, n. 41, at 367–69 (citing ALA. CODE § 12-21-227; D.C. CODE ANN. § 14-306; GA. CODE ANN. § 24-9-23; MASS. GEN. LAWS ANN. CH. 223, § 20; and MO. ANN. STAT. § 546.260, which codify adverse testimony privileges without any exception for crimes committed by one spouse against the other—and GA. CODE ANN. § 24-9-21; N.H. R. EVID. 504; N.C. GEN STAT, § 8-57(c); S.C. CODE ANN. § 19-11-30; and W. VA. CODE ANN. § 57-3-4, which codify spousal-communications privileges without such an exception). There are a lot of nuances to how the spousal privileges apply—and those details extend beyond our immediate concern here. For the specifics regarding how these privileges frustrate law enforcement in the domestic violence context, *see* Cassidy, *supra* chap. 2, n. 41. Federal courts tend to create an exception for joint criminal enterprises. *See* REGAN, *supra* chap. 2, n. 11, at 91 (citing United States v. Marashi, 913 F.2d 724, 730–31 (9th Cir. 1990); United States v. Sims, 755 F.2d 1239, 1243 (6th Cir. 1985); United States v. Broome, 732 F.2d 363, 365 (4th Cir. 1984)). Some states have followed suit. *See* State v. Witchey, 388 N.W.2d 893, 895–96 (S.D. 1986); Wolf v. State, 674 S.W.2d 831, 841–42 (Tex. App. 1984). *But see* Johnson v. State, 451 So. 2d 1024, 1024 (Fla. Dist. Ct. App. 1984); State v. White, 480 A.2d 230, 232 (N.J. Super. Ct. Law Div. 1984). We endorse that exception because it speaks directly to our fourth consideration, namely, that the privileges risk creating more successful criminal activity.
9. *Need for Parent/Child Privilege*, 22 CHAMPION 10, 11 (Apr. 1998) (proposal by the National Association of Criminal Defense Lawyers for enactment of a statutory parent-child communication privilege by Congress and state legislatures).
10. 553 F. Supp. 1298, 1326 (D. Nev. 1983).
11. *Id.* at 1304 (quoting Wisconsin v. Yoder, 406 U.S. 205, 232 (1972)).
12. *Id.* (citing Susan Levine, Comment, *The Child-Parent Privilege: A Proposal*, 47 FORDHAM L. REV. 771, 782–83 (1979)).
13. Jessica Perry, Note, *The Parent-Child Testimonial Privilege: An Argument for Qualified Recognition*, 37 BRANDEIS L.J. 97, 106 (1998/1999).
14. *Id.*

15. *Id.*
16. *In re Agosto*, 553 F. Supp. at 1326.
17. The generally acknowledged purpose of the attorney-client privilege is "to encourage 'full and frank communication between attorneys and their clients and thereby promote broader public interests in the observance of law and the administration of justice.'" Swidler & Berlin v. United States, 524 U.S. 399, 403 (1998) (quoting Upjohn Co. v. United States, 449 U.S. 383, 389 (1981)); *see also* RESTATEMENT (THIRD) OF THE LAW GOVERNING LAWYERS § 68 cmt. c (2000) ("The rationale for the [attorney-client] privilege is that confidentiality enhances the value of client-lawyer communications and hence the efficacy of legal services.").
18. United States v. Ismail, 756 F.2d 1253, 1258 (6th Cir. 1985) (suggesting that the parent-child privilege could be analogized to the marital privileges insofar as they both contribute to family "harmony").
19. Another option some have pursued is to claim the privilege under the First Amendment. *See In re* Greenberg, 11 Fed. R. Evid. Serv. 579, 1982 WL 597412, at *1 (D. Conn.) (recognizing a parent-child privilege under the Free Exercise Clause because of the Jewish law's prohibition from having parents testify against their children); *see also* Grand Jury Proceedings of John Doe v. United States, 842 F.2d 244, 248 (10th Cir. 1988) (rejecting the claim of a fifteen-year-old Mormon who invoked the Free Exercise Clause to avoid testifying against his mother). *But see* Smilow v. United States, 465 F.2d 802, 804 (2d Cir. 1971) (refusing to grant such a privilege because the court was skeptical of the genuinely religious basis of the claim despite claimant's invocation of potential "divine punishment" and "ostracism from the Jewish Community"). Some have also suggested that the Fifth Amendment privilege against self-incrimination should be held to protect people from being forced to testify against their family members. *See, e.g.*, Margaret Carlson, *Should a Mom Rat on Her Daughter?*, TIME, Feb. 23, 1998, at 25.
20. Courts routinely apply the criteria adumbrated by John H. Wigmore in his evidence treatise. 8 WIGMORE, *supra* chap.1, n. 2, § 2192. The "Wigmore Test" considers four factors: (1) the communication must originate in confidence that it will not be disclosed; (2) this element of confidentiality must be essential to the full and satisfactory maintenance of the relation between the parties; (3) the relation must be one which in the opinion of the community ought to be sedulously fostered; and (4) the injury that would inure to the relation by the disclosure must be greater than the benefit thereby gained for the correct disposal of the litigation. *Id.*
21. All of these arguments appear in *In re Grand Jury*, 103 F.3d 1140, 1144 (3d Cir. 1997).
22. *Developments in the Law*, *supra* chap. 1, n. 9, at 1474.
23. For an effort to think through how we might furnish testimonial privileges to friends, *see* Sanford Levinson, *Testimonial Privileges and the Preferences of Friendship*, 1984 DUKE L.J. 631, 643–54. Levinson argues that it might be a good idea if people could choose to give a limited number of "privilege tickets" to whomever they want—thereby, deciding for themselves where they most need

a relationship of trust. *See id.* at 654–62. The value of friendship and family in political and legal life is further explored in Ethan J. Leib, *The Politics of Family and Friends in Aristotle and Montaigne*, 31 INTERPRETATION: J. POL. PHIL. 165 (2004), and Ethan J. Leib, *Friendship & the Law*, 54 UCLA L. REV. 631 (2007) [hereinafter Leib, *Friendship*], in which Leib argues that many areas of the law should confer upon the friend special status and consideration.

24. It is worth noting that at least one commentator would like a "qualified" parent-child privilege that would apply only in criminal contexts rather than civil contexts because the "stress placed on the family bond would be greater where criminal punishment was at stake." Perry, *supra* chap. 3, n. 13, at 114. In our view, precisely because much more tends to be at stake in the pursuit of criminal justice, the familial privileges are especially inappropriate in the criminal context.
25. "[I]t hath been resolved by the Justices that a wife cannot be produced either against or for her husband." 1 E. COKE, A COMMENTARIE UPON LITTLETON 6b (1628); *see also* 8 WIGMORE, *supra* chap. 1, n. 2, § 2227.
26. *See* 8 WIGMORE, *supra* chap. 1, n. 2, § 2227.
27. *See Developments in the Law*, *supra* chap. 1, n. 9.
28. Logan, *supra* chap. 2, n. 31, at 347. *See generally* Malinda L. Seymore, *Isn't It a Crime: Feminist Perspectives on Spousal Immunity and Spousal Violence*, 90 NW. U. L. REV. 1032 (1996). There are exceptions, both at common law, and today in many jurisdictions, for crimes against spouses or others in the household. *See* Cassidy, *supra* chap. 2, n. 41, at 361 n.170, 367 n.205 (citing AK. R. EVID. 505(A); ARIZ. REV. STAT. ANN. § 13-4062; CAL. EVID. CODE § 970; COLO. REV. STAT. § 13-90-107; CONN. GEN. STAT. ANN. § 54-84A; HAW. REV. STAT § 626-1; IDAHO CODE ANN. § 19-3002; KY. R. EVID. 504; MD. CODE ANN., CRTS. & JUD. PROC. § 9-106; MICH. COMP. LAWS ANN. § 600.2162; MINN. STAT. ANN. § 595.02; NEB. REV. STAT. § 27-505; NEV. REV. STAT. § 49.295; N.J. STAT. ANN. § 2A:84A-17; N.C. GEN. STAT. § 8-57; OHIO REV. CODE ANN. § 2945.42; OR. REV. STAT. § 40.255; 42 PA. CONS. STAT. § 5913; TEX. R. EVID. 504(B); VA. CODE ANN. § 19.2-271.2; WASH. REV. CODE ANN. § 5.60.060 (1); W. VA. CODE ANN. § 57-3-3; WYO. STAT. ANN. § 1-12-104); *see also* State v. Taylor, 642 So. 2d 160, 166 (La. 1994) (creating an exception by judicial construction); Stubbs v. State, 441 So. 2d 1386 (Miss. 1983) (same); State v. Benson, 712 P.2d 252 (Utah 1985) (same). Still, as Cassidy notes, a number of jurisdictions permit no such exception. Cassidy, *supra* chap. 2, n. 41, at 367–68 (citing Alabama, the District of Columbia, Georgia, Massachusetts, and Missouri).
29. *See* Cassidy, *supra* chap. 2, n. 41, at 352 (describing how *Crawford v. Washington*, 541 U.S. 36 (2004), makes it much more difficult to prosecute domestic abusers).
30. 8 WIGMORE, *supra* chap. 1, n. 2, § 2192. *See generally* United States v. Bryan, 339 U.S. 323, 331 (1950).
31. United States v. Nixon, 418 U.S. 683, 710 (1974).
32. We are indebted to Michael O'Hear for this point.
33. We are somewhat skeptical of the capacity for decision-rule doctrines in the law of evidence and crimes to influence most people's primary conduct. *See* Paul H. Robinson & John M. Darley, *Does Criminal Law Deter? A Behavioral Science*

Investigation, 24 OXFORD J. LEGAL STUD. 173 (2004). But there might be pockets in the population that are especially susceptible to these rules, such as the families involved in organized crime; these families are repeat players and can obtain counsel to guide their conduct.

34. Neal Kumar Katyal, *Conspiracy Theory*, 112 YALE L.J. 1307, 1333 (2003).
35. REGAN, *supra* chap. 2, n. 11, at 91.
36. Mary Coombs mentioned, in her comments upon an earlier version of this argument, that although we emphasize that the spousal privileges are family ties benefits, we disregard the reality that the state cannot take a neutral position in this context: if the state did not give the "innocent" spouse a testimonial privilege, the state's prosecutors would have an extra tool (and an extra sharp one, at that) in coercing testimony from a defendant because the state could always leverage pressure against the innocent spouse. We think that there remain two neutral positions, neither of which the state adopts in its current solicitude for family status. Either the state could afford testimonial privileges to a wide circle of persons that extend beyond the spousal context or it could afford no one such privileges. We prefer the latter approach because we see no reason to give criminals access to confessors, who may both help defendants evade capture and avoid confession to law enforcement. We do not see this preferred neutral policy as a burden on family status because any defendant who trusts any intimate will give the prosecutors a tool for coercion all the same. Most important for our purposes here is not neutrality as between defendant and state but neutrality as between defendants with family networks and those without.
37. MD. CODE ANN. CTS. & JUD. PROC. § 9-106(a) (West 2006); *cf.* CAL. CODE CIV. PRO. 1219(c) (West 2007) (sentencing victims of domestic violence guilty of contempt for counseling or community service).
38. *See* Louis Kaplow & Steven Shavell, *Legal Advice About Information to Present in Litigation: Its Effects and Social Desirability*, 102 HARV. L. REV. 567, 597 (1989) (questioning the merits of the attorney-client privilege); *see also* JEREMY BENTHAM, *Rationale of Judicial Evidence*, *in* 7 THE WORKS OF JEREMY BENTHAM 473–75, 477, 479 (J. Bowring ed., 1842) (arguing that the attorney-client privilege serves to let the guilty go free).
39. *See* Chapter 1.
40. *See* Charles Daniels & Teresa Storch, *Criminal Law*, 14 N.M. L. REV. 89, 105 (1984) (citing WAYNE LAFAVE, CRIMINAL LAW 716 (4th ed. 2003)).
41. *See* State v. Mobbley, 650 P.2d 841, 843 (N.M. Ct. App. 1982) (Lopez, J., dissenting).
42. State v. C.H., 421 So. 2d 62, 65 (Fla. Dist. Ct. App. 1982).
43. United States v. Hill, 279 F.3d 731, 737 n.17 (9th Cir. 2002).
44. The Florida court recognized the issue that "some immunized family members might render assistance to an offender for reasons other than familial affection" but simply noted this did not render the statute "fatally overinclusive" under its constitutional analysis. *C.H.*, 421 So. 2d at 65.
45. Callanan v. United States, 364 U.S. 587, 593 (1961).
46. *See, e.g.*, Thomas, *supra* chap. 2, n. 32, at 293 (describing the maltreatment of children from ancient Greece through twentieth-century America).

47. *See, e.g.*, PLECK, *supra* chap. 1, n. 67, at 6; Judith G. McMullen, *Privacy, Family Autonomy, and the Maltreated Child*, 75 MARQ. L. REV. 569, 572–81 (1992).
48. *See* Franklin Zimring, *Legal Perspectives on Family Violence*, 75 CAL. L. REV. 521, 523–24 (1987) (using a hypothetical to suggest that if a stranger slapped a child, it would be considered assault and battery, but the matter would be treated very differently by the legal system if a mother slapped her own child).
49. *See* Thomas, *supra* chap. 2, n. 32, at 293 (noting "our reluctance to believe that parents—whom we expect to love and protect their offspring—could maltreat or abuse their own children, sometimes even fatally"). Thomas further notes that "[o]ur laws and legal systems have developed over hundreds of years around the notion that parents will love and protect." *Id.*
50. *See, e.g.*, Ira Lupu, *The Separation of Powers and the Protection of Children*, 61 U. CHI. L. REV. 1317, 1324 (1994) ("[I]t is now clear that the psychological influences at play in family life are not limited to the positive sentiments of affection and concern."). For example, the National Clearinghouse on Child Abuse and Neglect Information concluded that there were approximately one thousand four hundred child abuse and neglect fatalities in the United States in 2002, although that number is in all likelihood too low because these cases are traditionally underreported. *See* ADMIN. FOR CHILDREN & FAMILIES, DEP'T OF HEALTH & HUMAN SERVS., CHILD MALTREATMENT 51 (2002), *available at* http://www.acf.hhs.gov/programs/cb/pubs/cm02/cm02.pdf.
51. *See* Pollard, *supra* chap. 1, n. 68, at 621–22.
52. *Id.* at 621.
53. *Id.* at 602–13.
54. *See* Marc MILLER & RONALD WRIGHT, CRIMINAL PROCEDURES: PROSECUTION AND ADJUDICATION, CASES, STATUTES AND EXECUTIVE MATERIALS 104 (3d ed. 2007) (discussing studies and statistical evidence of effect of release on acquittal rates and sentences).
55. Raeder, *A Primer*, *supra* chap. 1, n. 152, at 8 ("Where are the children? Although it is estimated that nearly 20 percent of women are arrested in the presence of their children, relatively few police departments have developed protocols for child-sensitive arrest practices. Whether or not a woman had her child with her when she was arrested, jurisdictions vary widely about obligations of police and Child Services. Thus, although not typically thought of as a function of defense counsel, it is important to find out whether the female defendant has minor children, and, if so, their location, because many of these women are not in intact families. In other words, counsel should assume that many women will not have voluntarily revealed to the police that they have children or disclosed their whereabouts, given the realistic fear that their children may become involved in the foster care system, triggering the ASFA timeline leading to termination of family rights. Ascertaining that a woman's children are safe will both let her focus on assisting in her defense, and ensure that she does not face child endangerment charges if no one is at home or someone unreliable is watching the children.") (citation omitted); *id.* (encouraging lawyer to see if there "are any programs that will house both mother and child"). *See also* CLARE M. NOLAN, CAL. RES.

BUREAU, CHILDREN OF ARRESTED PARENTS: STRATEGIES TO IMPROVE THEIR SAFETY AND WELLBEING (2003), *available at* http://www.library.ca.gov/crb/03/11/03-011.pdf.

56. United States v. Booker, 543 U.S. 220 (2005).
57. *See, e.g., supra* chap. 1 (discussing *Johnson* case at text accompanying note 123).
58. As previously urged by one of us (Markel), the competence criterion must be satisfied at the time of the criminal offense, the trial, and during the punishment to satisfy the moral requirement that punishment be intelligible to the offender. Specifically, the offender must have freely undertaken the criminal action and known (or reasonably should have known) that his conduct was unlawful at the time he committed the crime; at the time of adjudication, the offender had to either freely and knowingly plead guilty or have the competence to assist in the preparation of his case for trial; and at the time at which the punishment is inflicted, he had to be able to understand that he is being punished for his unlawful actions. *See* Markel, *Against Mercy, supra* chap. 2, n. 57, at 1445–46; *see also* Dan Markel, *Executing Retributivism*, 103 NW. U. L. REV. (forthcoming 2009), *available at* http://ssrn.com/abstract=1263683 (addressing offender competence in the context of punishment theory). Moreover, the sentence would need to be within the proper bandwidth of proportionality compared to the severity of the offense and other offenders punished for a comparable offense.
59. Reducing the sentence or relieving liability may be appropriate if the offender had diminished capacity or if the crime was committed under duress because of a relationship with the primary offender or because of a history of domestic violence within the relationship. Similarly, if there can be a causal connection drawn between the feature of a person that elicits someone's compassion (*i.e.*, the mother was stealing to feed her children) and the choice to commit the crime, then that too might be a reason for a legitimate departure. Or, if there is some other reason related to the merits of the case that warrants less punishment: for example, the offender has reduced the social cost of his wrongdoing by coming forward to the government. Absent these considerations, we can insist on a meaningful distinction between factors about someone's background that, in the main, should not mitigate the sentence and factors surrounding someone's criminal action with which an attractive vision of criminal justice is properly concerned. Markel, *Against Mercy, supra* chap. 2, n. 57, at 1466–67. Of course, all this assumes there are no justifications or excuses for the offender either.
60. *See* Raeder, *Gender and Sentencing, supra* intro., n. 24, at 908–09; Raeder, *Remember the Family, supra* chap. 1, n. 106, at 251; Weinstein, *supra* chap. 1, n. 106, at 169.
61. *See, e.g.*, Philip M. Genty, *Damage to Family Relationships As a Collateral Consequence of Parental Incarceration*, 30 FORDHAM URB. L.J. 1671, 1680 (2003).
62. *See generally* Darryl Brown, *Cost-Benefit Analysis in Criminal Law*, 92 CAL. L. REV. 323, 343–48 (2003) [hereinafter Brown, *Cost-Benefit Analysis*]; Darryl Brown, *Third Party Interests in Criminal Law*, 80 TEX. L. REV. 1383, 1407 (2002).
63. *Cf.* Paul Butler, *Race-Based Jury Nullification: Case-in-Chief*, 30 J. MARSHALL L. REV. 911, 919 (1997) (arguing that "[parental] training prevents more crime

than the deterrent effect of prison"). On the related claim that lengthy terms of incarceration are criminogenic and counterproductive, *see* Brown, *Cost-Benefit Analysis*, *supra* chap. 3, n. 62, at 346.

64. *See* Dan Markel, *State, Be Not Proud: A Retributivist Defense of the Commutation of Death Row and the Abolition of the Death Penalty*, 40 HARV. C.R.-C.L. L. REV. 407, 459 (2005); Cass R. Sunstein & Adrian Vermeule, *Is Capital Punishment Morally Required? Acts, Omissions, and Life-Life Tradeoffs*, 58 STAN. L. REV. 703, 711–16 (2005).
65. Of course, we also think there are a variety of noncarceral punishments that might be appropriate for many nonviolent crimes. One of us (Markel) has written on this earlier. *See* Markel, *Shaming Punishments*, *supra* chap. 2, n. 63.
66. To prevent the offender from trying to delay sentencing indefinitely, we might want to restrict the length of the deferral. Thus, if the crime occurs at T1, and the defender only has one child who is four years old, the defendant would be permitted to defer sentencing for fourteen years. This limit would apply even if the defendant subsequently had more children after T1. During those fourteen years, the offender would effectively be on probation, such that if the offender violated other conditions of the delayed sentencing, the offender would then go to prison. This does not eliminate the imposition of harms on children but it reduces, in part, the likelihood of such harm being realized.
67. *See, e.g.*, Raeder, *A Primer*, *supra* chap. 1, n. 152, at 8–9. Indeed, Raeder herself typically centers her critique on the costs incarceration poses on nonviolent offenders.
68. *See id.* at 3–8.
69. A similar point may be made about the introduction of victim impact or defendant impact evidence. For example, some jurisdictions limit who may offer statements on behalf of victims or defendants to family members only. Although we are personally divided over the desirability of victim or defendant impact evidence, we all agree that statutes or policies that permit only family members to offer statements are too narrowly crafted.
70. Raeder refers to these programs as options for mothers with children. *See generally* Raeder, *Remember the Family*, *supra* chap. 1, n. 106; Raeder, *Gender and Sentencing*, *supra* intro., n. 24.
71. FED. BUREAU OF PRISONS, POLICY STATEMENT 7300.4A(a), VISITING REGULATIONS; *see also* GLASER, *supra* chap. 1, n. 136, at 362; AM. CORRECTIONAL ASS'N, *supra* chap. 1, n. 136, at 542; AM. PRISON ASS'N, *supra* chap. 1, n. 136, at 342; COMM'N ON ACCREDITATION FOR CORRECTIONS, *supra* chap. 1, n. 136, at 68; FED. BUREAU OF PRISONS, PROGRAM STATEMENT 5270.07, § 541.12(5), INMATE RIGHTS AND RESPONSIBILITIES (1987).
72. *See, e.g.*, Block v. Rutherford, 468 U.S. 576, 585 (1984); Bell v. Wolfish, 441 U.S. 520, 547–48 (1979); *In re* Dyer, 20 P.3d 907, 912 (Wash. 2001) (finding that prison authorities have wide discretion to administer an extended visitation policy because "[i]t is not in the best interest of the courts to involve themselves in the 'day-to-day management of prisons, often squandering judicial resources with little offsetting benefit to anyone. Courts ought to afford appropriate deference and flexibility to state officials trying to manage a volatile environment.'" (quoting Sandin v. Conner, 515 U.S. 472, 482 (1995))).

73. *See* BUREAU OF PRISONS, POLICY STATEMENT 7300.4A(1).
74. BRENDA MCGOWAN & KAREN BLUMENTHAL, WHY PUNISH THE CHILDREN? A STUDY OF CHILDREN OF WOMEN PRISONERS 50–53 (1978); Genty, *supra* chap. 3, n. 61, at 1680.
75. MCGOWAN & BLUMENTHAL, *supra* chap. 3, n. 74, at 50–53; Genty, *supra* chap. 3, n. 61, at 1680.
76. *See, e.g.*, 28 U.S.C. § 994(d) (2000).
77. Kelly Bedard & Eric Helland, *The Location of Women's Prisons and the Deterrence Effect of "Harder" Time*, 24 INT'L REV. L. & ECON. 147–49 (2004). Notably, Bedard and Helland are able to show that the "harder" time actually serves a deterrent effect; so what may look like a "tax" on families may in the end be an indirect way to keep the family together. *Id.* at 148–49. They conclude: "[t]he evidence suggests that an increase in average prison distance leads to a decrease in crime. A 40-mile increase in the average distance to a female penitentiary reduces female violent crime, property crime and murder rates by 6.9, 2.3 and 13.3%, respectively." *Id.* at 165.

    These results are very provocative and suggest that a "family sensitive" location policy may actually recommend having the state place women *far away from their families* as an indirect way to deter their participation in crime. The results of Bedard and Helland's study suggest how empirical work could usefully illuminate the relationship between family ties and criminal justice. Still, it is important to acknowledge that Bedard and Helland appreciate the externalities associated with using remote prison locations for their deterrent effect and do *not* ultimately endorse using "harder" time as a way to keep families together:

    > The evidence presented in this paper suggests remote prison locations and/or restricted visitation as low cost crime deterrence mechanisms. However, our estimates do not quantify the welfare implications of this change. Increasing the distance to women's prisons (or an outright ban on visitation) has clear externalities. There is ample evidence that a mother's incarceration has adverse effects on her children. It therefore seems quite likely, although not certain, that even more severe restrictions on maternal visitation would exacerbate an already bad situation for the children of female inmates. As such, the secondary effects therefore render the long-run general equilibrium effects of prison location on crime rates ambiguous.

    Id. at 166 (citation omitted).
78. These programs are particularly important because of the disproportionate harm that incarceration can visit upon mothers and their children. For example, women are more likely to face termination of parental rights if sent to prison than men, because women are more likely to have sole custody of their children and therefore not to have ready access to another suitable caregiver.
79. 28 U.S.C. § 994(d).
80. *See, e.g.*, *supra* chap. 2, n. 70.
81. *Cf.*, *e.g.*, Bedard & Helland, *supra* chap. 3, n. 77, at 165–66.

82. Elizabeth Scott and Amitai Aviram shared the reaction that average citizens may view certain family ties benefits as ways by which the state tries to induce compliance with the overall legal regime. *Cf.* Robinson & Darley, *supra* chap. 2, n. 15, at 497–99; Robinson, *supra* chap. 2, n. 15. In other words, absent these benefits and privileges, confidence in the legitimacy of the criminal justice system would erode precipitously. In some such situations, prosecutors might end up exercising their discretion to decline exacting "full justice" because they would face the threat of jury nullification. These suggestions are provocative—as far as they go. But we think that the elimination of the unjustified family ties benefits can be explained in a moral vocabulary (accuracy, equality, crime reduction) that would resonate with much of the population. Just as government has successfully disturbed and altered social norms involving racism or sexism, so too could institutions of criminal justice shape social norms and not just uncritically reflect them. In any event, it may turn out this concern about noncompliance is exaggerated; we need empirical work to study whether jurisdictions without family ties benefits are suffering from higher crime rates than those with them, and whether those jurisdictions that have either adopted or abandoned such benefits found any noticeable differences within their own jurisdiction.
83. For example, the punishment discounts given to parents, on the one hand, rupture equality norms and, on the other hand, may work to reduce harms that young children may endure in the absence of a parent.
84. For instance, we are aware that families often help in the reintegration of offenders into society, but we doubt that families would refuse to offer that help in the absence of family-specific privileges extended during the course of investigating, prosecuting, and punishing the predicate criminal activity.

Part 2. Punishing Family Status

1. Justin Boggs, *Parents of Slain Victorville Child Receive Long Prison Terms*, DAILY PRESS, Dec. 30, 2005. For examples of other recent cases where mothers have been prosecuted for failing to protect their children from harm inflicted by another, *see also* Bill Scanlon, *Mom Guilty in Baby's Death*, ROCKY MOUNTAIN NEWS, Dec. 22, 2007 (describing the case of Molly Midyette, whose ten-week-old son died after beatings inflicted by his father); Steven Ellis, *Court Upholds Murder Conviction for Failing to Protect Son*, METROPOLITAN NEWS-ENTERPRISE, Mar. 12, 2008 (describing the case of Sylvia Torres Rolon, who was convicted of second degree murder after failing to protect her one-year-old child from a horrific night of abuse inflicted by her boyfriend).
2. We recognize that this group of burdens may fall into something of a different category than parental responsibility laws or omissions liability, in the sense that a desire to enforce a certain vision of public morality might motivate a state's decision to utilize the power of the criminal law. We think it is important to recognize, however, that the state is promoting a certain vision

of family within *both* categories of burdens, in that it is essentially trying to foster an environment in which caregiving can flourish, and that we need to consider whether the use of the criminal law in these contexts in fact effectively serves that goal. In addition, these two categories of burdens are linked in the sense that the existence of a certain family relationship is a prerequisite for imposing liability, and thus both categories warrant analysis under our framework.

3. We acknowledge that, in some instances, victims may feel that they, as well as defendants, have been harmed by family ties burdens.
4. There are some exceptions—largely those associated with incest and obligations to pay parental support—that we discuss *infra* in Chapter 5.
5. We recognize this stands at odds with current constitutional doctrine that permits promiscuous use of severe criminal sanctions. *See generally* Sherry F. Colb, *Freedom from Incarceration: Why Is This Right Different from All Other Rights?*, 69 N.Y.U. L. REV. 781 (1994); Douglas Husak, *The Criminal Law As a Last Resort*, 24 OXFORD J. LEGAL STUD. 207 (2004).
6. *See* Frontiero v. Richardson, 411 U.S. 677, 684 (1973); LINDA K. KERBER, WOMEN OF THE REPUBLIC: INTELLECT AND IDEOLOGY IN REVOLUTIONARY AMERICA 138-55 (1980).

Chapter 4. An Overview of Family Status and Criminal Justice Burdens

1. That's not to say that vicarious and omissions liability are *only* triggered in the familial context. Some states authorize vicarious liability prosecutions against corporations for the crimes of their employees and omissions liability usually encompasses various situations beyond failure to rescue a family member.
2. For those readers wondering, our view is that state statutes criminalizing polygamy raise problems to those statutes prohibiting incest between consenting and competent adults. In the absence of a marital connection to a third person, *X* may marry *Y*. In states prohibiting polygamy, *X* may not marry *Y* on account of the prior relationship *X* entered into with *Z*.
3. In addition to creating criminal liability, family status is used in some jurisdictions as a basis for inferring a breach of trust that serves as an aggravating factor at sentencing. *See, e.g.*, R. v. Gladue, [1999] 1 S.C.R. 688, 740-41 (Can.) ("the offence involved domestic violence and a breach of the trust inherent in a spousal relationship. That aggravating factor must be taken into account in the sentencing").
4. *See* Diana Marrero & Shana Gruskin, *Mom Arrested in Child's Death; Police: Woman Ignored Danger by Leaving Daughter with Boyfriend*, FT. LAUDERDALE SUN-SENTINEL, June 21, 2002, at 1B. One of the fascinating aspects of this case is that the boyfriend was eventually acquitted in the child's death, so only the mother's omission was punished. *See* Susannah Nesmith, *3 Years Later, Man Cleared in Baby's Death*, MIAMI HERALD, Feb. 11, 2006, at B4.

5. WAYNE R. LAFAVE, CRIMINAL LAW § 6.2 (4th ed. 2003); *see also* David Hyman, *Rescue Without Law: An Empirical Perspective on the Duty to Rescue*, 84 TEX. L. REV. 653, 655 (2006) ("The common law approach is straightforward. Absent a limited number of specific exceptions, there is not duty to rescue, regardless of the ease of rescue and consequences of non-rescue.")
6. A very small number of states have adopted so-called "Good Samaritan" statutes, imposing criminal liability in limited circumstances upon those who fail to rescue persons in emergency situations. *See, e.g.*, VT. STAT. ANN. tit. 12, § 519; R.I. GEN. LAWS § 11-56-1 (1998).
7. 308 F.2d 307, 310 (D.C. Cir. 1962).
8. *See* State v. Walden 293 S.E.2d 780, 786 (1982) (denying "that parents have the legal duty to place themselves in danger of death or great bodily harm in coming to the aid of their children"); DRESSLER, *supra* chap. 1, n. 44, at 114; Andrew Ashworth, *The Scope of Criminal Liability for Omissions*, 105 L.Q. REV. 424 (1989) (discussing the requirement that the rescue must be an easy one).
9. Larry Alexander, *Criminal Liability for Omissions: An Inventory of Issues, in* CRIMINAL LAW THEORY: DOCTRINES OF THE GENERAL PART (S. Shute & A. Simester eds., 2002); *see, e.g.*, R. v. Conde, (1867) 10 Cox Crim. 547, 549 (Cent. Crim. Ct.).
10. At common law, other status relationships could trigger a duty to rescue as well, such as the duty of a ship captain to the passengers. *See generally* LAFAVE, 1 SUBST. CRIM. L. § 6.2 (2007); State v. Mally, 366 P.2d 868 (Mont. 1961).
11. *See* Alexander, *supra* chap. 4, n. 9.
12. *See, e.g.*, Muehe v. State, 646 N.E.2d 980 (Ind. 1995); *see also* Michelle S. Jacobs, *Requiring Battered Women Die: Murder Liability for Mothers Under Failure to Protect Statutes*, 88 J. CRIM. L. & CRIMINOLOGY 579, 586–87 (1998) (describing parents' duties to their children).
13. *See, e.g.*, State v. Schultz, 457 N.E.2d 336 (Ohio 1982) (upholding involuntary manslaughter conviction for mother who failed to protect her child during brutal beating by live-in boyfriend); Smith v. State, 408 N.E.2d 614 (Ind. 1980) (upholding conviction of involuntary manslaughter for mother who failed to protect her son from repeated abuse by her live-in boyfriend).
14. *See, e.g.*, People v. Beardsley, 150 Mich. 206 (1907).
15. *See* State ex rel. Kuntz v. Mont. Thirteenth Judicial Dist. Court, 995 P.2d 951, 956 (Mont. 2000).
16. *See* Alexander, *supra* chap. 4, n. 9.
17. *Compare* Leet v. State, 595 So. 2d 959, 963 (Fla. App. 1991) (holding that the live-in boyfriend of a child's mother owed a legal duty to the child to prevent abuse by the mother after establishing a "family-like relationship") *with* State v. Miranda, 878 A.2d 1118, 1131 (Conn. 2005) (overruling lower court's conclusion that live-in boyfriend had duty to rescue his girlfriend's child despite years of a "familial relationship with victim's mother;" the problem of not using crisp legal categories is it will be too tempting to assign liability to "other members of the extended family, to longtime caregivers who are not related to either the parent or victim, to regular babysitters, and to others with regular and extended relationships with the abusing parent and the abused victim").

18. *E.g.*, Cornell v. State, 159 Fla. 687, 32 So. 2d 610 (1947) (conviction of grandmother for manslaughter by gross negligence for death of grandchild turned on facts independent of status).
19. Jill Smolowe, *Parenting on Trial: A Couple Is Fined for a Son's Crimes*, TIME, May 20, 1996, at 50.
20. *Id.*; *see also* Pamela K. Graham, Note, *Parental Responsibility Laws: Let the Punishment Fit the Crime*, 33 LOY. L.A. L. REV. 1719, 1740-41 (2000).
21. *See* Leila Atassi, *Parental-Responsibility Law Strikes a Chord: Maple Heights' Stance Draws Broad Response*, CLEV. PLAIN DEALER, Apr. 30, 2006, at B1 (discussing widespread interest in a new parental responsibility law); *see also* Naomi Cahn, *Pragmatic Questions About Parental Liability Statutes*, 1996 WIS. L. REV. 399; Linda Chapin, *Out of Control? The Uses and Abuses of Parental Liability Laws to Control Juvenile Delinquency in the United States*, 37 SANTA CLARA L. REV. 621 (1997); J. Herbie DiFonzo, *Parental Responsibility for Juvenile Crime*, 80 OR. L. REV. 1 (2001); Susan S. Kuo, *A Little Privacy, Please: Should We Punish Parents for Teenage Sex?*, 89 KY. L.J. 135 (2000); Eve M. Brank et al., *Parental Responsibility Statutes: An Organization and Policy Implications*, 7 J.L. & FAM. STUD. 1 (2005); Tammy Thurman, *Parental Responsibility Laws: Are They the Answer to Juvenile Delinquency?*, 5 J.L. & FAM. STUD. 99 (2003).
22. More often, however, parents are targets via other avenues for the misdeeds of their children: "statutory civil penalties for property damage caused by their children, eviction from public housing if criminal activity has occurred in their homes, and increased exposure to civil lawsuits filed by victims of youth violence." DiFonzo, *supra* chap. 4, n. 21, at 3. A survey of the civil liability regimes around the country can be found in Brank et al., *supra* chap. 4, n. 21. For a discussion of these efforts to impose tort liability on parents for the acts of their children, see Rhonda V. Magee Andrews, *The Justice of Parental Accountability: Hypothetical Disinterested Citizens and Real Victims' Voices in the Debate Over Expanded Parental Liability*, 75 TEMP. L. REV. 375 (2002). *See also* Chapin, *supra* chap. 4, n. 21, at 629–638 (focusing on criminal statutes).
23. *See* Jerry E. Tyler & Thomas W. Segady, *Parental Liability Laws: Rationale, Theory and Effectiveness*, 37 SOC. SCI. J. 79, 79 (2000) (noting that the Massachusetts Stubborn Child Law of 1646 authorized the imposition of fines on parents whose children were caught stealing); *see also* Cahn, *supra* chap. 4, n. 21, at 405–06 (noting that "[s]tates have been enacting laws holding parents criminally liable for the delinquent acts of their children for almost a century," primarily through the enactment of statutes making it a criminal offense to contribute to the delinquency of a minor). Cahn adds that parents were frequently prosecuted in juvenile courts under these laws during the first half of the twentieth century. *Id.* at 406–07.
24. Leslie Joan Harris. *An Empirical Study of Parental Responsibility Laws: Sending Messages. But What Kind and to Whom*?, 2006 UTAH L. REV. 5, 6–7 ("This kind of law is more than one hundred years old, and lawmakers seem to 'discover' the idea of using parental responsibility laws to prevent teenage crime every couple of decades or so.").

25. Paul W. Schmidt, Note, *Dangerous Children and the Regulated Family: The Shifting Focus of Parental Responsibility Laws*, 73 N.Y.U. L. REV. 667, 675 n.62 (1998).
26. *Id.*
27. *See, e.g.*, N.M. STAT. ANN. § 30-6-3; OR. REV. STAT. ANN. § 163.577(1) (West 2003).
28. *Id.*; *see also* Brank et al., *supra* chap. 4, n. 21, at 9–10 (giving examples from Georgia and Iowa).
29. N.Y. PENAL LAW § 260.10 (criminal liability for parent who "fails or refuses to exercise reasonable diligence" in controlling child).
30. *See* Act of June 21, 1995, No. 702, § 2, 1995 La. Acts 1854, 1855-56 (codified at LA. REV. STAT. ANN. § 14:92.2 (West Supp. 1997)) ("Improper supervision of a minor by parent or legal guardian"). *See generally* LAFAVE, 2 SUBST. CRIM. L. § 13.4.
31. Schmidt, *supra* chap. 4, n. 25.
32. *See* OR. REV. STAT. § 163.577(1).
33. *See* Maple Heights Parental Responsibility Ordinance No. 648.20; No. 698.02 (providing for sentence of 180 days in prison).
34. Maple Heights v. Ephraim, No. 90237, slip op. at 7, (Ohio Ct. App. Sept. 11, 2008).
35. *See* Silverton, Oregon Criminal Code § 9.24, *available at* http://www.codepublishing.com/OR/silverton/silver09.html#9.24 (last visited Oct. 1, 2008).
36. *See* Leila Atassi, *Parents to Pay for Youths' Crimes*, CLEV. PLAIN DEALER, Apr. 19, 2006, at B1 (quoting Mayor Hector).
37. *See* IDAHO CODE § 32-1301 (authorizing counties and cities to establish ordinances based on failure to supervise a child). The Idaho legislature authorized strict liability but permitted affirmative defenses based on certain factors: whether the parent was the victim of the juvenile misdeed; whether the parent reported the misconduct; and whether the parent took reasonable precautions to supervise the child.
38. We have seen some estimates in the literature suggesting that in the last decade there were about seventeen states with criminal parental responsibility laws. But these numbers are misleading because some of the statutes cited are just general "contributing to the delinquency of a minor" statutes, which apply to all adults, not just parents or legal guardians.
39. *See* OR. REV. STAT. § 163.577; LA. REV. STAT. ANN. § 14:92.2. Louisiana subjects parents to up to six months' imprisonment for permitting an unlicensed minor driver to drive a vehicle if the minor ends up involved in an accident that resulted in death or serious bodily injury to another person. The statute also makes it a crime for a parent, "through criminal negligence," to permit "the minor to associate with a person known by the parent" to be a gang member, a convicted felon, or a drug dealer or user. A parent convicted under this particular provision faces up to thirty days in a jail and a $250 fine. *See* LA. REV. STAT. ANN. § 14:92.2 (defining the crime of the improper supervision of a minor by a parent or legal guardian). The statute allows a parent to escape liability under these latter provisions if the parent sought assistance from various agencies in modifying the child's behavior or if the parent referred "the child to appropriate treatment or corrective facilities." ***Id.***

40. *See, e.g.*, Corpus Christi, Tex., Code § 33-48 (1985) (parental duties include "[k]eeping illegal drugs and illegal firearms out of the home; [p]roviding reasonable supervision of the minor child; and [f]orbidding the minor from keeping stolen property, or illegally possessing firearms or illegal drugs" (subsection letters omitted)); Elgin, Ill., Mun. Code tit. 10, ch. 10.66 (1995) (punishing parents who "willfully, knowingly or recklessly permit any minor" to possess "illegal drugs or drug paraphernalia," or "commit an act tending to break the peace," violate curfew, or "engage in street gang related criminal activity"); *see also* Peter Applebome, *Parents Face Consequences As Children's Misdeeds Rise*, N.Y. TIMES, Apr. 10, 1996, at A1 (observing proliferation of "dozens" of ordinances in towns near Chicago in "last two years").
41. *E.g.*, Salt Lake City, Utah, Code §§ 11.60.010-.060 (1995); St. Clair Shores, Mich., Code of Ordinances § 20.565.
42. *See* Schmidt, *supra* chap. 4, n. 25, at 682 n.102 (1998) (providing examples).
43. *See* State v. Akers, 400 A.2d 38 (N.H. 1979); Doe v. Trenton, 362 A.2d 1200, 1203 (N.J. 1976).
44. *See* Akers, 400 A.2d at 39.
45. Trenton, 362 A.2d at 1203.
46. Williams v. Garcetti, 853 P.2d 507 (Cal. 1993).
47. *See* CAL. PENAL CODE § 272 (1988 amendment). The amendment was enacted in response to the perception that California was in the throes of a "gang crisis." *See* Williams, 853 P.2d at 510.
48. *Id.* at 509. The privacy challenge was dropped over the course of the litigation and not ruled upon by the California Supreme Court.
49. *See id.* at 511. The Court rather summarily rejected the overbreadth challenge. *See id.* at 516–17.
50. *See id.* at 513.
51. *See* Harris, *supra* chap. 4, n. 24, at 17 ("Anecdotal evidence shows these laws are almost never enforced and soon fall out of favor, only to be rediscovered in a few years. The next section of this Article reports on an empirical study of the enforcement of parental responsibility laws in Oregon that supports the anecdotal evidence."). Harris' study of Oregon shows that about one-third of the municipalities participating in the survey had parental responsibility laws, but they were rarely, if ever, enforced. *Id.* at 22–23.
52. *See* Schmidt, *supra* chap. 4, n. 25, at 684 (citing as example OR. REV. STAT. § 163. 577(3)-(4)).
53. Jeff Jacoby, *Hypocrisy on Adult Consent*, BOSTON GLOBE, Aug. 28, 2005, at C11 (quoting sentencing judge).
54. *Id. See also* Muth v. Frank, 412 F.3d 808 (7th Cir. 2005).
55. *See* Courtney Cahill, *Same Sex Marriage, Slippery Slope Rhetoric, and the Politics of Disgust: A Critical Perspective on Contemporary Family Discourse and the Incest Taboo*, 99 N.W.U. L. REV. 1543, 1546 (2005) ("[T]he very term 'incest' is a powerful way to provoke an almost visceral disgust toward any relationship to which it is compared.").
56. People v. Baker, 69 Cal. 2d 44, 49 (1968); State v. Scion Barefoot, 31 S.C.L. 209, 228–29 (S.C. App. 1845) (stating that at English common law, incest did not void

a marriage but made it voidable); Graham Hughes, *The Crime of Incest*, 55 J. CRIM. L. CRIMINOLOGY & POLICE SCI. 322, 323–25 (1964).

57. According to one recent survey, adult consensual consanguineous pairings are not prohibited in Rhode Island, Ohio, and New Jersey. Note, *Inbred Obscurity: Improving Incest Laws in the Shadow of the "Sexual Family,"* 119 HARV. L. REV. 2464, 2469–70 (2006) (discussing the three American jurisdictions) [hereinafter Note, *Inbred Obscurity*].
58. States can also prohibit marriage between various pairings of relatives through their domestic relations statutes, even if they do not attach criminal penalties to the relationship. *See* Margaret Mahoney, *A Legal Definition of the Stepfamily: The Example of Incest Regulation*, 8 B.Y.U. J. PUB. L. 21, 27 (1993) (noting "the ban on incestuous relationships is enforced under two types of state regulations": first, the civil laws denying recognition to marriages between certain relatives, and second, the criminal statutes that "punish attempted marriages, as well as sexual activity outside of marriage"). We focus here on the criminal statutes.
59. 41 AM. JUR. 2D Incest § 11 n.2 (providing citations). The defendant's awareness relates to his knowledge of the relationship, not his knowledge of the law that punishes incest.
60. Note, *Inbred Obscurity*, *supra* chap. 4, n. 57, at 2465 ("The criminal incest laws in the vast majority of states apply to [consensual] incest as well by making the crime distinct from the crime of rape.").
61. *See* Brett McDonnell, *Is Incest Next?*, 10 CARDOZO WOMEN'S L.J. 337 (2004) (compiling the various state laws on incest). Ohio only targets parental figures for criminal liability for incest, and New Jersey does not penalize the parties to incest when both are 18 or older. Note, *Inbred Obscurity*, *supra* chap. 4, n. 57, at 2469 nn.38–39.
62. *Id.* at 349.
63. *See, e.g.*, State v. Johnson, 670 NW.2d 802, 813 (Neb. App. 2003) (discussing Nebraska statute).
64. *See* McDonnell, *supra* chap. 4, n. 61 (compiling the various state laws on incest).
65. *Id.*
66. *See id.*
67. Elise Soukup, *After Gay Marriage, Polygamy Activism Rises*, NEWSWEEK, Mar. 20, 2006, at 52.
68. *See* 11 AM. JUR. 2D Bigamy § 1. Interestingly, some states don't require *X* to actually marry *Y* in order to be guilty of bigamy; extramarital cohabitation suffices to trigger liability. *See* Elizabeth F. Emens, *Monogamy's Law: Compulsory Monogamy and Polyamorous Existence*, 29 N.Y.U. REV. L. & SOC. CHANGE 277, 308 n.158 (2004). Some states also punish the single person who knowingly marries the spouse of another person. *See* 11 AM. JUR. 2D Bigamy § at §1-3. This type of legislation is not a family ties burden as we define it because the state is not treating defendant *X* any differently on account of *X*'s family status or connection; rather, it's because of *X*'s would-be spouse's prior family connection. That's not to say such legislation does not raise its own problems, but we are focused on those statutes that place burdens on persons because of *their* familial status.

69. We use bigamy to refer to the criminal laws prohibiting the practice of polygamy, or taking on more than one spouse, regardless of gender. For a collection of bigamy statutes, *see* Emens, *supra* chap. 4, n. 68, at 290 n.51.
70. *See, e.g.*, Kirk Johnson & Gretel C. Kovach, *Daughter of Sect Leader Gets Additional Protection*, N.Y. TIMES, June 4, 2008, http://www.nytimes.com/2008/06/04/us/04polygamy.html (discussing conviction of FLDS sect leader, Warren Jeffs).
71. Jonathan Turley, *Of Lust and the Law*, WASH. POST, Sept. 5, 2004, at B1.
72. This qualification is important because if anti-fornication laws exist in a given jurisdiction then adultery is not really a family ties burden but a redundancy—assuming that fornication is sexual relations between non-married partners and that adultery is defined as sexual relations between a married person and another person who is not the spouse. For our particular purpose, we are focused on adultery laws that operate in jurisdictions in which fornication (defined as sexual relations outside marriage) is not prohibited. To the extent that jurisdictions impinge on all consensual sexual relations outside marriage between mature individuals, there is no specific family ties burden, but it goes without saying that our liberal commitments would trigger hostility to such laws, which persist in various forms in ten states and the District of Columbia. *See* Emens, *supra* chap. 4, n. 68, at 290 n.49 (collecting statutes).
73. Adultery laws also occasionally raise issues like those discussed *supra* chap. 4, n. 68 because some jurisdictions retain laws punishing an unmarried person from engaging in sexual relations with a married person. Our analysis is restricted to those laws punishing only those married persons engaged in extramarital sex.
74. *See* Emens, *supra* chap. 4, n. 68, at 299 n.107 (citing study reporting that 35 percent of American married men and 20 percent of American married women have adulterous sex).
75. *See id.* at 290 n.49 (collecting the statutes of twenty-three states plus the District of Columbia that continue to criminalize adultery).
76. Lynn D. Wardle, *Parental Infidelity and the "No-Harm" Rule in Custody Litigation*, 52 CATH. UNIV. L. REV. 81, 95 n.57 (2002) ("According to the Washington Post/Kaiser/Harvard Survey Project in 1998, eighty-eight percent of Americans believe that adultery is immoral, while only eleven percent find it morally acceptable.").
77. *See* Emens, *supra* chap. 4, n. 68, at 290, n. 49.
78. *See* John F. Kelly, *Virginia Adultery Case Roils Divorce Industry: Conviction Draws Attention to Little Used Law*, WASH. POST, Dec. 1, 2003, at B1, B8; John F. Kelly, *Va. Man Challenges State's Adultery Law; ACLU Joins Appeal, Cites Privacy Issue*, WASH. POST, Feb. 26, 2004, at B8.
79. *See* Melissa Ash Haggard, *Adultery: A Comparison of Military Law and State Law and the Controversy This Causes Under Our Constitution and Criminal Justice System*, 37 BRANDEIS L.J. 469, 469–70, 476–77 (1998); James M. Winner, *Beds with Sheets but No Covers: The Right to Privacy and the Military's Regulation of Adultery*, 31 LOY. L.A. L. REV. 1073, 1073–74 (1998).
80. *See generally* C. Quince Hopkins, *Rank Matters but Should Marriage? Adultery, Fraternization, and Honor in the Military*, 9 UCLA WOMEN'S L.J. 177 (1999);

Military Gets New Rules on Adultery: It's Still a Crime, but Not All Cases Will Be Prosecuted, CHI. TRIB., July 29, 1998, *available at* 1998 WL 2880547.

81. *See, e.g.*, Bradley Graham, *Military Leaders Worry Privately About Impact: Some Troops Offended by Double Standard*, WASH. POST, Sept. 15, 1998, at A10, *available at* 1998 WL16556190.
82. *Cf.* Christopher R. Leslie, *Creating Criminals: The Injuries Inflicted by "Unenforced" Sodomy Laws*, 35 HARV. C.R.-C.L. L. REV. 103 (2000) (arguing that even unenforced laws are not harmless because they create a criminal class).
83. Outside of Massachusetts and Connecticut, same-sex marriage is illegal in the United States, and thus adultery laws probably apply as a class only against those who are married, i.e., heterosexuals. Jesse McKinley & Laurie Goodstein, *Bans in 3 States on Gay Marriage*, N.Y. TIMES, Nov. 5, 2008, at A1. In light of the recent events surrounding Proposition 8 in California, the status of same-sex marriage is still unresolved in that state, most especially for the 18,000 same-sex couples who were legally married before the passage of Proposition 8. Bob Egelko, *Anti-gay Marriage Group Steps Up for Prop. 8*, S.F. CHRON., Nov. 11, 2008, at B-2.
84. Press Release, Office of the Governor, State of Alaska, Parent Sentenced for Failure to Pay Child Support (Feb. 9, 1999), *available at* http://csed.state.ak.us./PressReleases/fisher.html.
85. *Id.*
86. Obviously, the failure to pay the government one's tax liabilities is criminal. But private parties cannot generally trigger the criminal justice system to enforce debts outside the child support context.
87. *See* Posting of Nate Oman to Concurring Opinions, Debt, Status and Fatherhood, http://concurringopinions.com/archives/2007/05/ (May 25, 2007, 12:34 EST); *see also* Ronald K. Henry, *Child Support at a Crossroads: When the Real World Intrudes upon Academics and Advocates*, 33 FAM. L.Q. 235, 240 (1999) (stating that "the collection tactics practiced for child support debt are tolerated for no other form of debt in American society").
88. 18 U.S.C. § 228 (2000).
89. Deadbeat Parents Punishment Act, Pub. L. No. 105-187, 112 Stat. 618 (1998).
90. SCOTT SUSSMAN & COREY MATHER, CENTER ON FATHERS, FAMILIES, AND PUBLIC POLICY, CRIMINAL STATUTES FOR NON-PAYMENT OF CHILD SUPPORT BY STATE 1 (2003), www.cffpp.org/publications/pdfs/crimstat.pdf. States have also tried a number of other measures to enforce child support orders, from garnishing wages to suspending drivers' licenses to booting cars. *See* Solangel Maldonado, *Deadbeat or Deadbroke: Redefining Child Support for Poor Fathers*, 39 U.C. DAVIS L. REV. 991, 1000 (2006) (describing various efforts); *see also* Jennifer Goulah, Comment, *The Cart Before the Horse: Michigan Jumps the Gun in Jailing Deadbeat Dads*, 83 U. DET. MERCY L. REV. 479, 486 (2006) (describing how some states post "wanted" posters of deadbeat dads and others send birthday cards, reminding parents of their child's birthday and urging them to pay).
91. *See generally* Ann Britton, *America's Best Kept Secret: An Adult Child's Duty to Support Aged Parents*, 26 CAL. W. L. REV. 351, 351–52 (1990); Shannon Frank Edelstone,

Filial Responsibility: Can the Legal Duty to Support Our Parents Be Effectively Enforced, 36 FAM. L.Q. 501 (2002); Katie Wise, *Caring for Our Parents in an Aging World: Sharing Public and Private Responsibility for the Elderly*, 5 J. LEGIS. & PUB. POL'Y 563 (2002); Andrea Rickles-Jordan, *Filial Responsibility: A Survey Across Time and Oceans*, 9 MARQ. ELDER'S ADVISOR 183 (2007); Matthew Pakula, *A Federal Filial Responsibility Statute: A Uniform Tool to Help Combat the Wave of Indigent Elderly*, 39 FAM. L.Q. 859, 860 (2005); Seymour Moskowitz, *Filial Responsibility Statutes: Legal and Policy Considerations*, 9 J.L. & POL'Y 709, 710 (2001).

92. *See* CAL. PENAL CODE § 270c (1999); CONN. GEN. STAT. ANN. § 53a-4 (2007); IND. CODE ANN. § 35-46-1-7 (2004); KY. REV. STAT. ANN. § 530.050 (2007) (Kentucky); MD. CODE, FAM. LAW §§ 13-101, 13-102, 13-103 (2006); MASS. GEN. LAWS ch. 273, § 20 (2000); MONT. CODE ANN. § 40- 6-301 (2007); N.C. GEN. STAT. § 14-326.1 (2005); OHIO REV. CODE § 2919.21 (2003); R.I. GEN. LAWS §§ 15-10- 1 (2006); VT. STAT. ANN. tit. 15, §§ 202, 203 (2006); VA. CODE ANN. § 20- 88 (2007). *See generally* Rickles-Jordan, *supra* chap. 4, n. 91.
93. *See* Terrance A. Kline, *A Rational Role for Filial Responsibility Laws in Modern Society?*, 26 FAM. L.Q. 195, 196 (1992) (noting that "no state appears to enforce" filial responsibility laws).
94. *See* CAL. PENAL CODE § 270c (2008).
95. MASS. GEN. LAWS ch. 273, § 20 (2007).

Chapter 5. A Framework for Analyzing Family Ties Burdens

1. *Cf.* JOHN RAWLS, A THEORY OF JUSTICE 10-15 (rev. ed. 1999).
2. *Cf. e.g.*, R. v. Gladue, [1999] 1 S.C.R. 688, 740-41 (Can.) (discussing the breach of trust associated with violence against one's spouse as an aggravating factor in determining culpability).
3. *But cf.* Jennifer M. Collins, *Crime and Parenthood: The Uneasy Case for Prosecuting Negligent Parents*, 100 NW. U. L. REV. 807 (2006) (discussing results of a study showing that in practice, parents who lose children because of their negligent conduct are often treated more leniently than unrelated caregivers who cause death).
4. As we discuss in the next Chapter, one can design policies to accommodate these concerns in several ways.
5. *See* FLETCHER, *supra* chap. 2, n. 9, at 3 (1993).
6. *See* Meir Dan-Cohen, *Responsibility and the Boundaries of Self*, 105 HARV. L. REV. 959 (1992).
7. *See* Regan, *supra* intro., n. 24; REGAN, *supra* chap. 2, n. 11.
8. *See* Hills, *Constitutional Rights*, *supra* chap. 2, n. 14, at 147.
9. Of course, in cases in which family ties burdens are liability-creating statutes on the basis of status—such as bigamy, incest, or nonpayment of child support—these family burdens are creating a new class of criminals: persons without family status

engaged in this conduct would not be criminals. But this kind of criminogenesis is different from the way in which some of the family ties benefits created incentives to perpetrate misconduct that *would* be punishable regardless of the defendant's family status.

There is also a plausible story to tell in which family ties burdens increase systematic inaccuracy in the criminal justice system. Because proving the elements of these crimes will often turn family members against one another, it may be harder to achieve truth-telling by relevant players, increasing judicial error rates. Yet this is not the sort of inaccuracy we generally had in mind in the first Part of the book; we weren't talking about systemic inaccuracy there but inaccuracy in individual cases.

10. *See generally* Markel, *Against Mercy*, *supra* chap. 2, n. 57.
11. On heteronormativity, *see, e.g.*, Nancy J. Knauer, *Heteronormativity and Federal Tax Policy*, 101 W. VA. L. REV. 129 (1998).
12. *See generally* Laura T. Kessler, *Transgressive Caregiving*, 33 FLA. ST. U. L. REV. 1 (2005).
13. *See, e.g.*, Katherine M. Franke, *Theorizing Yes: An Essay on Feminism, Law, and Desire*, 101 COLUM. L. REV. 181, 183–84 (2001); Symposium, *The Structures of Care Work*, 76 CHI.-KENT L. REV. 1389 (2001); Martha T. McCluskey, *Caring for Workers*, 55 ME. L. REV. 313 (2003); *cf.* Sasha Roseneil, *Why We Should Care About Friends: An Argument for Queering the Care Imaginary in Social Policy*, 3 SOC. POL'Y & SOC'Y 409, 411 (2004); Mary Becker, *Care and Feminists*, 17 WIS. WOMEN'S L.J. 57 (2002).
14. *Cf.* Larry Alexander, *Consent, Punishment, and Proportionality*, 15 PHIL. & PUB. AFFAIRS 178 (1986) (analyzing a "consensual theory of punishment" that "substitute[s] consent for moral desert as the justification for imposing punishment on specific individuals").
15. *Cf.* ERIC POSNER, LAW AND SOCIAL NORMS 24 (2000) (discussing how an actor's willingness to bear certain costs or consequences can be a way of "establishing or preserving one's reputation").
16. *See, e.g.*, Williams v. State, 664 P.2d 137, 139 (Cal. 1983) ("As a rule, one has no duty [under tort law] to come to the aid of another."); 3 FOWLER V. HARPER ET AL., THE LAW OF TORTS § 18.6 (2d ed. 1986); WAYNE R. LAFAVE, CRIMINAL LAW § 6.2 (4th ed. 2003).
17. The metaphor here reaches a bit too far since admittedly we don't live life as single adults whom the state is otherwise and implicitly always watching closely, ready to step in at any point as part of its own duty to rescue or support. Nonetheless, with every marriage or choice to parent, the actors are explicitly or implicitly stating their intention to care and support the other person in the relationship.
18. For disturbing counter-examples, consider the allegations made against Warren Jeffs, who was charged in a scheme of forcing young girls into marriages with older men, some of whom were closely related to the brides. *See, e.g.*, John Dougherty, *Polygamist Is Indicted in Assault of a Child*, N.Y. TIMES, July 23, 2008, at A14; John Dougherty & Kirk Johnson, *Sect Leader Is Convicted as an Accomplice to Rape*, N.Y. TIMES, Sept. 26, 2007, at A18.

19. *See generally* HENDRIK HARTOG, MAN AND WIFE IN AMERICA: A HISTORY (2000) (charting changes in law and its effects on the American institution of marriage).
20. *See, e.g.*, Ruthann Robson, *Assimilation, Marriage, and Lesbian Liberation*, 75 TEMP. L. REV. 709, 777-800 (2002) (explaining why marriage might be viewed as compulsory).
21. *See* Rhonda V. Magee Andrews, *The Justice of Parental Accountability: Hypothetical Disinterested Citizens and Real Victims' Voices in the Debate over Expanded Parental Liability*, 75 TEMPLE L. REV. 375, 415 (2002) ("Parents, generally speaking, have made a choice to parent... This choice, in most cases, represents voluntary action....").
22. Some have argued that women have little freedom to reject society's expectations that they will choose to mother. *See, e.g.*, ELIZABETH BARTHOLET, FAMILY BONDS: ADOPTION, INFERTILITY AND THE NEW WORLD OF CHILD PRODUCTION 35 (1993) ("Women are taught from birth that their identities are inextricably linked with their capacity for pregnancy and childbirth and that this capacity is inextricably linked with mothering."); Robson, *supra* chap. 5, n. 20, at 814. Others may perceive a religious obligation to procreate and parent despite their desire to do otherwise.
23. *See* Ethan J. Leib, *A Man's Right to Choose (an Abortion?)*, 28 LEGAL TIMES 60 (2005) [hereinafter Leib, *Right to Choose*]. Although it is undoubtedly true that most "deadbeat" fathers are not individuals who had children against their will—in the sense that they attempted to use birth control, had semen stolen from them in a sexual act without vaginal penetration, or were encouraged in sexual situations by partners who were dishonest about their fertility status—it is still likely true that many fathers have support obligations to children that they affirmatively would have chosen not to have were the reproductive freedom choice solely within their discretion.
24. Michael M. O'Hear, *Yes to Nondiscrimination, No to New Forms of Criminal Liability: A Response to Collins, Leib, and Markel*, 88 B.U. L. REV. 1437 (2008)
25. Roderick M. Hills, Jr., *Do Families Need Special Rules of Criminal Law?*, 88 B.U. L. REV. 1426 (2008) [hereinafter Hills, *Families*].
26. 18 U.S.C. §1346.
27. We do not disagree with Professors Hills and O'Hear that even paradigmatic cases of choice or consent in relationships—like the parent-child and spouse-spouse relationship—leave us with line drawing problems in some individual cases. Since we think of our analysis as primarily targeted at legislators designing these types of liabilities, we think the arguments of Professors Hills and O'Hear trying to undermine the choice involved with being a parent are perfectly admissible to that audience. Still, we continue to think that, difficulties notwithstanding, we can impute voluntariness to the parent-child relationship in a world where access to birth control, abortion, and adoption exist. Professor Hills may be right that there are implicit "normative goals that lead us so easily to infer that consent exists" in these relationships. *See id.* But that does not vitiate our understanding of them as voluntary nor does it undermine our attribution of meaning and value to that voluntariness, complicated though that

voluntariness may be. *See generally* Ethan J. Leib, *Responsibility and Social/Political Choices About Choice*, 25 LAW & PHIL. 453 (2006) [hereinafter Leib, *Responsibility*]. Moreover, whatever problems there are with imputing voluntariness to parenthood, three of the seven burdens—adultery, bigamy, and duty to rescue—are also implicated in the spousal context, where imputing voluntariness is generally less troublesome.

28. The age of the person matters as does the mental competence; we can imagine excluding from criminal liability those whose competence was below a minimum standard.
29. We use the term *covenants* instead of contracts, because we do not think there has to be bilateral exchange or consideration to make the declaration of intent to care for another legally binding in this context.
30. One of us has written that an opt-out should be available to fathers before birth under certain circumstances. *See* Leib, *Right to Choose*, *supra* chap. 5, n. 23. But this is a very special case—and it presumes a lack of consent on the part of the father of ever entering the relationship of father-child. Obviously, different concerns are presented when an adult consents to care for a child—and then attempts to withdraw such consent.
31. For a provocative discussion of what parents owe their children (which also explains why parents cannot opt out), *see* Elizabeth S. Scott & Robert E. Scott, *Parents As Fiduciaries*, 81 VA. L. REV. 2401 (1995). One of us has also argued for a mandatory duty to rescue for friends within tort law. *See* Leib, *Friendship*, *supra* chap. 3, n. 23, at 685–87. Because of the liberty interests implicated by the criminal law, it does seem useful to have a registry for these purposes.
32. For more details on how one such registry could function, *see, e.g.*, David L. Chambers, *For the Best of Friends and for Lovers of All Sorts, A Status Other than Marriage*, 76 NOTRE DAME L. REV. 1347 (2001). Vermont and Hawaii already have "reciprocal beneficiary" statutes that cover some of this territory. *See* HAW. REV. STAT. ANN. §§ 572c-1 to -7 (LexisNexis 2005); VT. STAT. ANN. tit. 15, §§ 1301–06 (2002). To our mind, the state could create a legal registry that could easily be configured to signal who is in one's circle of care and what obligations one has assumed.
33. *See, e.g.*, Marin Roger Scordato, *Understanding the Absence of a Duty to Reasonably Rescue in American Tort Law*, 87 TUL. L. REV. 1447, 1452-55 (2008). We may disagree with the no-duty-to-rescue pattern for other reasons, but if we are to have it and its exceptions, as they are, the doctrine should at least be operationalized in a way that better promotes the underlying interests.
34. O'Hear, *supra* chap. 5, n. 24.
35. By rejecting unilateral voluntariness, it's unclear whether Professor O'Hear would also forbid bilateral exchanges that conventionally create omissions liability, such as when *X* hires *Y* to be his private nurse. There is also an irony here: O'Hear gives us a hard time for purportedly *expanding* criminal law liability, but it is his alternative model of "vulnerability and proximity" without a voluntariness

side-constraint that might very well expand liabilities even further than our model.

36. So, for example, when children grow up, there might not be a basis for uncritically extending these duties anymore, at least according to Professor Markel. But to Professors Collins and Leib, there are some situations in which the vulnerability persists, such as with incest. Yet, even in these cases, the voluntariness of the relationship still plays a role too in assessing whether it makes sense to criminalize status-based obligations.
37. Given the tradeoffs involved, we are open-minded about a general duty to perform costless rescues. We recognize that such a law would violate our voluntariness requirement but we are less concerned about that prospect because a *general* duty to rescue would not use status-based characteristics to impose criminal liability, our principal concern in this book.
38. We put aside the standard cases in omissions liability in which *X* creates the peril to *Y* or *X* waves *Z* away from rescuing *Y*. But one standard case, that of contract, does warrant more emphasis. We were puzzled by Professor Hills's suggestion that the criminal law of omissions treats families differently from contractually bound "providers of caregiving services." Hills, *Families, supra* chap. 5, n. 25. This is not a correct statement of the law, as we discussed in Chapter 4. If someone hired a nurse or even a neighbor for the purpose of caregiving, that contract would in fact be a sufficient basis for criminal liability in many jurisdictions if that person failed to perform an easy rescue. In some sense, that person is no different than *X* who waves *Z* away from rescuing *Y*.
39. We acknowledge Professor O'Hear's concern that the opt-in registry discussed in the piece is unlikely to be widely used, especially among the lower socioeconomic strata of society. *See* O'Hear, *supra* chap. 5, n. 24. That, perhaps, shows a limit of the registry. But the fact that not all poor homosexual couples may enjoy the *ex ante* benefit of a duty to rescue via a registry is not itself a reason to deny that benefit to those poor homosexual couples who do (or, more importantly, their children). Thus, something like the registry is still necessary to avoid the facial discrimination and inequality that results without it. Moreover, we are somewhat puzzled at why the registry would not provide sufficient information to subscribing parties about their duties, as O'Hear laments. *See id.* Signing up is actually quite likely to force that information—and would furnish the state with the opportunity to instruct parties about their responsibilities.
40. Hills, *supra* chap. 5, n. 25.
41. *See supra* chap. 2; Markel, Collins & Leib, *Family Ties, supra* chap. 1, n. 161, at 1187–88.
42. We should note that one can be a liberal about the criminal justice system—meaning here, concerned with consent—but status oriented in other areas of the law, such as family or civil law. More importantly, to adopt a moral theory about obligation that is non-liberal in the context of family and other close relationships does not decide the question about how the related legal system should be designed. When one takes to institutional design, the choice about how much

to build off of voluntarism and how much to build off of a relational obligation is very much contingent on context. *See* Leib, *Responsibility*, *supra* chap. 5, n. 27. For more on building a moral theory of obligation relationally rather than from consent, *see* Samuel Scheffler, *Relationships and Responsibilities*, 26 PHIL. & PUB. AFFAIRS 189 (1997).

43. JOHN RAWLS, A THEORY OF JUSTICE 220 (rev. ed. 1999) ("Each person is to have an equal right to the most extensive system of equal basic liberty compatible with a similar system for all"); J.S. MILL, 21 COLLECTED WORKS OF JOHN STUART MILL 262 (J. M. Robson ed., 1963) ("[T]he burden of proof is supposed to be with those who are against liberty; who contend for any restriction or prohibition.... The a priori assumption is in favour of freedom.").
44. The phrase "*equally effective*" is important. We acknowledge that the criminal law involves powers of norm expression; therefore, we must assess carefully whether non-criminal alternatives affecting social norms carry similar expressive force.
45. Richard S. Frase, *Excessive Prison Sentences, Punishment Goals, and the Eighth Amendment: 'Proportionality' Relative to What?* 89 MINN. L. REV. 571(2005); Alice Ristroph, *Proportionality as a Principle of Limited Government*, 55 DUKE L.J. 263 (2005); Youngjae Lee, *The constitutional Right Against Excessive Punishment*, 91 VA. L. REV. 677 (2005).
46. *Cf. generally* Douglas Husak, *The Criminal Law as a Last Resort*, 24 OX. J. LEGAL STUD. 207 (2004); DOUGLAS HUSAK, OVERCRIMINALIZATION 55 (2008); Nils Jareborg, *Criminalization as Last Resort (Ultima Ratio)*, 2 OHIO ST. J. CRIM. L. 521, 524 (2005).
47. If the burden was not imposed on individuals based on their family status, it is not a family ties burden in the sense we mean, even if the policy ends up substantially hurting those with families. We again refer the reader to our earlier stated conviction that most problems that have a disparate impact on families are best regarded as problems that need to be addressed in the criminal justice system for all those concerned, regardless of whom they affect. So if one has a particular problem, for example, as we do, with the war on drugs and how it often leads to over-incarceration, the solution is not to have a band-aid for families but rather to fix the underlying policy of over-incarceration.

Chapter 6. Application of the Framework to Family Ties Burdens

1. Prince v. Commonwealth of Massachusetts, 321 U.S. 158, 166 (1944) (noting that "the family itself is not beyond regulation in the public interest.... And neither rights of religion nor rights of parenthood are beyond limitation. Acting to guard the general interest in [a] youth's well-being, the state as *parens patriae* may restrict the parent's control.... [T]he state has a wide range of power for limiting parental freedom and authority in thing's affecting the child's welfare").

2. *See* Sherry F. Colb, *When Oral Sex Results in a Pregnancy: Can Men Ever Escape Paternity Obligations?*, FINDLAW, Mar. 9, 2005, http://writ.news.findlaw.com/colb/20050309.html.
3. One's response here hinges on whether one believes that a person who takes precautions against pregnancy still assumes the risk of being commandeered into parenting by the state and the other partner. It might be a remote but foreseeable risk; thus, the question then is whether it is just to impose this consequence on the person. Perhaps one should be able to insure against the risk though it raises moral hazard issues. Professor Collins is of the view that a man should be on the hook unless his sperm was effectively purloined through deception or coercion. Professors Leib and Markel think a man should not be commandeered into parenting obligations by the criminal law's apparatus if he takes due care prior to and during sex: *e.g.*, he discusses the issue with a partner in advance of sexual relations using reliable birth control methods, and the woman agrees then that if birth control fails, the man will not be responsible for more than his fair share of a post-conception abortion.
4. June Carbone, *The Legal Definition of Parenthood: Uncertainty at the Core of Family Identity*, 65 LA. L. REV. 1295 (2005).
5. Indeed, the child at issue in *Jones*, 308 F.2d at 307, resided with a family friend at the time of his death.
6. *See generally* Laura Rosenbury, *Between Home and School*, 155 U. PA. L. REV. 833 (2007).
7. In establishing the criteria to answering this question, legislators, prosecutors, or courts may want to consider a variety of factors including: co-residence between the defendant and the minor, whether the defendant provides financial support to child, whether the defendant has formally terminated parental rights or instead makes statements to the public or the government regarding the relationship for purposes such as taxes or other government benefits. On the features that generally trigger legal recognition of parenthood, *see* David D. Meyer, *Parenthood in a Time of Transition: Tensions Between Legal, Biological, and Social Conceptions of Parenthood*, 54 AM. J. COMP. L. 125, 132–43 (2006).
8. The other aspects of the omissions liability doctrine should attach: *e.g.*, the rescue has to be one that is actually achievable and doesn't pose undue risks to the rescuer.
9. *Cf.* Carol Sanger, *A Case for Civil Marriage*, 27 CARDOZO L. REV. 1311 (2006); Edward A. Zelinsky, *Deregulating Marriage: The Pro-Marriage Case for Abolishing Civil Marriage*, 27 CARDOZO L. REV. 1161, 1164 (2006).
10. 75 AM. JUR 2D *Trespass* § 157 (2008).
11. Zucht v. King, 260 U.S. 174, 176 (1922).
12. Selective Serv. Sys. v. Minnesota Pub. Interest Research Group, 468 U.S. 841, 854-55 (1984).
13. *See* Hyman, *supra* chap. 4, n. 5.
14. We leave aside for now whether the age of majority for this purpose should be dropped from 18 to a lower age, such as 16.

15. The problem with this rationale is it might be said about any norm of responsible behavior; there really is not a single unified theoretical account that adequately explains what the boundaries of criminal law are. *See* Antony Duff, *Theories of Criminal Law*, *in* STANFORD ENCYCLOPEDIA OF PHILOSOPHY. Still, that most parents will comply is not a good reason not to have the law. Will the law "crowd" out otherwise trust-based conduct, as some have suggested?

    It is hard to see how it would, even if there is some value in compliance outside the law. For discussion of the "crowding" thesis—and its rejection, *see* Ethan J. Leib, *Friends As Fiduciaries*, 86 WASH. U. L. REV. 665 (2009) [hereinafter Leib, *Friends As Fiduciaries*]; Ethan J. Leib, *Friendship As Relational Contract* (forthcoming 2009); Frank Cross, *Law and Trust*, 93 GEO. L.J. 1457, 1545 (2005) ("Whatever the intuitive appeal of the claims that legalization undermines trust, they cannot be sustained once they are subjected to scrutiny and empirical testing.").
16. On latitude to parenting, *see* Murray, *supra* chap. 1, n. 100.
17. Mississippi prohibits "[a]doption by couples of the same gender." MISS. STAT. § 93-17-3(2). Florida goes further and prohibits all "homosexuals" from adopting, whether coupled or not. *See* FLA. STAT. ch. 63.042(3). However, about half the states "now permit same-sex couples to raise children together through second-parent adoptions or through entry into marriage or a marriage-like union." David D. Meyer, *supra* chap. 6, n. 7, at 135.
18. That's not to deny that *ex ante* Larry may feel denigrated on the basis of sexual orientation discrimination.
19. Of course, some opponents would rely on more attenuated causal theories of harm if children are entrusted to the care of homosexual couples or those in polyamorous unions. *E.g.*, Press Release, Christian Inst., Blair's Gay Adoption Plans Will Harm Children (May 7, 2002), http://www.christian.org.uk/pressreleases/2002/may_7_2002.htm.
20. The fact that a mother is often charged in the failure to protect scenario is a powerful example of the "mother-blaming" phenomenon that affects not only our legal institutions, but also our cultural norms about parenting. As Professor Becker states, "[M]others are expected to be much better and more powerful parents than fathers, always putting their children's needs above their own and protecting their children from all harm." *See* Mary E. Becker, *Double Binds Facing Mothers in Abusive Families: Social Support Systems, Custody Outcomes, and Liability for the Acts of Others*, 2 U. CHI. L. SCH. ROUNDTABLE 13, 15 (1995); *see also* Naomi Cahn, *Policing Women: Moral Arguments and the Dilemma of Criminalization*, 49 DEPAUL L. REV. 817, 822 (2000) (arguing the criminal justice system treats mothers more harshly); JANE SWIGART, THE MYTH OF THE BAD MOTHER: THE EMOTIONAL REALITIES OF MOTHERING 6 (1991) ("[W]e live in a society that simultaneously idealizes and devalues the mother.").
21. *See* Murray, *supra* chap. 1, n. 100.
22. We are grateful to Professor Murray for alerting us to this point.
23. *Cf.* Carol Sanger, *Separating from Children*, 96 COLUM. L. REV. 375 (1996); Erik Eckholm, *Older Children Abandoned Under Law for Babies*, N.Y. TIMES, Oct. 3, 2008,

at A21 (showing parents abandoning children well past infancy when they are promised immunity from prosecution for neglect).

24. *See* Nancy S. Erickson, *Battered Mothers of Battered Children: Using Our Knowledge of Battered Women to Defend Them Against Charges of Failure to Act, in* 1A CHILDREN AND FAMILIES: ABUSE AND ENDANGERMENT 197, 199 (Sandra Anderson-Garcia & Robert Batey eds., 1991) ("[B]ased on sheer numbers alone, one could predict that women will be prosecuted for this category of failure to act more frequently than men.").
25. One commentator has argued that "society particularly expects that the mother will be the child's protector" and that "[t]he mother is expected to suppress any individual needs or identity of her own in order to serve and protect the needs of her child." Jacobs, *supra* chap. 4, n. 12, at 587; *see also* Becker, *supra* chap. 6, n. 20, at 15 (arguing that "[t]here is a profound tendency in our culture to blame mothers (not fathers) for all problems children face (and all problem children)").
26. Naomi Cahn, *Policing Women: Moral Arguments and the Dilemmas of Criminalization*, 49 DEPAUL L. REV. 817, 822 (2000).
27. *See* Bernardine Dohrn, *Bad Mothers, Good Mothers, and the State: Children on the Margins*, 2 U. CHI. L. SCH. ROUNDTABLE 1, 3–4 (1995) (discussing domestic violence and child abuse as strong predictors of each other).
28. *Cf.* Nicholson v. Scopetta, 344 F.3d 154 (2d Cir. 2003) (disapproving of a city agency's practice of removing children from a custodial parent based on a parental failure to prevent the child from witnessing domestic violence).
29. *See* Becker, *supra* chap. 6, n. 20, at 19 (noting that women are sometimes murdered after leaving an abusive spouse).
30. *See id.*
31. *See id.* at 31–32 (urging the provision of stronger "safety nets" for women in abusive situations); *see also* Linda Gordon, *Feminism and Social Control, in* WHAT IS FEMINISM? 63, 69 (Juliet Mitchell & Annie Oakley, eds., 1986) ("Good social policy could address the problem of wife beating in part by empowering women to leave abusive situations, enabling them to live in comfort and dignity without men.").
32. Becker, *supra* chap. 6, n. 20, at 32. It is important to note that Becker also argues that "we must also change other parts of the social and legal system to make it easier for women to escape abusive households with their children." *Id.*
33. *See id.* at 21 (arguing that the mother "is in a much better position than the child to prevent abuse and owes a duty of care to her children").
34. As Mary Becker has written, "[T]he assumption should be that the adult who was not literally a hostage—not literally coerced at every available second—*could* have acted to end abuse," at least by picking up the phone and calling 911. Becker, *supra* chap. 6, n. 20, at 55.
35. There may be some cases in which the more passive parent is just as culpable as the actual abuser, by providing active encouragement or a weapon or the like.
36. *See, e.g.*, Nina Callaway, Your Wedding Vows: Samples of Wedding Vow Wording, ABOUT.COM, http://weddings.about.com/cs/bridesandgrooms/a/vowwording.htm

(traditional language wording includes "to have and to hold from this day forward, for better or for worse, for richer, for poorer, in sickness and in health, to love and to cherish; from this day forward until death do us part.") (last visited Sept. 28, 2008).

37. *Cf.* MICHAEL SANDEL, LIBERALISM AND THE LIMITS OF JUSTICE.
38. *See, e.g.*, People v. Beardsley, 150 Mich. 295, 113 N.W. 1128 (1907) (reversing manslaughter conviction of man who failed to aid his lover after she overdosed on morphine because he owed her no legal duty). Indeed, some states have recently recognized that limiting liability to formal legal relationships would be plainly underinclusive. State v. Caton, 739 N.E.2d 1176, 1181 (Ohio Ct. App. 2000) ("Whether a person stands in *loco parentis* is a factual question. The term does not signify a formal investiture...." (citation omitted)); Leet v. State, 595 So. 2d 959, 963 (Fla. App. 1991) (concluding that the live-in boyfriend of a child's mother owed a legal duty to the child to prevent abuse by the mother after establishing a "family-like relationship" for an extended and indefinite period). We believe all states need to move in this direction and have a proposed a clear mechanism by which they could do so.
39. Another reading, which we find somewhat implausible, is that it exhibits special faith in the spouses of black persons that they are more motivated to undertake rescues without the threat of legal sanction for failure to do so. *Cf.* O'Hear, *supra* chap. 5, n. 24.
40. In light of the extent of discrimination against gay individuals in this country, we think it far too risky just to hope that courts in all states would extend the same protections and obligations to individuals in a homosexual relationship as they would to individuals in heterosexual relationships. As a point of comparison, states are split about whether to allow same sex partners to recover in tort for wrongful death or infliction of emotional distress. *See* D. KELLY WEISBERG & SUSAN APPLETON, MODERN FAMILY LAW: CASES AND MATERIALS 404 (3d ed. 2006).
41. We note that some civil union laws, such as Vermont's, offer same-sex couples the same panoply of rights and responsibilities that exist with heterosexual marriages. *See* VT. STAT. ANN. tit. 15, § 1204 (2002). In such a situation, we think there is still a residual discrimination on the basis of sexual orientation by denying the word *marriage* to such partnerships but that discrimination does not extend to our core area of concern, the criminal justice system, because the obligations run on the same tracks. That said, the discrimination persists against those involved in voluntary and committed polyamorous relationships or in non-sexual unions who nonetheless seek to enter covenants of care with each other. *Cf. generally* Leib, *Friendship, supra* chap. 3, n. 23; Laura Rosenbury, *Friends with Benefits?*, 106 MICH. L. REV. 189 (2007) (arguing that a failure to recognize friendship impedes the elimination of state supported gender role expectations).
42. By decoupling omissions liability and marriage, we do not run the risk of punishing what amounts to a purely private breach of contract through criminal law. Since there is no bilateral exchange or consideration with

our omissions registry but only a declaration to the state with binding consequences, the state may decide to punish those who make false claims to the state or those who lull the state's agents into complacency *vis-à-vis* a particular person. The lulling notion, of course, applies only to those few situations in which the state already has reason to be mindful of the vulnerability of a particular person.

43. At least one of us has some sympathy with the idea that voluntary friendships can trigger substantial legal duties. *See* Leib, *Friendship*, *supra* chap. 3, n. 23; Leib, *Friends As Fiduciaries*, *supra* chap. 6, n. 15. Few of these envisioned duties for friendship are criminally punishable upon breach but, admittedly, some are. Leib's approach to friendship—and his resistance to registries in that context—is, in some ways, inconsistent with the approach taken here. To the extent that the approaches differ, Leib is willing to concede that the use of a registry for criminal law liability may be the better way to allocate friendship's burdens. But the private, civil law is another story.
44. Brank *et al.*, *supra* chap. 4, n. 21.
45. *E.g.*, IDAHO CODE ANN. § 32-1301 (2006); LA. REV. STAT. ANN. § 14:92:2 (2004).
46. Brank et al., *supra* chap. 4, n. 21, at 3 (noting that "all of the states have some form of civil parental liability"); Chapin, *supra* chap. 4, n. 21, at 633–34 (discussing compensation and deterrence rationales of civil liability statutes).
47. United States v. Pinkerton, 328 U.S. 640 (1946).
48. *See* Alex Kreit, *Vicarious Criminal Liability and the Constitutional Dimensions of* Pinkerton, 57 AMER. UNIV. L. REV. 585 (2008).
49. *See, e.g.*, Paul Marcus, *Criminal Conspiracy Law: Time to Turn Back from An Ever More Expanding Ever More Troubling Area*, 1 WM. & MARY BILL RIGHTS J. 1, 7 (1992) (criticizing *Pinkerton*).
50. Kreit, *supra* chap. 6, n. 48.
51. *See* Posting of Dan M. Filler to Concurring Opinions, Strict Liability for Parents, http://www.concurringopinions.com/archives/2006/07/strict_liabilit.html (July 6, 2006) (stating that these proposals raise questions both about effectiveness and morality). There apparently have been few recent empirical studies assessing the effectiveness of these laws. *See* Juvenile Justice Reform Initiatives in the States 1994-1996, http://ojjdp.ncjrs.org/pubs/reform/ch2_d.html (bemoaning the lack of data about whether these statutes are effective) (last visited Sept. 28, 2008); *see also* Chapin, *supra* chap. 4, n. 21, at 653–54.
52. *See* Posting of Dan M. Filler, *supra* chap. 6, n. 51.
53. Harris, *supra* chap. 4, n. 24, at 5.
54. *See* Courtney L. Zolman, Comment, *Parental Responsibility Acts: Medicine for Ailing Families and Hope for the Future*, 27 CAP. U. L. REV. 217, 229 (1998) (citing statement by Nia Keeling, a family outreach worker); *see also* Tyler & Segady, *supra* chap. 4, n. 23, at 80 (citing the statement "[s]how me a bad kid and I'll show you a bad parent," made at a city council meeting in Southfield, Michigan, that ultimately authorized a parental responsibility ordinance).
55. *See* Chapin, *supra* chap. 4, n. 21, at 624.

56. For a discussion of whether poor parenting is in fact a substantial contributing factor to juvenile delinquency, *see id.* at 664–71.
57. *See* DiFonzo, *supra* chap. 4, n. 21, at 44; *see also* Cahn, *supra* chap. 4, n. 21, at 425–27 (identifying other causes of juvenile delinquency, such as "deficiencies in early childhood education, peer pressure, and inadequate job opportunities"); Amy L. Tomaszewski, Note, *From Columbine to Kazaa: Parental Liability in a New World*, 2005 U. ILL. L. REV. 573, 582–85 (discussing how factors like the media and biology might contribute to juvenile delinquency).
58. DiFonzo, *supra* chap. 4, n. 21, at 47; *see also* Cahn, *supra* chap. 4, n. 21, at 416 (suggesting that some parents do such a poor job of parenting, such as engaging in physical abuse, that their children might reject their supervisory efforts).
59. DiFonzo, *supra* chap. 4, n. 21, at 48. *See also* Eckholm, *supra* chap. 6, n. 23.
60. *Id.* DiFonzo also argues that jailing a parent deprives the youthful offender and any siblings of a parental influence in the home; this criticism is less persuasive if the parenting at issue was truly inadequate or even affirmatively harmful.
61. Asymmetrical dependency refers to relationships where one person possesses substantial authority and responsibility over another person who is largely dependent for his or her well-being on the authority-wielding person. Martha Fineman elaborates upon this notion. *See* MARTHA ALBERTSON FINEMAN, THE NEUTERED MOTHER, THE SEXUAL FAMILY, AND OTHER TWENTIETH CENTURY TRAGEDIES 8 (1995). Our vision of who stands in relationships of asymmetrical dependency does not rest necessarily upon *residency*, but we recognize its general significance.
62. *See* U.S. SENTENCING GUIDELINES MANUAL § 3B1.3 (1992) (providing a sentencing enhancement for abusing a position of trust). Notice that use of sentencing enhancements this way are fine under our framework: they are not family ties burdens because they apply to all positions of trust. More, they would usefully undercut one way in which this burden is actually used to benefit intrafamilial sex abusers, as we suggested in Part I. Leib discusses how this provision can be used to protect friendship as a caregiving relationship in Leib, *Friendship*, *supra* chap. 3, n. 23, at 690 n.324.
63. *E.g.*, Carolyn S. Bratt, *Incest Statutes and the Fundamental Right of Marriage: Is Oedipus Free to Marry?*, 18 FAM. L.Q. 257, 259 (1984). This may help explain why adopted children are sometimes excluded from such prohibitions.
64. *See* Cahill, *supra* chap. 4, n. 55, at 1569. Cahill cites a number of courts that referenced these rationales in upholding incest laws. *See, e.g.*, *In re* Tiffany Nicole M, 571 N.W.2d at 878 (citing both the possibility of "genetic mutation" and the need "to protect children from the abuse of parental authority"); State v. Kaiser, 663 P.2d 839, 843 (Wis. Ct. App. 1983) (same). McDonnell cites a related concern of preventing the family from becoming "oversexualized," with family members viewing other members as potential sexual partners. McDonnell, *supra* chap. 4, n. 61, at 353.
65. *See* Note, *Inbred Obscurity*, *supra* chap. 4, n. 57, at 2464 n.10 (citing Benton v. State, 461 S.E.2d 202, 205 (Ga. 1995) (Sears, J., concurring) (on point of reducing rivalry); *id.* at 2465 n.13 (citing CLAUDE LÉVI-STRAUSS, THE ELEMENTARY STRUCTURES OF KINSHIP 479 (Rodney Needham ed., James Harle Bell & John Richard von Sturmer trans., 1969)).

66. *See* McDonnell, *supra* chap. 4, n. 61, at 352 (describing how many incestuous relationships pose no genetic problems and suggesting that states could take a more narrow approach by allowing incestuous couples to marry but making it illegal for them to have children). McDonnell does not grapple with the question whether such a statute would be constitutional. Margaret Mahoney makes the point that the genetic issue also cannot justify those state statutes criminalizing relationships between stepparents and stepchildren. *See* Mahoney, *supra* chap. 4, n. 58, at 28.
67. *See* Cahill, *supra* chap. 4, n. 55 (discussing how disgust and revulsion drive much of incest regulation).
68. *See* Mahoney, *supra* chap. 4, n. 58, at 28 (describing how "community norms" and religious history serve as common rationales for incest legislation).
69. As we noted above, three states do not punish consensual adult sibling sexual conduct.
70. Professors Collins and Leib would add that persons who once had a relation of asymmetric dependence should be precluded from future relations not involving asymmetry. Professor Markel disagrees; in his view, genuine and mature consent may plausibly exist even between adults who were once in a relationship of asymmetric dependence.
71. *See* Note, *Inbred Obscurity, supra* chap. 4, n. 57, at 2469–70 (detailing the confusing pattern of incest laws).
72. In other contexts, Professor Markel suggests possibilities including registering the relationship with the government if it fits into a certain category of risk and requiring participants to the relationship to take a sex-education course. *See infra* chap. 6, n. 84. These might be appropriate in this context as well.
73. Here we largely agree with the observation from Justice Scalia's dissent in *Lawrence v. Texas*, 539 U.S. 558, 597 (2003), in which he noted that the reasoning of the Court's majority opinion makes it difficult to resist the conclusion we draw regarding consensual adult relations.
74. *See* Posting of Dan Markel to PrawfsBlawg, The Sex-Ed License, Redux, http://prawfsblawg.blogs.com/prawfsblawg/2008/02/the-sex-ed-lice.html (Feb. 19, 2008) (discussing shadow effects of incest, adultery, and polygamy laws); Kay L. Levine, *The Intimacy Discount: Prosecutorial Discretion, Privacy, and Equality in the Statutory Rape Caseload*, 55 EMORY L.J. 691 (2006) (lamenting shadow effects on consensual activity in statutory rape context).
75. *See* Cahill, *supra* chap. 4, n. 55, at 1569. Cahill cites a number of courts that referenced these rationales in upholding incest laws. *See, e.g., In re* Tiffany Nicole M, 571 N.W.2d 872, 878 (Wis. Ct. App. 1997) (citing both the possibility of "genetic mutation" and the need "to protect children from the abuse of parental authority"); State v. Kaiser, 663 P.2d 839. 843 (Wis. Ct. App. 1983) (same).
76. *See* Note, *Inbred Obscurity, supra* chap. 4, n. 57 (developing this argument).
77. *See, e.g.*, State v. Thompson, 792 P.2d 1103 (Mont. 1990) (concluding that a high school principal who threatened to block a student's graduation unless she consented to sexual intercourse could not be convicted of the crime of "sexual intercourse without consent").

78. We recognize that some proponents of incest laws may be sincerely motivated by religious views or other comprehensive moral views, but those views, in a liberal society sensitive to the rights of minorities, are not necessarily views that a liberal criminal justice system must abide by. We also recognize there is an important and complicated separate issue of whether any incestuous marriages should be permitted. Our focus here is on whether currently criminal conduct should be decriminalized or reformed, and we will restrict our discussion to that subject.
79. While a sentence enhancement may, to some, signal that one victim seems to be "worth more" than another victim, we think there is less reason to be worried about that message since an offender in that context has voluntarily created the trust relationship, and the breach of it makes the underlying conduct plausbily more reprehensible from society's perspective.
80. Note, *Inbred Obscurity, supra* chap. 4, n. 57, at 2468 n.31 ("The likelihood that offspring of very closely related partners (parent-child and siblings) will have a genetic disease is about 13%, which is much greater than the likelihood that two strangers, with no family history of the disease, will have a child with such defects, which is 0.1%. Two less closely related partners, such as first cousins, have a slightly greater than 3% chance of having a child with a genetic defect.") (citations omitted).
81. Note, *Inbred Obscurity, supra* chap. 4, n. 57, at 2468.
82. As to how these concerns are addressed outside the criminal justice system, we are more ambivalent. We recognize that some might try to distinguish eugenics (which might be thought to perfect a given gene pool) from genetics-based fears about incest, which are trying to avoid harms to future humans, as opposed to perfecting them. The problem with this distinction is that it assumes a moral baseline of non-incestuous relationships; if a community had endorsed incestuous relationships historically, then efforts to ban such relationships would be viewed by that community as "eugenics" by virtue of the goal of trying to improve the general issue of the community.
83. Indeed, to the extent that incest laws produce sentencing discounts to sexually abusive family members, the incest regime is complicit in extending a family ties "benefit" with no adequate justification for under-punishing those who sexually abuse their dependents.
84. Professor Markel, for instance, holds the view that if someone aged fifteen to eighteen invites and chooses consensual relations with another person aged fifteen or higher, then that person should be able to engage in that relationship provided certain (admittedly difficult) conditions are satisfied. For example, a state could have a policy by which sex education courses would be a prerequisite for sexual activity in the same way that driver education in some jurisdictions is a prerequisite for permissible driving. On this view, all persons under eighteen wishing to have sex without fear of prosecution would have to secure a sex-education license, which they could get from a variety of possible private or public sources. *See* Posting of Dan Markel to PrawfsBlawg, Is Teen Sex Like Teen Driving? The Uneasy Case for the Sex-Ed License, http://prawfsblawg.blogs.com/prawfsblawg/2008/02/is-teen-sex-lik.html (Feb. 15, 2008). The education

would foster awareness of pregnancy, birth control techniques, genetic risks, disease, and physical and psychological coercion. Additionally, even with such a sex-education license, adult-minor or minor-minor sex (regardless of consanguinity) could be presumptively or categorically prohibited when there is a relationship of asymmetrical dependence or cohabitation or supervisorial relationship in school, work, or extracurricular activities. Last, in relationships where there is a substantial age difference, which raises suggestions of coercion, the relationship's sexual turn would have to be declared in advance to a regulatory agency (or designated authorities) to certify that these conditions have been satisfied. Prosecution for statutory rape would be threatened in the absence of compliance. *See also* Posting of Dan Markel to PrawfsBlawg, Sex with Minors, Sex Between Minors, http://prawfsblawg.blogs.com/prawfsblawg/2008/02/sex-with-minors.html (Feb. 7, 2008); Posting of Dan Markel to PrawfsBlawg, Marriage of Minors, Marriage Between Minors, http://prawfsblawg.blogs.com/prawfsblawg/2008/02/marriage-of-min.html (Feb. 8, 2008).

85. However, one could permit or require the fact finder to infer that coercion is present in certain circumstances: *e.g.*, does one person serve in a caregiving or supervisorial role to the other? But that question would cut across family status bloodlines. For Markel, concerns about medical risks and pregnancy would be addressed through the use of a sex-ed license, which would help secure a safe harbor from prosecution.

86. *See, e.g.*, Lawrence v. Texas, 539 U.S. 558, 590 (2003) (Scalia, J., dissenting) (suggesting that the constitutionality of laws prohibiting adult incest were called into question by the Court's decision in *Lawrence*); Cahill, *supra* chap. 4, n. 55, at 1544 (describing statement by Senator Rick Santorum, who asserted that "If the Supreme Court says you have the right to consensual [gay] sex within your home, then you have the right to bigamy, you have the right to polygamy, you have the right to incest, you have the right to adultery. You have the right to do anything."); Cass Sunstein, *What Did Lawrence Hold? Of Autonomy, Desuetude, Sexuality, and Marriage*, 55 SUP. CT. REV. 27, 60–65 (2003) (discussing the implications of *Lawrence* for incest laws). The same slippery slope concerns about incest were also raised by opponents to the legalization of interracial marriage. For a very interesting discussion on that topic, *see* Cahill, *supra* chap. 4, n. 55, at 1554–57.

87. Bigamy is also increasingly on the agenda. *See* Jeffrey Michael Hayes, *Polygamy Comes out of the Closet: The New Strategy of Polygamy Activists*, 3 STAN. J. CIV-R. CIV-LIBERTIES 99 (2007).

88. *See, e.g.*, Sunstein, *supra* chap. 6, n. 86, at 62 (noting it cannot be said that incest "prohibitions run afoul of some emerging national awareness."). One organization, however, is seeking to liberalize cousin marriage. *See* Cousin Couples, http://www.cousincouples.com (last visited Sept. 27, 2008).

89. *See, e.g.*, McDonnell, *supra* chap. 4, n. 61, at 352–53; Note, *Inbred Obscurity*, *supra* chap. 4, n. 57, at 2465–66.

90. *See* Christine McNiece Metteer, *Some "Incest" is Harmless Incest: Determining the Fundamental Right to Marry of Adults Related by Affinity Without Resorting to State Incest Statutes*, 10 KAN. J.L. & PUB. POL'Y 262 (2000); *see also* Bratt, *supra*

chap. 6, n. 63. At least one state supreme court has agreed with this general proposition. *See* Israel v. Allen, 577 P.2d 762 (Colo. 1978) (striking down state statute prohibiting marriage between brother and sister related only by adoption as unconstitutional).

91. Robson, *supra* chap. 5, n. 20, at 762.
92. *Id.*
93. *Id.* at 764.
94. For some historical background on American bigamy laws, *see generally* Late Corp. of the Church of Jesus Christ of Latter-Day Saints v. United States, 136 U.S. 1 (1890); Murphy v. Ramsey, 114 U.S. 15 (1885); Reynolds v. United States, 98 U.S. 145 (1878).
95. *See* Shayna M. Sigman, *Everything Lawyers Know About Polygamy Is Wrong*, 16 CORNELL J. L. PUB. POL'Y 101, 106 (2006) ("The full case has not been made for criminalization of polygamy, it has been assumed. The harms of polygamy have been assumed, as have the effects of criminalization. The accepted rationale is that polygamy will spring up wherever it is permitted, harming women, children, and the very foundations of free society."). Sigman's article and some others provide an exception to this pattern of neglect. *See also* Keith E. Sealing, *Polygamists out of the Closet: Statutory and State Constitutional Prohibitions Against Polygamy Are Unconstitutional Under the Free Exercise Clause*, 17 GA. ST. U. L. REV. 691, 737–57 (2001); Emens, *supra* chap. 4, n. 68; Maura I. Strassberg, *The Challenge of Post-Modern Polygamy: Considering Polyamory*, 31 CAP. UNIV. L. REV. 439, 439 (2003).
96. *See* Hayes, *supra* chap. 6, n. 87, at 105.
97. This was a particular problem with the community of the recently convicted Warren Jeffs, who married off barely post-pubescent girls in his community and at the same time effectively banished teenage boys from the community to "make more girls available for marriage to the elders." Julian Borger, *Hellfire and Sexual Coercion: The Dark Side of American Polygamist Sects*, GUARDIAN, June 30, 2005, at 15.
98. *See* sources cited *supra* chap. 5, n. 18.
99. *See, e.g.*, Geoffrey Fattah, *Bigamy Law Debated*, DESERET NEWS (Salt Lake City), Feb. 3, 2005, http://deseretnews.com/article/1,5143,600109729,00.html (debating the application of a bigamy law to a man with a "spiritual" third wife).
100. *But see* State v. Holm, 137 P.3d 726, 732 (Utah 2006) (holding that the bigamy statute in Utah covers both state-sanctioned marriages and those that are not state sanctioned).
101. *See, e.g.*, Feminist Majority Foundation, *Utah: Plural Wife Is First Woman Charged in Polygamy Case*, FEMINIST DAILY NEWS WIRE (Oct. 16, 2002), http://feminist.org/news/newsbyte/uswirestory.asp?id=7073.
102. Maura Strassberg, *The Crime of Polygamy*, 12 TEMP. POL. & CIV. RTS. L. REV. 353, 371–74 (2003).
103. *See* Sigman, *supra* chap. 6, n. 95, at 151-55 (considering the various economic theories which may encourage polygamy).
104. *See* Emens, *supra* chap. 4, n. 68, at 315–17.

105. *See* Sigman, *supra* chap. 6, n. 95, at 152 n. 430; *see also* ROBERT WRIGHT, THE MORAL ANIMAL: THE NEW SCIENCE OF EVOLUTIONARY PSYCHOLOGY 96–99 (1994).
106. We presume most people will not be comfortable with this solution. But we're not convinced there is a problem of welfare exploitation to solve in the first place; if there is, this is one possible conclusion among others.
107. The Koran actually instructs Muslim men not to take on more wives than they can afford to keep in equal comfort. *See* Sigman, *supra* chap. 6, n. 95, at 158 n.485 (citing THE QUR'AN: A NEW TRANSLATION 4:34 (M.A.S. Abdel Haleem trans., Oxford Univ. Press 2004)).
108. It's important to note that the official Mormon institutions no longer support or encourage polygamy, but there are communities that are Mormon-inspired and continue these practices; it is largely on these offshoots that Professor Strassberg focuses. Strassberg, *Crime of Polygamy*, *supra* chap. 6, n. 102, at 354.
109. Strassberg, *The Crime of Polygamy*, *supra* chap. 6, n. 102, at 405–12.
110. Professor Strassberg has also emphasized the harm of polygamous communities to liberal democracies on different grounds. Drawing on a Hegelian perspective, for example, Strassberg indicated that polygamous marriage cultivates despotism or inhibits the development of liberal values such as equality among persons. *See, e.g.*, Maura I. Strassberg, *Distinctions of Form or Substance: Monogamy, Polygamy and Same-Sex Marriage*, 75 N.C. L. REV. 1501, 1537 (1997) (noting that monogamous marriage is "peculiarly suited to cultivate the freedom to pursue particular ends and the freedom of self-governance by rational ethical principles which must be characteristic of citizens of a free state"). In response, Professor Sigman persuasively notes that the social science literature does not "significantly substantiate the theory that polygamy bars the development of romantic love within a private intimate sphere, that polygamy causes despotism, or that monogamy causes the development of the liberal state." Sigman, *supra* chap. 6, n. 95, at 176 (examining various studies). From a theoretical perspective, moreover, we are puzzled why Professor Strassberg would be willing to tolerate the decriminalization of laws limiting polyfidelity involving mature individuals if these Hegelian concerns were paramount. *See* Strassberg, *supra* chap. 6, n. 102, at 429 (concluding that there is little evidence to justify bans on polyamory when it involves mature individuals). Additionally, our sense is that liberal regimes retain their credibility by reducing the instances in which they use the criminal law to interfere with the autonomous and consenting choices of the individuals involved. Taking a firm stand against polygamy requires liberal regimes to abandon their commitment to respect most forms of private ordering in the absence of obvious and substantial negative externalities.
111. *E.g.*, United States v. Reynolds, 98 U.S. 145 (1878).
112. Martha Ertman, *The Story of Reynolds: Federal "Hell Hounds" Punishing Mormon Treason*, *in* FAMILY LAW STORIES 51 (Carol Sanger ed., 2007); Kerry Abrams, *Polygamy, Prostitution, and the Federalization of Immigration Law*, 105 COLUM. L. REV. 641 (2005).
113. Historical opposition to polygamy sometimes invoked explicitly racist rationales, for example, that polygamy was something that was "almost

exclusively a feature of the life of Asiatic and of African people," not something that was appropriate "among the northern and western nations of Europe." Reynolds v. United States, 98 U.S. 145, 164 (1878); *see also* Francis Lieber, *The Mormons: Shall Utah Be Admitted into the Union?*, 5 PUTNAM'S MONTHLY 225, 234 (1855).

114. It seems that much of the historical American animus against polygamy is rooted in religious discrimination against the Mormon faith tradition and its adherents. *See, e.g.*, Martha M. Ertman, *"They Ain't Whites, They're Mormons": An Illustrated History of Polygamy as Race Treason*, available at http://papers.ssrn.com/sol3/papers.cfm?abstract_id=1270023. Additionally, many Christians traditionally viewed polygamy with disdain and continue to do so today. Sigman, *supra* chap. 6, n. 95, at 142-43.

115. Sigman helpfully explains why polygamy may be more marginally abusive to women but also why these claims are suspect. *See* Sigman, *supra* chap. 6, n. 95, at 172–73. She notes

> (1) polygamy invites secrecy, undermining women's ability to get help if needed; (2) the structure of polygamy suggests that the husband will not have sufficient time to devote to each wife or their children; (3) the treatment by other wives may be abusive; and (4) the types of people who voluntarily choose polygamy may be attracted to the uneven power dynamic.
>
> However, there is no evidence that polygamy per se creates abuse or neglect. Having sister wives can be a support network. The status of senior wives versus junior wives and the relationships among these women vary between cultures. In fact, by banding together, women sometimes wield more power to change their husband's problematic behavior. Yet sometimes co-wives are perpetrators [of the abuse against women].

Id.

116. Cheshire Calhoun, *Who's Afraid of Polygamous Marriage? Lessons for Same-Sex Marriage Advocacy from the History of Polygamy*, 42 SAN DIEGO L. REV. 1023, 1039 (2005) ("What these historical details remind us is that gender inequality is a contingent, not a conceptual, feature of polygamy.").

117. Sigman, *supra* chap. 6, n. 95, at 161–63 (summarizing research explaining the rareness of polyandry).

118. *See id.* at 163–64 ("Rather than the gender biased monolith some have made it out to be, polygyny is a multi-faceted choice of family structure, rooted in the economic, sociological, cultural, and biological particulars of a given society."); *see also* Remi Clignet & Joyce A. Sween, *For a Revisionist Theory of Human Polygyny*, 6 SIGNS 445 (1981) (demonstrating diversity of polygynous marriages).

119. *E.g.*, Strassberg, *supra* chap. 6, n. 109, at 1589 ("[M]onogamous marriages in nineteenth-century America were based on the same patriarchal ideas about women's nature and gender roles as polygamous Mormon marriages.").

120. *See* Sigman, *supra* chap. 6, n. 95, at 173 nn.595–96 (citing studies); *see also* Hayes, *supra* chap. 6, n. 87, at 107 n.47 ("If there are crimes being committed,

and underage child brides, that needs to be prosecuted... [But,] what's the difference between that and other lifestyles with children in them?" (citing Interview with Nancy Perkins, Reporter, Deseret Morning News (Apr. 12, 2006))).

121. *See* Hayes, *supra* chap. 6, n. 87, at 107 (quoting interview with a wife in polygamous relationship who reports that "[w]e are labeled as criminals and treated as criminals for the purpose of [Division of Child and Family Services] investigations").
122. *Cf.* Janet Elliott et al., *CPS Calls Sect Its Largest Case Ever*, Houston Chron., Apr. 8, 2008, at A1 (describing the adversarial custody hearings which would begin for each child found in a polygamous compound).
123. *See* Sigman, *supra* chap. 6, n. 95, at 164.
124. *See id.* at 172.
125. *See* sources *supra* chap. 6, n. 9.
126. *See* Nancy L. Rosenblum, *Democratic Families: 'The Logic of Congruence' and Political Identity*, 32 HOFSTRA L. REV. 145, 162 (2003).
127. *Cf.* Randall Kennedy, McCleskey v. Kemp: *Race, Capital Punishment and the Supreme Court*, 101 HARV. L. REV. 1388 (1988) (describing similar options in context of distribution of death penalty based on race of the victim).
128. Actually, it is hard to say whether a rule that defaults to decriminalization of bigamy would be a penalty default rule or a market-mimicking rule. Although the overwhelming majority of Americans oppose polygamy, the pattern of non-prosecution in some jurisdictions over the years suggests (weakly) that there's not much support for enforcing polygamy bans. *See* Sigman, *supra* chap. 6, n. 95, at 140–41 (noting lack of prosecutions over much of the last fifty years and general apathy among Utah law enforcement to prosecute polygamists); *see also* Dirk Johnson, *Polygamists Emerge from Secrecy, Seeking Not Just Peace but Respect*, N.Y. TIMES, Apr. 9, 1991, at A22 ("[I]n recent years, as state law enforcement officials have adopted an unwritten policy of leaving them alone, polygamists have gone public.").
129. *Cf.* Leah Sears Ward, *A Case for Strengthening Marriage*, WASH. POST, Oct. 30, 2006 at A17.
130. AEI STUDIES IN PUBLIC OPINION, ATTITUDES ABOUT HOMOSEXUALITY AND GAY MARRIAGE 51 (July 6, 2004).
131. *See* Joanna Grossman, *Punishing Adultery In Virginia: A Cheating Husband's Guilty Plea Is a Reminder of the Continued Relevance of Adultery*, FINDLAW, Dec. 3, 2003, http://writ.news.findlaw.com/grossman/20031216.html.
132. Indeed, many states have a multitude of civil law mechanisms that they use to signal disapproval of adultery and encourage monogamy. In North Carolina, for example, spousal support laws are used to send very powerful messages: if a judge finds that the "supporting spouse" engaged in act of "illicit sexual behavior," the judge *must* award alimony to the dependent spouse. On the other hand, if the dependent spouse engaged in sexual misconduct, the judge *cannot* award alimony, no matter how destitute the dependent spouse may be. *See* N.C. GEN. STAT. § 50-16.3A. North Carolina, along with a few other states, also retains the torts of seduction and alienation of affections, providing an avenue for

the wronged spouse to obtain recompense through tort law. We take no position in this paper on the merits of these mechanisms; we simply note they are available.

133. Some have argued that the United States military actually has an implicitly gendered approach to prosecuting adultery within courts martial. *See* Hopkins, *supra* chap. 4, n. 80. Because none of us has sufficient understanding of military legal culture, we really can't say what the military should do in its adultery regulations. Our general argument here would tend to suggest that the government should not criminalize consensual adult sexual behavior. But because our framework enables the government to proffer compelling interests to overcome our presumption against family ties, we can't be sure how to analyze military policy in this regard. Our instinct is to be suspicious, but we would defer to military law experts on this one.

134. *See generally* Mary Anne Case, *Marriage Licenses*, 89 MINN. L. REV. 1758, 1778 n.87, 1779 (2005) (suggesting that perhaps marriage one day could "mov[e] closer to a system of default rules in which couples could structure their own lives," for example by choosing to have "reliance or expectation damages" available for the breach of certain promises).

135. As with our approach to polygamy, it is hard to say whether decriminalization of adultery works to create a penalty default rule or a market-mimicking default rule. It is a penalty default rule if we assume most people want their marriages to look more like "covenant marriages," which require higher entry and exit costs. *See generally* Steven L. Nock, Laura Sanchez, Julia C. Wilson, & James D. Wright, *Covenant Marriage Turns Five Years Old*, 10 MICH. J. GENDER & L. 169, 170–72 (2003) (describing the terms of covenant marriage and analyzing satisfaction rates of those who have chosen them). If couples want exclusivity, the law will force them to take active steps to communicate and discuss that preference. On the other hand, it may be possible to infer (based on patterns of non-prosecution for adultery and assuming prosecutorial responsiveness to majoritarian will) that most people don't want to have prosecutors enforce these matters even if they view adultery laws in low regard. In that respect, the statute serves as a market-mimicking default rule. One flag of caution we want to raise is that if a jurisdiction adopted a default rule of decriminalization, it has to be aware of how default rules can be "sticky," and how such stickiness might affect the prospect of law's ability to affect behavior. For example, if we create a rule that defaults to allowing extramarital sex without any legal stigma, it might actually encourage that behavior even if the goal of the default rule is simply to encourage partners to have conversations and agreements about the scope of their relationship to each other. Of course, this result might occur if we simply decriminalized adultery without giving the opportunity for partners to secure promises of exclusivity through marital agreements. On "sticky" default rules, *see generally* Ronald J. Mann, *Contracts—Only* with *Consent*, 152 U. PA. L. REV. 1873 (2004); Brett H. McDonnell, *Sticky Defaults and Altering Rules in Corporate Law*, 60 SMU L. REV. 383 (2007).

136. We note that Professor Emens, after weighing various costs and benefits, ultimately preferred simple decriminalization of adultery statutes, noting the possibility that these statutes might be unconstitutional after *Lawrence*. Emens, *supra* chap. 4, n. 68. On the particular issue of post-*Lawrence* constitutionality, our sense is that if adultery statutes are drafted to be more respectful of the autonomous choices of individuals opting into a regime of regulation to prevent the kinds of harms that might materialize both to betrayed spouses and to any children of such a marriage, then it is likely they would survive constitutional scrutiny. Nonetheless, we too prescind from "contractual criminal law regulation" but principally for reasons having to do with fairness and externalities.
137. That said, if the sanctions were capped by a sentence of community service with no collateral consequences, it would dramatically reduce the concern of a socially costly punishment.

    We also note that there are some cases that have invalidated various contracts made between spouses, but the agreements we are discussing here are antenuptials; those are usually enforced if both parties are informed by counsel and reflect a basic fairness in exchange between the parties.
138. The family law implications of these proposals for property distribution or other issues are matters beyond the scope of our criminal law focus here. However, our liberty-respecting framework for polygamy raises important and interesting questions about the reach of family ties benefits, such as whether a person with several spouses should be entitled to spousal privileges with all of them, etc.
139. The "outside" person (*X*) is (knowingly or unknowingly) intruding upon the marital space between *Y* and *Z*. Our analysis of what penalty should attach to *X* is contingent upon *X*'s marital status. If *X* is unmarried, no penalty should attach, in our view, assuming *X* is a competent and mature individual. If *X* is married, his situation should be contingent upon whether his marital contract calls for exclusivity.
140. *Cf.* William J. Stuntz, *The Pathological Politics of Criminal Law*, 100 Mich. L. Rev. 505, 529-30 (2001) (stating that legislators have a great incentive to appeal to voters by both generating outcomes and taking symbolic stands).
141. *See* sources cited *supra* chap. 4, n. 90.
142. *See id.*
143. *Cf.* Markel, *Shaming Punishments*, *supra* chap. 2, n. 63 (discussing the use of alternative sanctions).
144. Maldonado, *supra* chap. 4, n. 90.
145. *See, e.g.*, WEISBERG & APPLETON, *supra* chap. 6, n. 40, at 700–01 (describing various enforcement mechanisms).
146. DAVID CHAMBERS, MAKING FATHERS PAY: THE ENFORCEMENT OF CHILD SUPPORT 84 (1979). Chambers studied enforcement efforts in Michigan between 1972 and 1975. *See also* Drew Swank, *The National Child Non-Support Epidemic*, 2003 MICH. ST. DCL L. REV. 357, 375–78 (2003) (citing the author's own studies for proposition that jailing was effective).

147. *See* Swank, *supra* chap. 6, n. 146, at 378.
148. A woman has been jailed for failing to pay child support in at least one case. *See* David Stout, *In Rare Role Reversal, Mother Is Jailed for a Failure to Pay*, N.Y. TIMES, July 26, 1995, http://query.nytimes.com/gst/fullpage.html?res=990CE7D9113EF935A15754C0A963958260.
149. It is critical to remember that in thinking about these burdens from an *ex ante* as opposed to an *ex post* perspective that we be especially mindful of how gender affects this particular context. Women can choose to have children or to choose another alternative (adoption/abortion), while men's options are significantly more limited in this regard. If the mother puts the child up for adoption, the father will not have to pay child support. But it is difficult for the man to contract out of his support obligations if the mother makes a unilateral decision to bring a fetus to term and raise the child herself. Perhaps that is as it should be—but it is relevant in policy design on subsidiary questions like the jailing of deadbeat dads.
150. An interesting complication arises in the context of blended families where children may find themselves raised by a number of different primary caregivers. If a father and stepmother divorce, should the stepmother, assuming she is financially able, be required to pay child support? We are uncertain—it might depend on whether there was a prenuptial agreement in some cases. But we all agree that the fairness of imposing *criminal* penalties on an individual in this position seems questionable, and thus the issues raised by blended families are another reason to favor non-criminal approaches.
151. *Cf.* Billingslea v. Texas, 780 S.W.2d 271 (Tex. Cr. App. 1989) (holding that an adult child's failure to seek medical care for ailing live-in parent does not constitute criminal negligence because there was no statutory duty to act).
152. Rickles-Jordan, *supra* chap. 4, n. 90, at 199 n.136.

Coda

1. We discuss this matter briefly in our Preface to Part II. In her reactions to a prior draft of Part I, Kate Bloch suggested to us that the privileges may be an effort to counterbalance the indirect harm and devastation the criminal justice system imposes on families. We were intrigued by such a suggestion but could find little evidence that policymakers thought about the privileges this way—and even if they had, we still had some trouble with the logical nexuses. However, at the very least, this type of reasoning might support some sentencing discounts, since lengthy incarceration terms undoubtedly take a large toll on many families.
2. In a recent paper, Steve Sugarman has drawn attention to the ways some governmental welfare policy areas have moved beyond defining the family in traditional (heteronormative and repronormative) terms. *See* Stephen D. Sugarman, *What Is a Family? Conflicting Messages from Our Public Programs*, 42 FAM. L. Q. 231 (2008). For the most part, the criminal law is still stuck in the 1950s in its distribution

of facial burdens and benefits to the institution of the family. We hope that changes—and soon.

3. For example, the city of Phoenix has a diversion program for domestic violence defendants, whereas the city of San Francisco excludes domestic violence defendants from its diversion program. *See. e.g.*, San Francisco Pretrial Diversion Project Guidelines, *available at* http://www.sfpretrial.com/eligibilitycriteria.html (excluding domestic violence offenders from a pretrial diversion program) (last visited Oct. 1, 2008); Domestic Violence Victim Information Center – FAQs, http://phoenix.gov/VICTIMSDV/dvfaq.html (explaining Phoenix's diversion program) (last visited Oct. 1, 2008).
4. *See* Ruth Colker, *Marriage Mimicry: The Law of Domestic Violence*, 47 WM. & MARY L. REV. 1841 (2006).
5. *See id.* at 1858.
6. *See id.* at 1859.
7. Deborah Tuerkheimer, *Recognizing and Remedying the Harm of Battering: A Call to Criminalize Domestic Violence*, 94 J. CRIM L. & CRIMINOLOGY 959, 959 (Summer 2004).
8. *See* Colker, *supra* chap. coda, n. 4, at 1882–83.

Index

C

D